PRESS LAW

AUSTRALIA
The Law Book Company Ltd.
Sydney: Melbourne: Brisbane

CANADA AND U.S.A.
The Carswell Company Ltd.
Agincourt, Ontario

INDIA
N.M. Tripathi Private Ltd.
Bombay

ISRAEL
Steimatzyky's Agency Ltd.
Jerusalem: Tel Aviv: Haifa

MALAYSIA: SINGAPORE: BRUNEI
Malayan Law Journal (Pte.) Ltd.

NEW ZEALAND
Sweet and Maxwell (N.Z.) Ltd.
Wellington

PAKISTAN
Pakistan Law House
Karachi

PRESS LAW

ROBIN CALLENDER SMITH, LL.B. (Hons.)

of Gray's Inn, Barrister

LONDON
SWEET & MAXWELL
1978

Published in 1978 by
Sweet & Maxwell Ltd. of
11, New Fetter Lane, London.
Photoset by Inforum Ltd of
Portsmouth and printed in
Great Britain by
Fletcher & Son Ltd., Norwich.

ISBN   hardback :   0 421   23440 7
        paperback :   0 421   23450 4

Contents

Preface

This book was born from a concern about the general level of legal ignorance amongst journalists. Some 10 years ago, as a reporter on the *Eastern Daily Press* and *Eastern Evening News*, too much of my own copy was written in a dangerous fashion. The accepted textbook in the field, while an excellent introduction to Press Law, avoided many of the specific queries I wished to have answered. A succession of tolerant senior colleagues imparted their wisdom, reinforced by the confidence of experience rather than by a real understanding of why what they suggested was correct.

Those good old days are fast running to a close. There have been major examinations of the laws on defamation, contempt, copyright, official secrets and privacy. Two Private Members' Bills have, in becoming Acts, created novel additions to the law of publications. One makes it potentially actionable to state the truth; the other provides a cloak of anonymity for an accused facing rape accusations.

Press law is riddled with anomalies. Implementation of some of the proposals in the reports mentioned above could remove the most manifest. One of the Faulks Committee recommendations was that legal aid should be available in filtered situations for defamation actions: such aid is not available at the moment. Further, that claims for less than £1,000 damages in defamation actions should be triable in the county court. That limited area could lead to radical adjustment of reporting at provincial and national levels.

The Younger Committee on privacy proposed a new cause of action where damage is caused by the use of information unlawfully acquired.

Despite stories of "gold-digging" actions with which the Press are threatened by the lunatic fringe, there are comparatively few defamation actions simply because the general reading public are unaware of the law in this area. Even given

advice, the money put at risk to obtain the remedy may out-
weigh the injury suffered. A change in this situation may lead
to injured readers being less content to accept an informal apology and being inclined, instead, to seek vindication through
the county court.

Complaints about an erosion of the freedom of the Press in
this specific area are scarcely tenable simply because the ordinary (rather than the professional) person is given the chance
to remedy the injury to a reputation.

If journalists are given the opportunity to understand the
law and then operate within it, the causes for complaint about
unsafe copy could diminish. I also believe that a journalist
should be prepared to and be capable of questioning critically
and constructively both the law he works within and the law
he observes.

To this end, certain statutes have been quoted in detail. If
their provisions seem obscure and unnecessarily complex,
journalists may be moved to question — rather than just to
accept passively — the general utility of "legalese."

It is a sincere hope that this book will give journalists the
fundamental information they must have to operate safely
within the law and, at the same time, kindle an interest in law
generally.

Some cases have been quoted to take the legal idea beyond
bare theory into the realm of practical application. The results
are not as logical, perhaps, as the façade presented by the legal
system would beg belief but there are many other areas of life
which share this defect.

If some of the detail seems daunting to the embryo journalist
(or to the experienced man who wants to find out what really
has been going on) there may be comfort in the fact that few
lawyers (without photographic memories) grasp and retain
such details easily. Skim-reading of sections two or three times
to grasp the general ideas will break the back of most of the
material so that later critical, concentrated study can establish
a foundation of residual knowledge. This can act as a touchstone, however unconscious, when writing copy so that legal
problems are avoided.

There is no intention in this book to turn journalists into
lawyers. However, if a legal reason exists for saying or not say-

ing a particular thing, it is part of the journalist's craft to appreciate this. The book is not offered as a weighty academic tome, each page loaded with footnotes. Its purpose is to bridge the gap between introductory material and the specialist works.

Since the major part of the text was written there have been some important developments. The Old Bailey trial of *Gay News* and its editor for blasphemous libel concluded with convictions which, at the time of writing, are the subject of an appeal to the Court of Appeal. The Royal Commission on the Press published its report. A summary of developments in these two areas is contained in the appendices which follow the main text.

It was possible at a late stage to include relevant provisions from the Criminal Law Act 1977 in the text.

An important case on the law of contempt may have been heard by the Divisional Court by the time the book is published. It concerns *The Journal* at Newcastle and Border Television. Reports of a trial at Carlisle mentioned that an accused had pleaded not guilty to certain theft counts and had then faced a jury trial pleading not guilty to handling counts. The trial had to be stopped because jurors could have realised that the accused had previous convictions (see p. 196). The information about the previous convictions came, of course, in open court but at a time before the jury was empanelled. The Phillimore Committee recommended that fair and accurate reports of proceedings in open court should not, of themselves, constitute contempt (see p. 132). The Attorney-General wished to have a clearer resolution of this important area and the decision of the Divisional Court will be of interest to both the Press and the public.

I am indebted to Professor Albert Pickerell of the U.C.L.A. School of Journalism at Berkeley, California, for certain material he had prepared on the operation of the Official Secrets Acts in the United Kingdom.

As more than a commonplace, I record my thanks to my former students, graduate and non-graduate: their comments on my abstractions helped me learn about what they wanted to know. My thanks are due to my legal, journalistic and teaching colleagues for comment and criticism at every stage, which has been heard but not necessarily acted upon.

The greatest debt, however, is to my wife, Leletta. Despite the supreme good fortune of being neither a lawyer nor a journalist, she made certain that the manuscript moved from being a mere idea to what is a reality.

ROBIN CALLENDER SMITH

October 5, 1977

TABLE OF CASES

TABLE OF STATUTES

xiv

PART 1

GENERAL MATTERS

1 Defamation and the Faulks Committee

Two definitions are set out below. The first, culled from case law, reflects the current classical view. The second, proposed as a statutory definition by the Faulks Committee on the law of defamation in 1975, may shortly become the touchstone for actions in this area. The differences between the two will be examined. It is important to grasp that defamation, whichever definition is used, is primarily a civil matter with the plaintiff seeking to recover damages for the tort (civil wrong) of injury to his reputation. If his reputation is not damaged but statements are made which affect him financially in his work, then he may have an action for the tort of injurious falsehood if he can prove the words were published maliciously and that the facts stated were untrue. In certain situations, defamatory matter may make the publisher liable to a criminal prosecution for criminal libel: this topic is dealt with separately.

Classical definition

Defamation is the publication to a third party of a statement which tends to lower a living person in the estimation of right-thinking members of society generally; or which makes them shun or avoid that person; or which disparages his reputation in relation to his work.

Statutory definition

Defamation shall consist of the publication to a third party of a matter which, in all the circumstances, would be likely to affect a person adversely in the estimation of reasonable people generally.

There was a traditional press definition, used as a rule of

thumb, that defamatory matter was copy which brought a person into "hatred, ridicule or contempt." While this is an element of either of the definitions quoted above, it is defective because it excludes the idea that a defamatory remark may cause damage because people avoid the injured person out of pity. For example:

> *Youssoupoff* v. *MGM Pictures Ltd.* (1934): in a film made by the defendants there was a suggestion that the plaintiff, a Russian princess, had either been raped or seduced by Rasputin. The princess was living in exile in Paris when the film appeared and she sued successfully because the defendants could not prove either of the suggestions they had made. They argued, however, that people seeing the film would not hate, ridicule or feel contempt for the princess. Their argument was rejected because she could show that certain friends avoided her out of mere pity to save her embarrassment if the allegations were true and that she was being shunned without any moral discredit on her part.

Both definitions stick to the idea of the reaction to the statement by the reasonable person. In law, this kind of test is known as the objective test. Currently, the jury decide whether, as a general group of 12 people, they would think less well of the plaintiff, considering the statements made. It is not enough that the plaintiff can only prove that a certain group think less well of him because, to allow this, would be to permit a subjective test which would add uncertainty to what is, already, a difficult area of the law.

> *Example:* X is a teacher, dedicated to classroom work and uninterested in school politics. He is criticised for not taking more part in sitting on committees dealing with the development of the school curiculum. His colleagues agree he is an excellent teacher in the classroom.
>
> It will be up to a jury to decide whether reasonable people think less well of him, as a teacher, because of his reluctance to give up his free time to do extra committee work. A specialised group — his colleagues — may think less well of him but the man in the street might think that X's approach, though perhaps selfish in a hard-headed way, has not lead to any real damage of his reputation as a teacher in the public sense.

The objective test does allow the law of defamation to change gradually: what the jury of 1900 might regard as defamatory might be considered not worthy of thought by the jury of 2000. This flexibility, while it may introduce some uncertainty and is generally conservative, allows the law in this area some development through successive decades and leaves the test to public feeling.

A Faulks Committee recommendation discussed later is that juries should be abolished in defamation actions, leaving the "reasonable man" decision to a single judge.

It may have been noted that, by the current definition, the defamatory statement refers to a living person. In other words, once a person dies — short of a criminal libel action — relatives have no right to take action to clear the name of the deceased. The Faulks Committee recommend that an action should be possible within five years of a person's death, not for damages but for a declaration in court that the deceased was defamed. The action could be brought by close relatives (the surviving spouse, children, brothers or sisters) and, if successful, the defendant would be liable to pay their legal costs for the action.

It is possible, under the present law, to defame a dead person and to set up a defamatory innuendo which relates to someone who is alive. The action brought by Madame Sukarno, discussed under "Criminal Libel," is one example.

At the moment there are two forms of defamation: *libel* and *slander*. The distinction is purely historical and England is one of the few countries in the world to retain the division.

Libel is a defamatory statement or representation in a permanent form (writing, pictures, etc.); radio and television broadcasts were categorised as libels by statute in the Defamation Act 1952, to clear up uncertainties and theatrical performances (except domestic ones given in private houses) fall within libel.

Slander is the form of action where the defamatory meaning comes from spoken words or gestures.

While the tort is defamation and the allegation is either libel or slander there are some important consequences of the distinction between the two categories.

(1) Libel, if it could provoke a breach of the peace, is a crime as well as a tort. There is no such thing as criminal slander, although slanderous words could lead to prosecutions for trea-

son, blasphemy or sedition.

(2) The injured party does not need to show any actual financial loss in libel. It is actionable *per se* (of itself) and the court presumes damage. Slander, however, requires proof of monetary loss (termed special damage) except in four cases:

    (a) an imputation of a criminal offence punishable with prison;

    (b) an imputation of a contagious or infectious disease which might prevent other people from associating with the plaintiff: this includes venereal disease, the plague and leprosy;

    (c) an imputation of adultery or unchastity relating to any woman or girl; and

    (d) words which disparage a man in relation to his office, trade, profession or calling.

> *Example:* X tells a reporter that his neighbour Y, is a persistent parking offender. If the words are untrue, Y has no action against X in slander unless he can prove he has suffered financial loss as a result of the remark. Parking offences are dealt with by fines, not imprisonment. Y could, however, sue the newspaper for libel because he does not need to show any kind of financial loss.

The distinction is unknown in Roman law and has been abolished in most Australian states and in New Zealand (countries which took Common Law systems from England). The Faulks Committee recommend that the distinction between libel and slander be abolished and that the rules adopted for defamation actions should be those for libel. In other words, damage would be presumed whether the offending words were spoken or written.

There is one further initial point. The current definition refers to the plaintiff being lowered, shunned or avoided or disparaged. The proposed statutory definition fixes as defamatory anything which would be likely to affect a person adversely. This adjective could cover a wider field of matter than the current definition. In addition, this crystallises the injury in defamation in terms which are easy to grasp.

What to do, however, with a newspaper publishing a picture or a cartoon of an individual in the nude? The Faulks Committee considered this specific point and emphasised that there was a difference between bad taste and defamation. The complaint related to a cartoon of a woman tennis player. They felt that no reasonable reader would have thought less well of her simply because an artist had, in effect, said: "this is what I think she looks like without any clothes on."

The Committee appear to have overlooked the full force of their proposed definition. While this type of case is undoubtedly more suitable for consideration by the Press Council, the circumstances of the publication would have to be considered. While cartoonists enjoy a decided latitude in their treatment of subjects, the injured woman could, on special facts, claim her reputation has been damaged adversely, particularly if she has never posed naked and her reputation as a professional tennis player requires some semblance of professional responsibility.

Taking the recent case of *Savalas* v. *Associated Newspapers* (1976), where it was incorrectly suggested that Mr. Telly Savalas — television's "Kojak" — could not function as a professional actor in the filming of a particular production because of his drinking and partiality for female company, it is clear that one reason why the jury awarded the £34,000 damages to him was because they felt his professional standing could have been damaged. This decision fell under the current law and perhaps more along the same lines would develop under the "adverse effect" rule.

Essentials of Defamation

What will be examined in this next section is, basically, what the plaintiff must be able to prove if he is to mount an action which is to have any chance of success. There are three hurdles:

(1) The words must *refer* to the plaintiff;

(2) They must be *published* (in some cases with malice); and

(3) They must be *defamatory* or capable of being defamatory.

These three essentials may be remembered by the mnemonic *repude* (as in repudiate), composed of the two letters beginning each essential component. The essentials will now be examined separately in more detail.

(1) *Reference to the plaintiff*

The cases discussed below are cited as examples of a plaintiff being able to show that he was thought, by reasonable people, to be the person referred to in the published work. For reasons which will become apparent when the defences are examined, the result of the first two cases could be the same now (despite s.4 of the Defamation Act 1952: unintentional defamation) and the sixth case, the most recent, is disturbing.

Hulton v. *Jones* (1910): Hulton's published a humourous account of a motor festival at Dieppe casting imputations on the morals of one Artemus Jones (a name invented by the author) who was supposed to be a churchwarden at Peckham. As printed, the whole article was supposed to be pure fiction. Hulton's were sued by a barrister named Artemus Jones who did not live at Peckham and had not gone to the Dieppe festival. Witnesses swore they thought the article referred to him. It contained the following passage:

"Upon the terraces marches a world, attracted by the motor races — a world immensely pleased with itself, and minded to draw a wealth of inspiration — and, incidentally, of golden cocktails — from any scheme to speed the passing hour .... 'Whist! there is Artemus Jones with a woman who is not his wife, who must be, you know, the other thing!' whispers a fair neighbour of mine excitedly into her bosom friend's ear. Really, is it not surprising how certain of our fellow-countrymen behave when they come abroad? Who would suppose, by his goings on, that he was a churchwarden at Peckham? No one, indeed, would assume that Jones, in the atmosphere of London, would take on so austere a job as the duties of a churchwarden. Here, in the atmosphere of Dieppe on the French side of the Channel, he is the life and soul of a gay little band that haunts the Casino and turns night into day, besides betraying a most unholy delight in the society of female butterflies."

The jury returned a verdict for Jones and awarded him £1,750 damages. On appeal, the House of Lords refused to disturb this finding. It was immaterial that Hulton's did not intend to defame him: it was sufficient that reasonable people thought he was the person referred to.

An irony behind the case was that the barrister had worked for Hulton's several years before. The editor noticed the name in the copy but thought that no one could think it referred to this former employee.

Newstead v. *London Express Ltd.* (1940): the defendants published a piece of copy which contained the following: "Harold Newstead, 30-year-old Camberwell man, was convicted of bigamy . . . ."

The copy was intended to refer to a Camberwell barman of that name and age. There was a barber with the same name and approximate age living in Camberwell and *that* Harold Newstead successfully sued and recovered damages (although only a farthing).

Identification of the plaintiff may take place, in a less foreseeable manner, by innuendo. Words may look quite innocent but, because of facts known to others, identification and a defamatory meaning may spring out of the most unlikely situations. If the plaintiff can prove the additional background facts which reveal the innuendo as being capable of referring to him in a defamatory sense, he may succeed in some startlingly unexpected situations.

A simple illustration is *Tolley* v. *Fry* (1931):

The plaintiff was a famous amateur golfer. The defendants published an advertisement showing a caricature of him with a bar of chocolate (their product) sticking out of his pocket. There was no argument about identification here and the style of the caricature was not, in itself, defamatory. Tolley successfully alleged, however, that there was the innuendo that he had prostituted his amateur status. Fellow golfers thought he had consented to and been paid for the advertisement apparently endorsing Fry's chocolate.

On identification by innuendo, the next three cases demonstrate the dangers.

Cassidy v. *Daily Mirror* (1929): at an Aintree race meeting Mr. Michael Cassidy went up to a *Mirror* photographer and asked him to take a picture of him with his fiancee. Cassidy had been, among other things, a general in one of the Mexican revolutions and was a race-horse owner. Unknown to the *Mirror*, he was also married. His wife, from whom he was separated, sued alleging that the published picture and caption was taken by her neighbours to mean that she was not Cassidy's true wife and that, while she had been calling herself Mrs. Cassidy, she was only his mistress. She succeeded and recovered £500.

Hough v. *London Express* (1940): copy about a boxer referred to his curly, fair-haired wife watching all of his fights from the ringside. Like Cassidy, Mr. Hough was married but separated. His wife, who did not have curly fair hair, sued on a similar innuendo and succeeded, recovering £650.

Morgan v. *Odhams Press* (1971): The *Sun* published an article which stated:
"A girl who is likely to be a key witness in a dog-doping scandal went into hiding yesterday after threats were made on her life. She left her lodgings in Shepherds Bush accompanied by two men. . . . She was kidnapped by members of the gang last week when they heard she had made a statement to the police. She was kept at a house in Finchley but was eventually allowed to leave when she promised she would return to Canada."

Morgan was a former wrestler who had retired to work as a freelance journalist and who was co-operating with a reporter on the *People*. He lived in Willesden and the girl had willingly stayed with him in his flat during the "last week" referred to in the copy. A policeman, a shopkeeper and a restaurant owner — all of whom knew Morgan well and who had seen him with the girl during that week — gave evidence that they thought the *Sun* item meant that he was one of the kidnappers and was involved in some way in the dog-doping. A jury awarded Morgan £4,750.

On appeal to the House of Lords, three of the five judges held that there was no rule that, before an article could be said to be defamatory, there must be some definite key or pointer indicating that the plaintiff, specifically, is referred to.

A new trial was ordered on the amount of damages in this case.

Lord Donovan, delivering one of the dissenting judgments in the House of Lords, stated:

"Cases such as *Cassidy* v. *Daily Mirror* and *Hough* v. *London Express* stand, I think, in a different category. When a newspaper publishes a statement concerning a man which necessarily implies that he is unmarried, the same statement necessarily implies that any woman holding herself out as his lawful wife is not entitled to that status. It is hardly surprising that there have been differences of judicial opinion whether, although the newspaper may be completely innocent of knowledge of the existence of the lawful wife, it must be regarded as having defamed her. But at least in such cases it can be said that a reasonable conclusion has been drawn from what the paper published. . . . I do . . . however, agree that in the present case there was no evidence justifying a reasonable conclusion that the article was defamatory of the plaintiff. . . ."

To counter arguments that the average reader of the *Sun* would have found nothing defamatory relating to Morgan in the copy, because Morgan's name was never included in the copy and because his flat was in Willesden not Finchley, the view of Lord Reid is representative in imposing liability on the newspaper:

> "What has to be decided is whether it would have been unreasonable for a hypothetical sensible reader who knew the special facts proved to infer that this article referred to the plaintiff. . . . If one must assume that he thinks and acts cautiously as a lawyer would do in his professional capacity then I have no doubt that he would say that that inference is not justified in this case. But if one is entitled to be more realistic and take account of the way in which ordinary sensible people do in fact read their newspapers and draw inferences then equally I have no doubt such people would quite probably draw this inference."

The effect of the majority judgments is to impose a harsh burden on the press. The speculations of individuals with special peripheral knowledge have been equated with the views and thoughts of the ordinary reader of a newspaper. The minority opinion that the *Cassidy* and *Hough* cases are different, in essence, because there is the pointer of the husband's name sets the logical limit of the innuendo: the judicial limit covers a broader area.

(2) *Publication*

Publication to a third party is an essential element in the *civil* law of defamation. It is not sufficient that the defendant writes a defamatory letter to the plaintiff: the contents of the letter must be published to others by the defendant. The plaintiff is not allowed to generate a civil action by causing the publication himself, showing it to others.

In *Hinderer* v. *Cole* (1977) an accountant received a letter from his brother-in-law sent to his office and addressed to "Mr. Stonehouse Hinderer." He was awarded £75 libel damages because his christian name was Alan and the letter was received when the M.P., John Stonehouse, had disappeared leaving debts.

The letter inside the envelope called Mr. Hinderer "sick, mean, twisted, vicious, cheap, ugly, filthy, bitter, nasty, hateful, vulgar, loathsome, gnarled, warped, lazy and evil." However, as these defamatory words were only published to the plaintiff and not to third parties (as in the case of the envelope), no action could be taken on them.

Publication has a broad meaning and is not limited to the printing of statements. A speaker publishes remarks to his audience: if a reporter takes notes and writes copy which appears, this is published to newspaper readers via the distributors, by the newspaper editor and proprietor.

Another case on publication, and when it is deemed to have occurred is:

Bryanston Finance Ltd v. *de Vries* (1975): the defendant believed the plaintiff's subsidiary company and its chairman, Mr. Smith, were acting irregularly. Documents were typed and photocopied by two of the defendant's employees. These included a circular to shareholders in the plaintiff company and covering letters to the Department of Trade and the Loan Committee of the Stock Exchange.

Copies of these documents were sent to S. with an accompanying letter threatening to reveal their contents to the authorities and to the press if a dispute was not settled by midnight. This threat was never carried out.

S sued for libel, claiming publication by the defendant of the defamatory material to the typist and photocopier. Damages totalling £500 were awarded against the defendant, who had pleaded qualified privilege in respect of these publications.

On appeal, the defence was permitted (destroying the plaintiff's claim) because:

(1) dictation to a typist and work by the photocopier was part of their normal work for the defendant (according to Lord Denning); or

(2) some of the recipients of the documents had a common interest in receiving the complaints and — if sent to them — there would have been qualified privilege. The process leading up to such (intended) publication received the same privilege (according to Lawton L.J.).

Express malice. It is usual for the plaintiff to allege, almost as a formality when the writ is served, that publication has been caused "maliciously."

Malice, in this area of law, means spite, ill-will, bad feeling, recklessness about the truth or falsity of the statement or some other personally injuring or discordant motive. The malice must be held by the defendant in relation to the plaintiff and lead to the publication.

The plaintiff has the burden of proving malice (if he feels it is relevant) using either the actual words published by the defendant or in background facts which show a campaign of harrassment on a personal level.

Proof of malice destroys the defences of:

(i) justification (truth) in relation to publication of "spent" convictions: see Rehabilitation of Offenders Act 1974;

(ii) unintentional defamation;

(iii) qualified privilege; and

(iv) fair comment.

Malice has no part to play in the defence of absolute privilege.

If the plaintiff can prove express malice then not only will the four defences above fail but he will generally recover higher damages because of the deliberate use of the bad motive in the publication.

(3) *Defamatory Words*

The meaning of the words in the item at issue is probably the most important single factor in any defamation action. It is from the meaning that the defamation occurs. The nature of any defence which the defendant might use depends on whether the words are statements of fact or expressions of opinion and also on the occasion which may have led to the publication.

Common abuse is generally not defamatory. To call someone a bastard rarely, now, implies illegitimacy but there may be circumstances where the plaintiff can show this meaning was intended.

The judge has an important function in this area:

(1) if he decides to leave the case to the jury, he must tell them what defamation means in law; but

(2) if he thinks no reasonable man could regard the words as defamatory, he must withdraw the case from the jury, killing the plaintiff's case.

Two examples of this second point are given below. The first case has been strongly criticised for its result but remains good as an expression of law, namely that judges have the duty to decide whether the words are capable of being defamatory. It is inevitable that, occasionally, they make mistakes. The second case, on appeal, produced an important piece of law for the press and one which — surprisingly — had not been resolved before.

Capital and Counties Bank v. *Henty* (1882): Henty and Sons were brewers and their customers generally paid by cheques drawn on the plaintiff bank. There was a squabble between Henty's and one particular bank manager. As a result, Henty's sent out a circular to their customers saying they would not "receive in payment cheques drawn on any of the branches of Capital and Counties Bank." There was a run on the bank and the plaintiffs sued Henty's for the alleged libel imputing insolvency. The House of Lords held (4-1) that the judge had correctly withdrawn the words from the jury as being incapable of being defamatory so, therefore, Henty's were not liable.

Lewis v. *Daily Telegraph* (1964): the defendants published a paragraph stating that City of London Fraud Squad officers were investigating the affairs of a company run by the plaintiff. Lewis alleged that the natural meaning of this paragraph was that the company (with him) had been conducting business fraudulently or dishonestly. The defendants admitted that the words were defamatory but denied they were defamatory in the particular sense alleged by Lewis. They argued that, while people might think less well of those being investigated by the police, they could justify this particular meaning. The Fraud Squad was investigating the company's operations. They denied, however, that the words could have the extended defamatory meaning that Lewis and the company were, in fact, acting fraudulently. The House of Lords agreed that the words were not capable of bearing the extended meaning which, as damages totalling £100,000 had been awarded by the jury against the *Daily Telegraph* (and, in another trial against the *Daily Mail* for a similar paragraph, damages totalling £120,000), had a significant practical effect.

In the *Lewis* case Lord Devlin, in the House of Lords, encapsu-
lised the matter:

> "If the ordinary sensible man was capable of thinking that
> wherever there was a police inquiry there was guilt, it would be
> impossible to give accurate information about anything: but in my
> opinion he is not."

As may be seen in the *Cassidy* and *Hough* cases, the defamatory meaning (that someone who is, in fact, married is thought
to be merely a mistress) may occur by innuendo. Defamation
by innuendo may also occur in references to professional people. To suggest that a barrister of 20 years' standing is so short
of work that he has been circularising solicitors implies that he
is professionally incompetent and that he is breaching the professional rules which forbid touting for business.

Since 1977, satire has had dangers which had been, if not concealed until then, relatively dormant. As a form of journalism
(and literature: the two are not necessarily divorced) there had
been a feeling that the full weight of the law of libel would not
descend on material which was obviously satirical and was not
intended to be understood literally.

In *Jenkins* v. *Socialist Worker and Foot* (1977) the material
complained of was headlined: "Spain? Fly me, I'm Clive."

> "Following the exciting electricians' union's scheme for holidays
> in Franco's Spain, disclosed in a recent issue, *Socialist Worker* can
> now reveal that A.S.T.M.S. (Association of Scientific, Technical
> and Managerial Staff) is in hot pursuit.
>
> The new A.S.T.M.S./Pickfords brochure carries a wide variety
> of scintillating cheap holidays in Spain. Best of all, but understand-
> ably slightly more costly, is the package which includes a visit to
> the cells normally occupied by the Carabanchel Ten and a ringside
> seat at the garrotting of Socialist militants.
>
> Your courier on this once-in-a-lifetime trip is none other than
> the genial A.S.T.M.S. general secretary. We understand even more
> exciting treats are in store for next year."

A jury awarded Clive Jenkins, the general secretary, £1,000 libel
damages (and £1,000 copyright damages for the reproduction of
his signature). They also awarded A.S.T.M.S. £100 libel damages
and £1,000 copyright damages (for the reproduction of its
emblem).

The magazine had also produced the following, with Mr. Jen-

kins' facsimile signature: 'Dear Colleagues, You know me, I'm in
the insurance business. I give talks to employers' organisations for
large fees. Well, I'm in the travel business as well. I would love to
take you to Spain, a country ruled by my fellow TUC General
Council member, Franco Chapple. What about it? Fly me, I'm
Clive.''

The jury presumably agreed that readers would believe that
Mr. Jenkins was a travel courier and Mr. Chapple was President of Spain.

The Defences

From a journalist's point of view, because the Press are the
most obvious defendants in libel actions, a knowledge of defamation defences is probably the most vital attribute in writing
safe copy. A clear understanding of exactly how the various
defences work permits potentially defamatory copy to reach
the public and to warn or inform them within the law. It is in
the defences to defamation that the law can be seen striking a
balance between the need to protect an individual's name from
unnecessary slurs and the right of individuals to hold and
express opinions or state facts which, perhaps, need publication.

If Mr. Lewis had succeeded in his action against the *Daily
Telegraph* (and also against the *Daily Mail*), basic information might never have reached the public. The Press would
have been powerless to report police investigations into the
affairs of Mr. John Poulson, to cite one recent example.

There are eight basic defences. The defendant need not rely
on one only: it is quite normal for two defences to be offered
and not unusual for there to be three.

The defences are:
(1) Consent
(2) Accord and satisfaction
(3) Apology and payment into court
(4) Unintentional defamation
(5) Justification (truth)
(6) Absolute privilege
(7) Qualified privilege
(8) Fair comment

(1) Consent (volenti non fit injuria)

A plaintiff in a civil action cannot complain about a matter to which he has consented, either directly or by implication.

> In *Moore* v. *News of the World* (1972), Dorothy Squires gave an interview to a *News of the World* reporter describing her relationship with her former husband, Roger Moore ("The Saint" and latterly "James Bond"). She thought the interview was to publicise her musical come-back. The article was written in the first person and purported to be "by" her "talking to" the reporter.
>
> She claimed she had not used the words in the article and that much of it was fiction and fabrication. She sued for libel and breach of copyright. The major libel allegation was that she was portrayed as a woman ready to wash her dirty linen in public.
>
> She recovered £4,300 when the defence pleas of justification and consent to publication failed.

(2) Accord and satisfaction

This occurs when the plaintiff gives up his cause of action because the defendant has paid an agreed settlement in damages and/or published an apology. As this is an effective contract, the plaintiff cannot later turn round and attempt to pursue the matter.

(3) Apology and payment into court

Created by section 2 of the Libel Act 1843, this defence is used rarely because of technical disadvantages. A simple payment into court has more utility.

The defendant must prove:

(a) the libel was inserted without malice or gross negligence;

(b) before the action began, or at the earliest opportunity afterwards, the defendant inserted in his newspaper or periodical a full apology or — if the publication appears at intervals exceeding one week — has offered to publish the apology in any other newspaper or periodical to be selected by the plaintiff; and

(c) the defendant has paid a sum of money into court for the plaintiff, by way of amends.

This defence can only be used for libels contained in public newspapers and periodicals. It should not be confused with the defence which follows.

(4) *Unintentional defamation*

Some of the foregoing examples must have indicated that a person may be defamed when the maker of the statement is totally innocent. This hardship led to section 4 of the Defamation Act 1952. The section provides a defence where the words are published innocently as defined within the section. The defendant may avoid liability to pay damages if he is willing to publish a correction and apology and to pay for the plaintiff's costs resulting from the publication. The defence's major weaknesses will be discussed after an outline of the requirements.

(1) The defence will only work if the words are published innocently. Innocent publication can occur when:

(a) the publisher did not intend to publish the words about the plaintiff and did not know of circumstances by which they might be understood to refer to him (*cf. Hulton* v. *Jones*); or

(b) the words are not defamatory on the face of them and the publisher did not know of circumstances by which they might be understood to refer to him (*cf. Cassidy* v. *Daily Mirror*); and, in either case,

(c) the publisher exercised all reasonable care in relation to the publication. ("Publisher," meaning any employee or agent of his who was concerned with the contents of the publication.)

To emphasise this first requirement, the defence is *either* no intention to defame *or* no knowledge of defamatory circumstances *plus* no negligence in either case.

(2) If the defendant claims the words were published innocently he may make an offer of amends to the plaintiff which must include an offer to publish or join in publishing a suitable correction and apology.

The offer of amends must be accompanied by an affidavit

which sets out the facts relied on to show innocent publication.

(3) If the offer of amends is accepted then proceedings for defamation in respect of the publication are barred: any question about the steps to be taken in fulfilling the offer can be decided by the court.

(4) If the offer of amends is rejected, the defendant has a valid defence if he can prove:

(a) innocent publication; and

(b) the offer was made as soon as possible after the complaint; and

(c) there was no negligence in the publication; and

(d) if he was not the author of the words complained of, the defendant can prove that the words were written by the author without malice.

(5) In support of the defence of innocent publication, the defendant is limited to the evidence specified in the affidavit which he sends with the offer of amends.

This is a complex defence and the Faulks Committee pointed to certain defects. When it became part of statute law, the object was to avoid the *Hulton* v. *Jones* and *Cassidy* v. *Daily Mirror* situation. Since 1952 there have only been two reported cases of litigation on the meaning of section 4. One was:

Ross v. *Hopkinson* (1956): £200 libel damages were awarded to the actress June Sylvaine (Ross) because her name was used for a character in a novel *The Sugar House*. The author had not taken steps to see whether or not there was someone of this name and, at the time, the actress had a play in the West End.

The criticisms are:

(1) the procedure required involves too much expense and formality. The defendant must collect the evidence and incorporate it in an affidavit which must be served with the offer of amends. This is time-consuming and expensive. It also puts the publisher in a dilemma: if he misses any evidence he cannot use it later because he is playing (in effect) a "sudden death" defence but if he tries to collect every piece of evidence he may need, the court may rule that he did not make the offer as soon as possible.

(2) the burden on the publisher, if he is not the author, to

prove that the author wrote the words without malice is onerous and (in the case of an anonymous letter) almost impossible
to discharge.

There is a further criticism that the Act is unsound in principle. Where the publisher can establish his own innocence, he
should not be precluded from using the defence simply
because he cannot establish that the original author was not
malicious. Although the standard of proof in civil cases is on
the balance of probabilities (more likely than not) rather than
the criminal standard of proof beyond reasonable doubt
(nearly certain), there is still a shift in the burden of proof
towards the defence.

The Faulks Committee, in clause 13 of their draft Defamation Bill, seek changes to make the idea behind section 4 work
properly. They advocate its repeal and replacement with a
more comprehensive section.

What they suggest would dispense with the need for an affidavit, allow argument about the offer of amends to be decided
by the courts, allow the defence to go beyond their original
statement of defence and, finally, abolish the requirement that
a publisher who was not the author of the words should have
to prove that the actual author was not malicious.

(5) *Justification (truth)*

Until July 1975, the defendant had a complete defence if he
could prove that his remarks were true in substance and in fact.
Then the Rehabilitation of Offenders Act 1974 came into
force. Section 8 of this Act states that, in relation to "spent"
criminal convictions, if the plaintiff can show the defendant
revealed such details with malice, the defence of truth fails.

Section 5 of the Defamation Act 1952 provides that:

"In an action for libel or slander in respect of words containing
two or more distinct charges against the plaintiff, a defence of justification shall not fail by reason only that the truth of every charge
is not proved if the words not proved to be true do not materially
injure the plaintiff's reputation having regard to the truth of the
remaining charges."

For example, a man is called a murderer, a cheat and a bad driver. The defence can prove the first two allegations but not the third. Section 5 allows the defence of justification to succeed because the remaining allegation, even though untrue, does not materially injure the plaintiff's reputation (unless he is a professional driver).

However, like section 4 and unintentional defamation, there are flaws in the operation of section 5. The plaintiff is the person who starts the action and, at the moment, he can pick and choose the words which he complains defame him. In the example above, he could leave the allegations of murder and cheating out of his statement of claim and sue solely on the driving allegation. If this kind of tactic were employed, the courts might only award derisory damages. In 1961, however, the House of Lords gave a ruling which comes dangerously close to encouraging the practice.

> *Plato Films* v. *Speidel* (1961): the plaintiff had been Supreme Commander of the Axis Land Forces in Central Europe. The defendants made a film about him which connected him with the murder of King Alexander of Yugoslavia and Monsieur Barthou in 1934 and indicated that he betrayed Field Marshal Rommel in June 1944. These were the points the plaintiff sued on. The bulk of the film, however, dealt with his war crimes and atrocities and the plaintiff did not deny these, or the truth of them, in his statement of claim. The House of Lords held that the defendants could not introduce this evidence either in defence or in mitigation of damages because he had not sued on this broader ground.

The Press Council have stated:

> "Under the law as it stands at present, a plaintiff can bring an action in respect of one untrue defamatory statement which he has selected from a number of others which were true. Plaintiffs do do this (. . . so s.5 does not work). if, however, the plaintiff had chosen to complain of all the defamatory statements, the defendant could rely on the truth of the majority of them to provide a good defence under the section."

As a result of what has been discussed so far in relation to section 5, the Faulks Committee recommend that:

(1) a defendant should be entitled to rely on the whole of the publication in answer to a claim by a plaintiff relating to only

a part of it; and

(2) the defence should not fail because the words complained of (or any other words in the same publication on which the defendant is entitled to rely) are not proved to be wholly true, if having regard to the extent that they are proved to be true they do not materially injure the plaintiff's reputation.

The committee further recommend that the whole defence be renamed "truth" because "justification", as a word, has too many misleading connotations (and the original defence was termed "veritas" which, translated, is truth).

Another statutory provision which enters the area of this defence is section 13 of the Civil Evidence Act 1968. Before this date, a criminal conviction was not even prima facie evidence of a civil plaintiff's guilt. This allowed convicted criminals to sue anyone who referred to their backgrounds and placed upon the defendants the onerous task of collecting up all the criminal trial witnesses and evidence (perhaps after 10 years) to attempt to justify the truth of what they had stated in a civil forum. This section of the Act provides that, in an action for libel or slander where the question of whether a person committed a criminal offence is at issue, proof that he was convicted is conclusive evidence that he did commit it.

As has been noted previously, the effect of this section is now considerably reduced by section 8 of the Rehabilitation of Offenders Act 1974. If the convicted criminal can show any bad motive in revealing his conviction (where spent) this malice will destroy the defence.

The defence, as may be appreciated, sounds solid but has a number of current defects. In addition to those already stated, there are a number of other points which make it an unpopular defence to run on its own.

(a) A writ alleging defamation can (at the moment) be issued any time within six years from the date of publication. Once issued, a writ stays "alive" for a year and a plaintiff could choose to serve it on the defendant 11 months and three weeks after it was first issued. The period allowed for pleadings between the parties may be quite substantial before the action is set down for trial. It would be possible for a period of at least eight years to elapse between the date of first publication and the action appearing in court. During this time, the witnesses the defence may wish to support the plea of truth may die, disappear or have their recollections seriously blurred by the passage of time. A time gap of a year can create serious problems for witnesses under cross-examination: seven more years can be disastrous.

(b) If it is the only defence used, and it fails, the jury may regard the defendant's conduct as reckless and return a verdict for heavier damages.

(c) It is for the jury to decide whether a minor inaccuracy defeats the defence. It is impossible to forecast, in advance, whether they will regard a slight inaccuracy as minor or not.

Some of these defects may be remedied if the Faulks Committee recommendations become law eventually. In particular, the committee has recommended that the time period for bringing an action for defamation should be reduced from six to three years.

As truth has a particular premium in the terms of this defence and in responsible copy generally, the statutory declaration may, on occasions, prove of value. Allegations are easy to make: if there is some substance, the maker of the statements should not object to a procedure which refines the burden of his remarks. Evidence may be taken down in the form of a written statement and drafted out for the informant's consideration. The agreed statement may be taken to a solicitor who, after asking the informant to swear to the truth of the contents, will witness the informant's signature for £1. Additional materials may be attached to the statement for minimal cost.

It is not suggested that this procedure is used regularly but, given substantial revelations, there are the advantages of preventing the source or sources back-tracking and of finding out, before an expensive action based on the truth of the words, what is fact and what is fantasy.

There is the additional advantage of such a declaration being admissible evidence even if the witness dies between publication and an action on the published words.

There are additional dangers in the republication of defamatory matter. Material, the subject of an action, may continue to exist in back numbers unless removed or properly obscured. The basic rule about publication to a third party of defamatory matter about the plaintiff is not avoided simply because there has been an action on the original words.

> *Example:* X is defamed inadvertently. The defence of unintentional defamation is used successfully and an offer of amends, complete with correction and apology, is accepted. The file copies remain unaltered. Eight years later Y sees the original defamatory remarks about X because they have not been removed. The paper cannot plead that it has taken all reasonable care and a second action, based on the republication, could be mounted with success.

Because reporters themselves write, there is a tendency to believe that what others write is the truth. Letters usually express the honest opinions of the writers. A check system is necessary to make certain, however, that the "writers" are bona fide because the newspaper will be liable if the facts stated are incorrect and the writer was motivated by malice. Thorough checking will eliminate most of the hazards in this area. Defamatory allegations are always worth a second look.

(6) *Absolute privilege*

Absolute privilege covers cases in which complete freedom of communication is regarded as so important that, no matter how outrageous or untrue the statement is, there is no legal redress. Qualified privilege, considered later, will also protect the maker of an untrue defamatory statement but only if the maker acted honestly and without malice. Malice has no part to play in the defence of absolute privilege. It is now the only defence with this distinction. Absolute privilege applies to:

(1) Judicial proceedings: anything said as part of the proceedings by the judge, counsel, witnesses or the parties. It does not cover interruptions from the public or other happenings which cannot be construed as part of the proceedings.

(2) Statements made in the course of parliamentary proceedings (*i.e.* Members of Parliament when they speak in a House of Commons debate) and statements contained in the official Reports of Parliamentary Debates (Hansard) by order of either House of Parliament. A newspaper report of a parliamentary debate carries only qualified privilege (see below). It is this privilege and its absolute effect which sometimes leads to Mem-

bers of Parliament being challenged to repeat the remarks "outside the House" (*i.e.* when this privilege does not exist.) It is worth noting that to issue a writ against a Member for remarks made during a parliamentary debate is a breach of parliamentary privilege and a contempt of the High Court of Parliament for which the offender, the defamed person, may be summoned to the Bar of the House for judgment.

(3) Communications between a solicitor and his client (and between counsel). This is known as legal privilege and exists not really for the lawyers but for the parties they represent.

(4) Fair and accurate reports of judicial proceedings, published contemporaneously, from courts within the United Kingdom.

It is this last category which is of primary importance to the Press and the problems and complexities merit detailed consideration. Before the words themselves are analysed, however, the history of this privilege must also be examined because of a number of accidents in its growth.

The origins are in section 3 of the Law of Libel Amendment Act 1888. There was a minor change in the Defamation Act 1952 to allow, rather belatedly, for the advent of radio and television. The net result is that Parliament has provided that "fair and accurate reports in newspapers or on radio or television of judicial proceedings publicly heard in the United Kingdom (if published contemporaneously) shall be privileged."

It is this final word which has created doubt. There is no substantial indication, from case law, as to whether the privilege is absolute or merely qualified.

There have been two reported cases where the courts seem to have assumed that the privilege was absolute (*Farmer* v. *Hyde* (1937) and *McCarey* v. *Associated Newspapers (No. 2)* (1965)). The matter was not argued in either case.

The majority opinion of the leading textbook writers is that the privilege is absolute.

Hansard (June 6, 1888) reveals the intention of Parliament but it is an intention to which the courts cannot refer. When English courts are faced with interpretation and construction of Acts of Parliament they can do little more than look at the enacted words. Matters debated in Parliament prior to the passing of the statute may not be cited to the court. Continental systems differ because all the debates prior to a particular enactment are considered relevant in the judicial interpretation.

The original Bill contained the word "absolutely" and this was deliberately struck out at the Committee stage. The result is that "privilege" stands in the final Act without any adjective.

The Faulks Committee (who recommend the whole situation be clarified by making such reports absolutely privileged) state ". . . that Parliament only meant the privilege to be qualified" and cite the striking out of the critical word as support for this view. They point, however, to two other facts:

(1) Under common law, regardless of the statute, such reports had qualified privilege even if not published contemporaneously. Unless the statute meant the privilege to be absolute, the section was achieving absolutely nothing.

(2) Under section 4 of the 1888 Act, certain reports of public meetings were privileged unless made maliciously. There is no reference to malice in section 3, so the privilege must have been intended to be absolute.

In the years since 1888 there has been no reported case in which it was suggested that a newspaper or broadcast report of United Kingdom judicial proceedings was published maliciously. The current situation is that such reports do carry absolute privilege. If this view is incorrect there is learned support for a declaration to make it correct. Either way, the issue has created no litigation on malice.

To examine the meaning of the key words in the section is the next task. Those words are: fair, accurate and contemporaneous.

Fair. A report is not fair if it does not state both sides of the proceedings before the court. It becomes unfair particularly when prosecution allegations are included in copy without (if they exist) defence rebuttals. The reporter must be aware of the difference between the prosecution outline of what they seek to prove (which is not evidence) and the actual evidence they present. Opening speeches may be used safely, providing that any deficiencies in their claims are noted during the course of a case in the copy: the defence counsel (or defence witnesses) would provide the necessary words. For reasons which will become apparent later, it is suggested that a brief summary of a statement in mitigation (however incredible) is included in copy when the defendant pleads guilty. If the defendant pleads not guilty, at least an outline of his defence must appear or the copy is unsafe.

Accurate. This requirement is, in practice, the one which creates the greatest problems. An inaccuracy, however slight, does destroy the privilege. As will be demonstrated, it is not just the parties and witnesses who appear before the court who may be aggrieved: the net spreads over a wider area.

> *Example:* Jon Sarjeant, a 47 year old labourer, of 132 London Road, Downtown, pleads guilty to a charge of theft before Downtown Magistrates' Court. On the court list he is described as John Sergeant of that address. The reporter used this form in his copy. Unknown to him, there is a John Sergeant who lodges there: he has been defamed (although the defence of unintentional defamation with a correction and apology may be of some avail).

It should be understood as something of critical importance that court lists carry no privilege whatsoever.

Using the same idea but with the reporter asking the clerk of the court for the information which, when given, is erroneous, the problem is still not solved. The information from the clerk, as it is not part of judicial proceedings, carries no privilege.

It is submitted that courts generally have a duty to establish clearly and audibly in public the exact identity of the accused for trial. It is the job of the clerk of the court to do this and to do it in a fashion which leaves no doubt about with whom the magistrates are dealing. Clerks in the courts above this level pose very few problems. It is when the establishment of identity becomes part of the proceedings that the privilege works properly. It does not matter that the accused maliciously says that he lives at an address other than his real one. It is merely sufficient that the reporter accurately reports the address the accused claims to have.

This view is reinforced by a Home Office circular (78/1967), which was recirculated in 1969. Justices' clerks were asked to consider court practice about oral identification of defendants following comments from the Press Council.

> "In many courts, both the name and address of the accused persons are stated in open court and privilege, under section 3 of the Law of

Libel Amendment Act 1888, is thus attracted to reports containing
names and addresses. In some courts, however, only the name of
the accused is mentioned in open court. If the address is not available from other sources, a report containing the name only may
cause hardship or embarrassment to persons of the same name. If
the address is available otherwise than by being mentioned in open
court, no privilege attaches to reports referring to it and a newspaper publishing it must bear the risk that the information was
incorrect. The result may be that in some cases, fortuitously and
without regard to the particular merits of the circumstances,
proper publicity is not given to the results of proceedings which
come before the court. It is one of the purposes of holding criminal
trials in open court that results should be widely known. . . . A person's address is as much a part of his description as his name.
There is, therefore, a strong public interest in facilitating press
reports that correctly describe the person involved.

The Secretary of State is aware that there are difficulties in any
absolute stipulation that addresses are to be mentioned orally, but
. . . in courts where it is not the practice to mention addresses in
open court, the practice could be reconsidered so that newspapers
are not inhibited from reporting accurate descriptions of persons
who come before the court.''

The circular also asked that court lists be made available to the
Press in advance of the proceedings.

What is strange is that the Faulks Committee do not suggest
that court lists should receive privilege. While the information
contained in them varies markedly from court to court, they
are of considerable importance. If the privilege was qualified,
subject to explanation or contradiction, innocently published
errors could swiftly be rectified.

A change in the previous example shows another aspect
where the Press, this time, creates the danger. Certain newspapers have a house rule that the street numbers should not be
included in copy. The truth being stranger than fiction, it is
often the case that there is more than one person with the same
name living in a street. By failing to particularise on the
address, newspapers are taking a dangerous course although
this may be made safer if ages and occupations are always
included in the copy. John Sergeant, the 40 year old insurance
salesman of London Road, Downton, cannot complain validly that people thought he was Jon Sarjeant, the 47-year-old

labourer of London Road.

Perhaps the classic dangers of inaccuracy come from outright misstatement or transposition. To say that a man has been convicted of dangerous driving when the conviction was only for careless driving is defamatory and without defence. The incorrect charge is more serious and inaccurate. There is no defence along the lines of "honest mistake." Transposition merits an example.

Mr A pleads guilty to unlawful possession of a firearm and is fined £50 by Downtown Magistrates' Court. Later in the list Mr. X is committed for trial at Downtown Crown Court on a similar charge.

The published copy has A committed for trial and X fined £50. X can successfully sue because he did not plead guilty and receive a fine and has therefore been defamed. His trial at the crown court has also been prejudiced and the newspaper may be liable, criminally, for this potential contempt.

If the example seems far-fetched, suffice it to say that it has occurred in a situation where the reporter was writing up a number of pieces of short copy from a busy morning's hearings.

Contemporaneity. This means that the report must be published in the first possible edition. For an evening paper, this may mean the following evening, depending on the copy deadlines; for a daily paper it means publication of court copy from the previous day. For a weekly, everything really depends on the day and time of the copy deadline. A weekly, printing on Thursday afternoon, should certainly have Wednesday's court copy included in it, if the copy is to be run at all.

This requirement encourages papers to publish the results of cases as soon as possible. If an individual has pleaded not guilty and is acquitted, he is entitled to have that fact (if it is published at all) published as soon as possible.

As will be seen in qualified privilege, if copy is innocently mislaid and appears slightly late there is still a defence, providing any suggestion of malice on the part of the newspaper can be rebutted. Providing the copy is fair and accurate the newspaper is not left totally defenceless.

Absolute privilege, in relation to what is said in court and reports of what is said, serves a serious purpose. There were suggestions by leading politicians during the early part of 1976 that this privilege should be curtailed. Mr. Jeremy Thorpe suggested that the bench should have power to warn witnesses who make irrelevant and defamatory statements about third parties that their testimony would not be privileged and that the Press should be subject to "certain civilised disciplines."

If witnesses in court proceedings were to lose this protection, the position of the accused person in a criminal trial could be seriously prejudiced. If an individual wished to dispute police evidence with a legitimate attack on prosecution witnesses he might, in the event of a conviction, face a defamation action from the police officers involved.

This could inhibit valid defences and perhaps lead to civil courts having to decide whether, in effect, a person had given perjured evidence. The issue would be for the payment of monetary damages. Some parties would, therefore, have an added interest in making certain that the original prosecution was succesful.

In raw terms, if a police officer planted drugs and could secure a conviction then, if his conduct had been questioned in court, he might gain from a civil action. The reverse flies out from the same Pandora's box. An accused, who is acquitted, might sue prosecution witnesses for what they said about him in the criminal court.

On the privilege attaching to what is said in court (as opposed to reports of court cases), the Faulks Committee recommend no change. The privilege exists as a matter of public policy, and the Committee felt it should not be lightly abandoned or modified.

There is a remedy for any member of the public wishing to contest a defamatory attack in court made in his absence. The Committee state: "It is open to anyone to apply to a court personally or by counsel for leave to make a statement in open court." The court does, however, have a discretion; it would not allow the procedure if the statement would harm the public or be unjust to the parties.

For court reports to have privilege, they must present a fair and accurate index of what took place in court. A reporter is not concerned about the absolute truth of the actual statements. If a newspaper had to check the facts alleged and the bona fides of every speaker in court before publishing testimony, the public would learn nothing.

There is, of course, a genuine hardship created by this privilege. For example:

> Three men appear before the local magistrates for stealing meat from the butchers where they work. They plead guilty but, in mitigation, tell the court they were only indulging in what everyone else in the shop practised. The shop has only three other employees who have not been doing anything criminal. They have been defamed but the accused have absolute protection and so has a newspaper report, providing it is a correct index of what the magistrates heard.

Reporters attend courts as members of the public on behalf of the public. Providing they relay for readers a correct and balanced account of the proceedings, such defamation protection is only logical.

Whether a court case is used is a matter of editorial policy. Many malpractices, actual or threatened, have been revealed by the Press via witness in court cases. To remove protection on allegations and reports of allegations in court could stifle the remarks and the public's awareness of the existence of the accusations. There has been an erosion since the Sexual Offences (Amendment) Act 1976 in that the identities of accused and complainant in rape cases initially may not be revealed but the substance of the allegations may still be revealed to the public from court proceedings.

The trigger for the attacks on the nature of absolute privilege in 1976 was a number of allegations made at a magistrates' court in the West Country by Mr. Norman Scott when he was facing criminal charges relating to social security payments. He alleged that he had had a homosexual relationship with Mr. Jeremy Thorpe.

During the *Poulson* case, attacks had been made on Mr. Reginald Maudling, the late Mr. Anthony Crosland and Lord George-Brown. These individuals, like Mr. Thorpe, were not present at or parties to the proceedings which generated the remarks which, in that instance, related to gifts.

(7) *Qualified privilege*

This privilege protects publications on the occasions outlined below, even if the statements are untrue, providing they are made without malice.

The basic concept of malice has already been discussed. There is one further aspect to be considered — infectious malice.

Infectious malice. If a person states something about another, for example to a reporter, and does so with deliberate spite or ill-will in indefensible defamatory terms, does the speaker's malice "infect" the reporter's innocent use in copy of what he has been told?

There is publication of the defamatory remarks to a third party (the reporter). There is re-publication and therefore a second cause of action when the reporter's copy appears in the newspaper.

The effect of infectious malice has been restricted: it had no part to play in the defence of absolute privilege and was excluded from the defence of qualified privilege in the second of the two cases mentioned below. The problems became evident in 1913.

> In *Smith* v. *Streatfield* (1913), printers were employed by a writer to produce a pamphlet. The pamphlet was circulated among people with a common interest in its contents. It contained statements which defamed the plaintiff and the writer was actuated by malice. This malice, it was held, defeated the defence of qualified privilege for the writer and for the printers when they were both sued.

The case was heavily criticised but judges continued to follow this "tottering authority" until 1965 when the Court of Appeal gave the necessary push (at least so far as qualified privilege is concerned).

> In *Egger* v. *Viscount Chelmsford* (1965), the plaintiff sued the assistant secretary and 10 members of a sub-committee of the Kennel Club for libel. She alleged this was contained in a letter written by the secretary, on the instructions of the committee, to a person interested, professionally, in its contents. The defendants, among other things, pleaded that the letter was written on an occasion of qualified privilege. The plaintiff alleged express malice because some of the committee members had been having rather a personal

dog-fight with her.

The jury found that the secretary and three members of the committee were not activated by any malice but that the other committee members were.

The Court of Appeal held that "a person who, without malice, publishes or takes part in publishing a defamatory statement on an occasion of qualified privilege (is not liable) because the privilege attaches to the individual publisher and not to the publication. ...."

The Appeal Court judges all had different reasons for this conclusion. The Faulks Committee recommend Lord Denning's view, which was:

"If the plaintiff seeks to rely on malice to aggravate damages, or to rebut a defence of qualified privilege, or to cause a comment, otherwise fair, to become unfair, then he must prove malice against each person whom he charges with it. A defendant is only affected by express malice if he himself was actuated by it: or if his servant or agent concerned in the publication was actuated by malice in the course of his employment."

The Faulks Committee recommend that the defences of qualified privilege and fair comment should not fail only because the speaker being reported is not expressing his genuine opinion or is taking improper advantage of the occasion. Particularly on the issue of fair comment this would lead to quite a considerable extension: if the comment appeared to be fair to a reporter in an interview situation then, providing the facts on which the comment was based were correct, malice on the part of the maker of the comment would not destroy the newspaper's defence. It would, of course, leave the maker of the statement open to an action for slander.

In brief, qualified privilege attached to:

(1) reports of parliamentary proceedings;
(2) judicial proceedings;
(3) statements made where there is a legal, moral or social duty;
(4) statements made to protect a trade interest;
(5) situations protected under section 7 of the Defamation Act 1952.

(1) Fair and accurate reports of parliamentary proceedings and extracts from parliamentary reports, papers and votes.

This is the Press privilege in relation to what is reported in Parliament and two cases illustrate its scope.

Wason v. *Walter* (1868): the plaintiff persuaded a member of the House of Lords to attack a judicial appointment on obviously false grounds. The Lord Chancellor, in answer to this attack in the House of Lords, described this tactic (in the actual debate) as a perpetual record of Wason's lying and malice. *The Times* accurately reported his remarks and Wason sued them. The action was dismissed (although the judgments make it clear that the court regarded these proceedings in Parliament as similar to judicial proceedings before any normal court).

Cook v. *Alexander* (1973): the subject matter of the proceedings was a parliamentary sketch in the *Daily Telegraph*. Complaints had been made about the running of an Approved School (Court Lees). The results of a Home Office inquiry were debated in the House of Lords and, during the debate, the Bishop of Southwark revealed that a master at the school, Mr. Cook, had sent boys for corporal punishment for misdemeanours, such as wearing socks in bed. The *Daily Telegraph* sketch concentrated on the Bishop's attack and included rebutting remarks from Lord Longford, describing the attack as monumentally unfair because Mr. Cook could not reply. The sketch concluded with a page reference where the full report of the debate could be read.

There was no evidence of malice and the question to be decided was whether the report was a fair one. The jury decided it was unfair and awarded £1,000 damages.

The Court of Appeal disagreed and decided the sketch was a fair report of the debate, protected by qualified privilege, because, in particular, of the reference to where the full report could be read in the newspaper.

(2) Fair and accurate reports of judicial proceedings which the public may attend.

This common law privilege has already been mentioned in connection with absolute privilege as providing protection if court reports are not published contemporaneously. It is more restrictive here, however, because the public must not have been denied the right of attendance at the proceedings. Further, "judicial" refers to a rather larger category of hearings than those envisaged under absolute privilege, providing the forum is not purely domestic and the public may attend.

This privilege also applies to foreign court proceedings, reported in England, where the subject matter is of legitimate interest to the English public.

Example: X is arrested in France on suspicion of the murder of his wife in France. X is a British subject and the Press interest in the case is that X is suspected merely because the French police cannot find another obvious suspect. In preliminary hearings before an examining magistrate in France, English reporters are permitted to attend but the public, generally, are excluded. The presentations to the examining magistrate are defamatory. Copy based on these proceedings, filed back to England for publication, would have no privilege even though it was fair and accurate.

Where the public may attend and the matter is of legitimate interest to the English reading public, qualified privilege does exist.

Webb v. *Times Publishing Company* (1960): the report here concerned a Swiss court case filed back to London. Donald Hume was charged with murdering a Swiss taxi driver. At his trial, he confessed to murdering a London car dealer, Stanley Setty. Hume had earlier been tried in England for Setty's murder, but acquitted on this charge. At the Swiss court hearing, Hume said he had killed Setty out of jealousy and sawn his body into pieces. Asked if he was married and had a child, Hume replied: "Yes, but it was not mine. The father was Stanley Setty." Mrs. Webb, Hume's former wife, sued for libel alleging that this contemporaneous report meant she had given perjured evidence at Hume's trial in 1950. The court held that *The Times* copy had qualified privilege because the subject matter was of legitimate interest to the English public and the allegation of Setty's fathering of the child was relevant to explanation of the motive behind the killing.

The increasing interchange of nationals of Common Market countries will inevitably lead to a growth in the importance of, and interest in, judicial proceedings heard abroad.

As a general point, qualified privilege is lost if publication of the details (*i.e.* prohibited details in juvenile court copy or from committal proceedings where reporting restrictions are not lifted) is forbidden by law. Salacious detail is restricted by the Judicial Proceedings (Regulation of Reports) Act 1926.

(3) Statements made in pursuance of a legal, moral or social

duty to a person who has a corresponding interest or duty to receive them.

This category covers such matters as employers' references for former employees and to statements made in certain commercial situations.

(4) Statements made to protect or advance an interest to a person with a common duty or interest in receiving the information: the interest at issue may be either private or public (as in the case of remarks made by a shareholder to others about the company's affairs).

(5) Statements privileged under section 7 of the Defamation Act 1952, as elaborated in the Schedule to the Act (Parts 1 and 2).

In this Schedule, Part 1 deals with statements which require no explanation or contradiction if a complaint is made; Part 2 (more extensive and, from the Press point of view, more important) covers situations where, for the privilege to be gained, a reasonable statement by way of explanation or contradiction must be given to the complainant if requested.

Part 1: Fair and accurate reports privileged without explanation or contradiction

This category includes reports from dominion courts, international courts, courts-martial held overseas and, in particular, "fair and accurate copies of or extracts from any register kept in pursuance of any Act of Parliament which is open to inspection by the public, or of any other document which is required by the law of any part of the United Kingdom to be open to inspection by the public."

This latter category includes extracts made from registers at Companies House, birth, marriage and death certificates and the like.

Part 2: Fair and accurate reports privileged subject to explanation or contradiction

This is the only area of English law to recognise the "right of reply" concept which has been considerably developed in America.

Reports within the following situations loose their privilege if the defendant unreasonably refuses a request to publish the reasonable statement indicated above. (An aggressive letter from a plaintiff's solicitor stating that, unless an apology was made, a writ would be issued was held not to be a sufficiently "special request": *Khan* v. *Ahmed* (1957).)

(a) A fair and accurate report of the findings or decision of any of the following associations, their committees or governing bodies, if the association:

(i) promotes or encourages art, science, religion or learning:

(ii) promotes or safeguards the interests of any trade, business, profession or industry or the people engaged there in; or

(iii) promotes or safeguards the interests of any game, sport or pastime carried on in public.

(b) A fair and accurate report of proceedings at any United Kingdom public meeting. A public meeting is defined as one held lawfully and in good faith for a lawful purpose for the furtherance or discussion of any matter of public concern. Admission to the meeting may be general or restricted.

The effect of this final specification allows meetings to be "public" even though tickets are required or certain groups are deliberately excluded from the meeting

(c) A fair and accurate report of the proceedings at any meeting or sitting in the United Kingdom of:

(i) any local authority or its committee;

(ii) any commission, tribunal, committee or person appointed for the purposes of any inquiry by statute or by the Administration;

(iii) any magistrate or magistrates acting otherwise than as a court exercising judicial authority;

(iv) any person appointed by a local authority to hold a local inquiry in pursuance of any statute; or

(v) any other tribunal, board, committee or body set up or acting under statute

providing that, in these cases, the admission of the Press and public to the meeting is not denied.

If a local authority or its committee resolves to exclude the Press and public under the Public Bodies (Admission to Meetings) Act 1960 or a planning inquiry decides to take evidence in private then such matter, if known, is not protected by this type of qualified privilege (though truth and fair comment might be of assistance).

(d) A copy or fair and accurate report or summary of any notice or information for the public issued by or on behalf of any government department, officer of state, local authority or chief officer of police. This includes statements made by the clerk of a local authority to the Press if he is acting for the council, and information gained on police "calls" if it is authorised (rather than off the record).

(e) A fair and accurate report of the proceedings at a general meeting of any public company.

It must be born in mind that this form of qualified privilege does have the additional requirement of entitling a person defamed, say, at a council meeting (and, in particular, in the newspaper's report of that meeting) to space, to explain or contradict what was reported of the defamatory remarks.

For instance:

There is a meeting of Downtown District Council's Sports and Recreation Committee. X is the chairman. A youth club in the town is organising a trip to Unterstadt, Downtown's German twin town. X indicates that he thinks the Council should be represented and suggests that he accompanies the club members.   Y, a member of the committe, interrupts and says: "The basic idea is good . . . but I don't think you should be the one to go."

X asks him why.

Y then states: "If you really want to know, I don't think someone with a conviction for indecent assault where a child was involved is the kind of person we want representing Downtown abroad. . . ."

Before a vote is taken to exclude the press and public and before a resolution to this effect is moved, X turns to the press bench and says: "Don't print a word of this. I'll sue anyone who suggests I'm a queer. This is scandalous. . . ."

The Press are later informed that Z will be going to Germany with the youth club.

Ethical considerations apart, there is qualified privilege on a

fair and accurate account of the meeting until the vote is taken
to exclude the Press and public. Y may or may not have slan-
dered X: his position is considered in the case which follows.
So far as the newspaper is concerned, providing X is permitted
space to explain or contradict Y's allegation and providing X
cannot prove malice against the newspaper, there is full protection from qualified privilege.

Y's position is a little more complex. Common law qualified privilege attaches to statements made in pursuance of a
legal, moral or social duty to people who have a corresponding
interest or duty to receive them. It is this aspect of privilege
which protects people like councillors, when speaking as
such, providing their remarks are not made maliciously.

The following case hinged on whether a councillor, who
defamed another during a meeting, had been malicious. The
malice alleged was recklessness about the truth or falsity of the
allegations he made.

Horrocks v. *Lowe* (1974): In 1961, Bolton Borough Council
bought a plot of land from a company of which Horrocks was the
chairman and majority shareholder. The sale was subject to a condition that the land would be left as open space. In 1968, when Horrocks was chairman of the Council's Finance and Management
Committee, (and a member of the Conservative majority in the
Council), the land was leased to Bolton Conservative Club for 99
years as a site for them to construct a club house. When the building was almost complete, the restriction on the use of the land was
re-discovered. The building had to be abandoned and the Council
had to pay £17,500 compensation.

The situation can be viewed diagrammatically. (See p. 40.)

Lowe, a former mayor, and an alderman member of the Council
with the Labour minority attacked Horrocks' position at a Council meeting (at which Horrocks was not present) as follows: "I
don't know how to describe his attitude, whether it was brinkman-
ship, megalomania or childish petulance. . . . I suggest he has misled the Committee, the leader of his party and his political and
club colleagues, some of whom are his business associates. I therefore request that he be removed from the committee. . . ."

Lord Denning M.R., in the Court of Appeal, gives a little of the
background. "Mr. Lowe went to the town clerk's office to obtain
information. He was given a timetable giving the dates of the letters that had passed between the borough solicitor and Mr. Hor-

Land Development & Building Ltd.
(Chairman: Horrocks) sells the
plot of land to Bolton Council
but retains a restrictive covenant

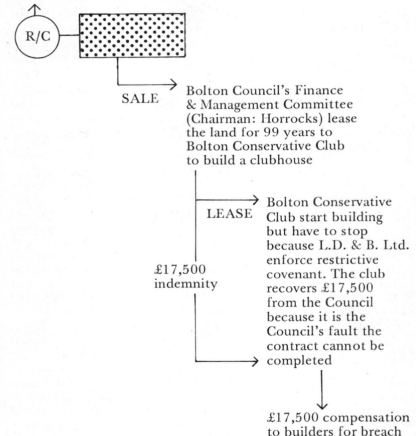

SALE

Bolton Council's Finance
& Management Committee
(Chairman: Horrocks) lease
the land for 99 years to
Bolton Conservative Club
to build a clubhouse

LEASE

£17,500
indemnity

Bolton Conservative
Club start building
but have to stop
because L.D. & B. Ltd.
enforce restrictive
covenant. The club
recovers £17,500
from the Council
because it is the
Council's fault the
contract cannot be
completed

£17,500 compensation
to builders for breach
of contract

rocks' solicitor: he was not shown the actual letters; nor was he told of their contents. He was only given the dates. He used this material to prepare notes for his speech. At the meeting, Mr. Lowe kept closely to his notes. Most of his speech was factually accurate. But he used words which were defamatory of Mr. Horrocks."

The local paper reported the meeting and used some of the remarks from the meeting. Horrocks issued a writ against Lowe claiming damages for slander and another writ against the paper alleging libel.

From a close inspection of the Court of Appeal judgment, it appears that the newspaper did not claim qualified privilege but, instead, argued that the words they actually printed were not defamatory. The claim against them was dismissed by the High Court judge, who tried the action, but it is difficult to understand why they did not rely on their section 7, Part 2 privilege. Compliance with the defence would have saved them a court appearance at all. Instead they chose a longer and more risky method which, in the event, was successful.

Mr. Lowe's defence was one of qualified privilege (as previously discussed) together with the defences of justification and fair comment. The judge held that the words were defamatory, that they were not justified but that the occasion was privileged. He found that the defendant was guilty of express malice (defeating the defence of qualified privilege) but did not rule on the issue of fair comment. This latter defence would have failed anyway because the facts on which Lowe commented were apparently incorrect and the defence of justification failed because of this.

The trial judge found expressly that "Mr. Lowe believed and still believes that everything he said was true and justifiable ..." but that, because of his anxiety to have Horrocks removed from the Management and Finance Committee, his state of mind was one of "gross and unreasoning prejudice." He ordered the defendant, who conducted his own case, to pay £400 damages.

The House of Lords affirmed the Court of Appeal decision to reverse the result of the case. They held that as the defendant believed that everything he said was true, there could be no express malice.

There is, however, an important difference between the

House of Lords' judgment (in the main from Lord Diplock)
and statements in the Court of Appeal from Lord Denning.
  Lord Denning said:

> "It is accepted that the occasion was privileged. It is of the first
> importance that the members of a local authority should be able to
> speak their minds freely on a matter of interest in the locality. So
> long as they honestly believe what they say to be true, they are not
> to be made liable for defamation. They might be prejudiced and
> unreasonable. They may not get their facts right. They may give
> offence to others. But so long as they are honest, they go clear. No
> councillor should be hampered in his criticisms by fear of an
> action for slander. He is not to be forever looking over his shoulder
> to see if what he says is defamatory. He must be allowed to give his
> point of view, even if it is hotly disputed by others. This is essential
> for free discussion. The one qualification on his freedom is that he
> must not be actuated by malice ... he is not to be held malicious
> merely because he was angry or prejudiced, even unreasonably prej-
> udiced, against the plaintiff so long as he honestly believes what he
> said to be true. Such is the law as I have always understood it to be."

In the House of Lords, Lord Diplock was not quite so enthu-
siastic about the clarity of the issue. He said:

> "The judgment of Lord Denning has been criticised in your Lord-
> ships' House as being based upon too broad a proposition of law.
> It is true that there are passages in this *extempore* judgment which
> might be read as suggesting that where on a privileged occasion a
> defendant publishes defamatory statements which he believes to be
> true he can only loose the protection of privilege on proof that he
> was actuated by personal spite against the person defamed. But the
> Court of Appeal were not embarking on a general exposition of the
> law of privilege in actions for defamation. Their attention was con-
> centrated upon the particular facts of the instant case as they had
> been found in the judgment of Stirling J. Upon those facts, the
> Court of Appeal's decision that Mr. Lowe's belief, that everything
> he said was true, entitled him to succeed on his defence of privilege,
> was in my view correct."

It becomes evident, from a later passage of Lord Diplock's judgment, that the major piece of "malice" relied on by Stirling J.,
was Mr. Lowe's refusal to apologise to Mr. Horrocks two days
after the meeting. The House of Lords regarded this as too trivial and insignificant. Lord Diplock concluded:

"However prejudiced the judge thought Mr. Lowe to be, however irrational in leaping to conclusions unfavourable to Mr. Horrocks, this crucial finding of Mr. Lowe's belief in the truth of what he said upon that privileged occasion entitles him to succeed in his defence of privilege."

The various judgments in the case create a slight conflict. No apology is made for quoting from the case extensively: it is from these words and this type of reasoning that the law emerges, develops and changes in emphasis. Lord Diplock states that the Court of Appeal was not "embarking on a general exposition of the law of privilege in actions for defamation" but it would appear that this, in fact, was the case. Lord Denning's remarks may have been *obiter dicta* (words spoken by the way rather than direct findings, which are known as *rationes decidendi*) but they may have more force than Lord Diplock is prepared to concede.

The Faulks Committee have a recommendation with a bearing on this case. They state:

"Under the present law a plea of qualified privilege will be defeated if the plaintiff can establish that the defendant was actuated by malice in making the publication complained of. The essence of malice in this context is that the defendant took improper advantage of the occasion which gave rise to the qualified privilege by making statements which he did not believe to be true, or for the purpose of venting his spite or ill-will towards the plaintiff. We, therefore, recommend an amendment of the law providing that a defence of qualified privilege shall be defeated if the plaintiff proves that the defendant, in making the publication complained of, took improper advantage of the occasion giving rise to the privilege."

Shortly after *Horrocks* v. *Lowe* was concluded in the House of Lords, Mars-Jones J., hearing a defamation action, developed the law in relation to qualified privilege in another direction.

The status of remarks made after a meeting, the substance of which attracted common law qualified privilege, had been uncertain. If a speaker at the meeting has apparently made defamatory remarks but, because of the acoustics or interruptions, the reporter is unable to hear exactly what they were, does the privilege from the meeting extend to explanations

and repetition after the meeting to clear up doubts about what
was said?

It is an important point. The newspaper's statutory qualified privilege only covers reports of such meetings if the report
is fair and accurate. A newspaper account of apparently defamatory remarks which were, in fact, misheard would have no
protection at all within qualified privilege. The report would
be neither fair nor accurate.

In this case, two former local government officers brought a
defamation action against a councillor. They alleged that the
councillor had called one of them a liar during debate and then
repeated the remark to a reporter after the meeting.

The judge held that common law qualified privilege did
extend to remarks after the meeting made in response to reporters' questions to check the accuracy of their notes.

The judgment in this unreported case is limited. It relates
only to the checking of what was said, not to a broadening of
allegations and additional defamatory material. It is a first
instance decision but of sufficient status to create a precedent
unless another High Court judge can find a legitimate way of
avoiding or distinguishing the judgment or unless the Court
of Appeal or House of Lords subsequently overrule the decision.

Mars-Jones J. appears to have adopted an eminently sensible approach in his direction to the jury. To have held otherwise would have been to discourage accuracy at the expense of
technicality.

The Committee also recommend that qualified privilege
should be extended to Common Market courts and tribunals,
to Press conferences, to company matters generally and to
reports of foreign courts generally.

It was argued before the committee that there should be a
special statutory privilege for reports or statements where:

(1) the matter is of public interest; and

(ii) the publisher believes the statement of fact to be true; and

(iii) the publisher exercises all reasonable care in relation to
the facts; and

(iv) in so far as the publication consists of comment the comment is capable of being supported by any facts which the
publisher believes to be true after exercising all reasonable care

to establish their truth and the comment is made is good faith.

This defence approximates to a combination of fair comment (see next topic) and the existing statutory defence of unintentional defamation, but without the requirements for a correction and apology.

The arguments for this statutory privilege were rejected. It would have put the Press in a special position whereby there would have been a right to publish false defamatory "facts" which ultimately turned out to be without foundation. Such a situation could arguably have been more damaging to the Press in the long run than beneficial. A free Press could have become a protected and slightly irresponsible Press, against which aggrieved persons had little or no remedy.

Lord Goodman, the then Chairman of the Newspaper Publishers Association, crystallised the matter:

> "A great newspaper, if it believes that some villainy ought to be exposed, should expose it without hesitation and without regard to the law of libel. If the editor, his reporters and advisers are men of judgment and sense, they are unlikely to go wrong; but if they do go wrong, the principle of publish and be damned is a valiant and sensible one for a newspaper and it should bear this responsibility. Publish and let someone else be damned, is a discreditable principle for a free press."

This defence would also have forced the Press to reveal their sources so that the bona fides of their informants could be ascertained. The Press Council commented: "It could be, therefore, that if the law required the disclosure of sources in order for a newspaper to avail itself of this defence, the defence would be generally ineffective."

(8) *Fair comment*

The defence of fair comment protects expressions of opinion on any matter of public interest. The defence probably originated in the late eighteenth century and is now recognised as an essential element for basic freedom of speech. As will become apparent, it is one of the most misleadingly-named defences and, on this particular point, the Faulks Committee recommend changes which would bring the substance of the defence into line with its title (they recommend a title of "comment"). Of the common law defences to defamation this one, especially, has an encrustation of technical components and has suffered, over the years, from heavy and not particularly worthy defence by-pass techniques. The substance of the defence has been preserved by the judges and is of use to the individual as much as to the Press.

There are four elements to the defence which will be outlined and then examined separately in more detail.

(1) The opinion expressed must be fair (*i.e.* one that an honest, though prejudiced, man could hold, however violent or exaggerated his views are). The word "fair" is misleading and "honest comment" is a more accurate reflection of the substance of this defence.

(2) It must be comment (opinion) rather than pure fact. For stated facts, the defendant would plead justification. But the "facts" on which the comment is based must be correct. There is no protection for comments based on incorrect or misapprehended facts. The "facts" relied on must have been known to the defendant when he made the comment.

(3) The subject matter of the comment must be of public interest. It is up to the judge to decide whether or not something is of public interest. The judicial test is "could the public legitimately be interested in the matter."

(4) The defendant must not have published the comments maliciously.

"Fair" The test is not whether the comment is correct nor is it necessary for the court to agree with it.

> "Mere exaggeration, or even gross exaggeration, would not make the comment unfair. However wrong the opinion expressed may be in point of truth or however prejudiced the writer, it may still be within the prescribed limit. The question which the jury must consider is this: 'Would any fair man, however prejudiced he may be, however exaggerated or obstinate his views, have said that which this criticism has said of the work which is criticised?'" (An extract from the judgment of Lord Esher M.R. in *Merivale* v. *Carson* (1887).)

The defence, therefore, protects unfair comments (if an objective test is used) and this is an initial confusion which is no longer justified. It is for this reason that the Faulks Committee want the defence to be re-named "Comment" although the requirements of this first test would remain unaltered.

An example of the kind of comment permitted comes from:

> Levene v. News of the World (1972): X was convicted of rape. The newspaper described him as a "vicious pest" who had subjected his victim to a "night of terror." X sued, unsuccessfully. Mr Justice Melford Stevenson said: "It would be a sad day if newspapers were forbidden to publish, and comment on, matters of public interest and the facts leading to important convictions. They are entitled to comment provided they do so fairly and without malice."

But, in Brooks v. I.P.C. Newspapers (1974), this plea (allied with justification) failed in relation to an article describing a solicitor who spanked women's bottoms as a "public menace." The plaintiff, however, recovered only contemptuous damages of ½p.

Comment v. Facts. The defence must establish that the facts (if any) on which the comments are based are true. Such facts may exist in the copy or be implicit from the headline. An example of untrue "facts" in the copy destroying the defence came recently in the following case:

> Bernstein v. Observer Ltd (1976): The Observer's City Editor had written a piece about Lord Bernstein headlined "The £25 million Barranquilla Scandal." The article said that, in recent years, parcels of shares in Barranquilla Investments had "moved across the City landscape with the smoothness of well-guided chips across a poker table . . . since Lord Bernstein joined the game with gusto in 1962 . . . the net apparent worth of Barranquilla shares had soared from under £5 million to £25 million"; and that "the ordinary investor . . . has as much chance of the action as he has of hitting the jackpot on Ernie . . . because the big boys have got all but 3.4 per cent. of Barranquilla's share capital tied up. Lord Bernstein now owns 64.2 per cent. through his master company, Granada Group, as well as having the lion's share of the 7.4 per cent. personally owned by the Barranquilla board. . . ." Lord Bernstein was portrayed in the article as a gambler, who had succeeded in getting into his hands or control, nearly all the share capital of Barranquilla to h so that the average investor had no chance of sharing in it. The defence argument was that the words were not defamatory: it had merely been asserted that, within a company, there were too

many shares in too few hands so that the average investor was frozen out.

The words of Lord Denning, when the *Observer* appealed against damages of £35,000 awarded by the jury, put the points concisely:

"It (is) essential that a newspaper must get its facts right. Here the newspaper had failed utterly. Lord Bernstein personally did not own a single Barranquilla share. The Granada company itself owned 64.2 per cent, but it was not Lord Bernstein's company at all. Nor was he the master of it. He was chairman but he personally owned less than one per cent. of the voting shares of the Granada Group. He did not own Granada or Barranquilla. The trustees of his children's trust owned 7.4 per cent. All the assertions were proved to be wrong."

A more complex case, involving a fact implicit in a headline, comes from:

Kemsley v. *Foot* (1952): In an article in the *Tribune* headlined "Lower than Kemsley" by Michael Foot, the copy ran: "The prize for the foulest piece of journalism perpetrated in this country for many a long year, and that is certainly saying something, must go to Mr. Herbert Gunn, editor of the *Evening Standard,* and all those who assisted him in the publication of an attack on John Strachey last week." The article proceeded with a savage attack on the *Evening Standard,* a paper with which Viscount Kemsley had no connection at all, although he was a well-known proprietor of other newspapers. Kemsley alleged that the words meant (in the headline and with the copy) that he used his position as a director of newspaper companies to force the publication of statement he knew to be false and that the headline suggested his name was a byword for this kind of action.

The House of Lords held that the defence of fair comment was open to Foot because, in the circumstances, the conduct of the Kemsley Press as publishers was sufficiently indicated as a fact on which comment was made. If the jury found the comment could have been made by an honest, though prejudiced man, the defence would succeed.

An example of the requirement that the comment must be made on facts known to the maker is:

Cohen v. *Daily Telegraph* (1968): the newspaper had commented on the "sad state of affairs" of a company. When sued, it was unable to use the defence of fair comment in relation to this remark and a later resolution to put the company into liquidation. The resolution came after the newspaper's comment.

A problem occurs when there is a suggestion of dishonourable or corrupt motives. If Lord Esher's test was allowed its full force, when defamatory facts are correctly stated, then imputations on motive by way of comment, if honestly believed, should also be protected.

> *Example*: Z, a well-known opponent of apartheid, accepts a job as a columnist on a paper noted for its support of South African policies. Y writes an article which states that the high salary offered to Z for the job was sufficient inducement to make a hypocrite out of the man.

The current state of the law is that a man's conduct may be open to ridicule but if it is suggested that he acted dishonourably or corruptly then the jury must decide:

(a) whether the defendant had an honest belief in what he said; and

(b) whether this belief was correct in fact.

In the example above, Y would only succeed with the defence of fair comment if he could prove Z had, in fact, acted dishonourably.

The double hurdle in this area mixes the nature of the defence. It requires first that a subjective test be applied and then sets this against an objective test. This creates a conflict which is not only confusing but undesirable and moves the defence closer to the requirements of justification.

The Faulks Committee recommend that only (a) above should be necessary for the defence to succeed. The plaintiff would only win if he could prove that this was not the genuine opinion of the defendant.

There is a statutory provision which enters this area: section 6 of the Defamation Act 1952. This provides:

> "In an action for libel or slander in respect of words consisting . . . partly of expression of opinion, a defence of fair comment shall not fail by reason only that the truth of every allegation is not proved if the expression of opinion is fair comment having regard to such of the facts alleged or referred to in the words complained of as are proved."

The defect in this situation is similar to that already discussed in relation to section 5 and the defence of justification. It will only work if the plaintiff complains about the whole of the article: if he chooses selectively, the defendant faces some problems.

To correct any ambiguity, the Faulks Committee recommend:

> "In an action for defamation in respect of words including or consisting of expression of opinion, a defence of comment shall not fail by reason only that the defendant has failed to prove the truth of every relevant assertion of fact relied on by him as the foundation for the opinion, provided that such of the said assertions as are proved to be true are relevant and afford a foundation therefore."

Public interest. Matters which the judge may rule are within this topic range from the conduct of the Prime Minister to the administration of the local flower show committee. What is vital is that the subject is one in which the public may be legitimately interested and this will vary from factual situation to situation. An affair between a married man and a woman is not, on the face of it, something the public could legitimately be interested in: if the man is a local councillor, given to making statements about the sanctity of marriage and the family, the situation changes.

Malice. The spite, ill-will or bad motive may be obvious:

> *Thomas* v. *Bradbury Agnew* (1906): *Punch* used a review of Thomas's book which was savage. The review appeared as a separate article in the body of the magazine. It was more of an attack on the author than on what he had written and the writer of the review, a man called Lucy, showed his extreme dislike of Thomas before the jury at the trial. Thomas was awarded £300 damages: the malice was obvious.

It is not sufficient for the plaintiff to show a general ill-will between the defendant and himself : he must actually show that the article complained of was positively actuated by malice. Thomas could do this in the case cited above.

> *Lyon* v. *Daily Telegraph* (1943): the newspaper published a letter

criticising radio comedies involving the Lyon family generally and the plaintiff in particular. The letter was signed "A. Winslow" from an address at "The Vicarage, Wallingford Road, Winchester." There was no such place in Winchester, neither was there an "A. Winslow" in Crockford's *Clerical Directory*. The Court of Appeal held that the comment itself was fair and that malice was not established simply because the author did not sign his correct name.

The Faulks Committee recommend that the word "malice" should no longer be used in relation to this defence. They prefer the idea of a "genuine" expression of opinion (or proof that the opinion expressed was not genuine). The plaintiff would need to show that the comment was not the defendant's honestly held belief and also give particulars of why he alleges this, before the trial.

Juries in Defamation Actions

In civil actions generally, juries are the exception rather than the rule. They are not used unless:
(a) there is an allegation of fraud in a civil case; or
(b) it is a defamation action.
The Faulks Committee heard arguments for retaining jury trials in defamation actions and for their abolition. These arguments are summarised below:

Retain Juries	*Abolish Juries*
1. Jury made up of all sorts whereas judge has narrow experience.	Judge better at giving legal reasons for his decision and can build up steady precedents.
2. Jury represents ordinary, reasonable people: judge rather isolated from slang expressions.	Jury too emotional about trivial factors: judge can understand technicalities.
3. Jury better at assessing whether someone's honour and integrity has been damaged.	The law in this area is so complex that juries can rarely understand what is going on.

4. Jury service brings the public into the law and jury verdicts are more publicly acceptable.

If the plaintiff has a weak case he will be told that he is more likely to succeed with a jury than before a single judge. The results of jury trials are unpredictable.

5. A jury's decision is anonymous but a single judge's is personal.

A jury's award of damages will be higher than a judge's award because of their inexperience in assessing damages.

6. Juries fight for the man in the street.

Jury trial is more expensive because it is more lengthy than trial before a single judge.

7. Losers more often accept jury verdicts and, because they do not give reasons for their decisions, the possibilities of expensive appeals are lessened.

Non-jury trial by agreement in defamation actions increasing and juries too often assume that admitted antagonism between the parties equals malice.

A variety of solutions were put forward.
(a) Trial by jury should be at the discretion of the court; or
(b) as above, but only in cases where public figures or public servants are involved; or
(c) the jury's duty should be limited to deciding whether the case is proved or not, without assessing the damages; or
(d) jury trials should be abolished completely; or
(e) defamation actions should be tried by a judge alone, sitting with lay accessors; or
(f) leave things as they are.
The committee recommend (a) and (c). In other words, trial by jury in defamations actions should be at the discretion of the court and, if allowed, the jury's function should be limited to deciding liability, not the actual amount of damages to be awarded. Juries should, if they find for the plaintiff, add riders that the damages should be substantial, moderate, nominal or contemptuous and leave it up to the judge to fix the amount within these categories. If a jury trial is refused, there should be an appeal as of right against this decision to the Court of Appeal.

This recommendation will be the subject of renewed debate if the proposals move towards actual legislation. As a former Lord Chancellor, Lord Gardiner, told the committee: "English is a living language and juries know better than judges, I am sure, what words mean."

The topicality of this subject was reinforced by two cases in 1976. In the first, already discussed under the defence of fair comment, Lord Bernstein was awarded £35,000 by a jury and the Court of Appeal upheld this as an award which a reasonable jury could have determined. In the second, *Savalas* v. *Associates Newspapers Ltd.*, a jury awarded the actor in the television series "Kojak" £34,000.

> In this case, the *Daily Mail* had described Savalas as "a big amiable beast of a man" and a former bit-part actor who could not cope with super-stardom. The report stated that Berlin night-life with Mr. Savalas's "slightly unsavoury ensemble" of cronies and girls led him to forget his lines on the set the next day and keep James Mason, his co-star, waiting.
>
> Savalas, while admitting his life was that of an extrovert, claimed that important film producers, who read this article, thought his capability as an actor might have diminished. He had not, in particular, ever kept his co-star waiting.
>
> The jury's award was followed by a letter to *The Times* by the foreman of the jury. He indicated that the jury panel, having found the allegations proved as defamatory, had no clear idea of how to assess the amount to award the plaintiff.

Exemplary damages

There is another aspect of defamation damages — the awarding of punitive or "exemplary" damages — which needs some exploration.

If the defendant has published defamatory matter with the calculated intention of making a profit it is open to the jury, in addition to the amount awarded to the plaintiff for the injury to his reputation, to fix an additional amount to penalise the defendant for his conduct. This is almost in the nature of a fine.

There has been considerable legal argument about the judicial rationale behind permitting "fines" in an area of civil law.

The matter came to a head in the case of:

> Broome v. *Cassell* (1972): in a book *The Destruction of Convoy P.Q. 17,* the author described the disaster which befell a convoy sailing for Russia during the Second World War. The author had been warned by authoritative sources that passages in the book were defamatory but he took the view that it was possible to say "some pretty near the knuckle things" about the plaintiff and others "but if one says it in a clever enough way, they cannot take action."
>
> The manuscript was rejected by one publishing house. Cassells took it on knowing of the rejection and libel dangers. They published the book, advertising it as a sensational interpretation of a naval disaster.
>
> The trial jury awarded the plaintiff £15,000 compensatory damages and £25,000 exemplary damages.
>
> Cassells and the author appealed but the House of Lords held that exemplary damages could be awarded when the defendant's conduct was calculated to make a profit which might well exceed the compensation payable as normal damages.

In defamation, to fall within this rule, the plaintiff had to show that the defendant (1) knew the proposed course was against the law or was reckless about this; and (2) decided to continue because the material advantages outweighed the possible material loss.

The Faulks Committee recommend that such damages should not be possible in defamation actions.

The Whitford Committee, which examined the law of copyright and reported in 1977 (see the section on Copyright) felt that exemplary damages should be retained for deliberate and profitable breaches of copyright.

It remains to be seen what Parliament will do with either or both recommendations.

Legal aid

Legal aid is not available to mount a defamation action. It is the only area of law bearing this restriction. The reasons, restated in 1967, are basically:

(1) too many trivial claims would appear and the increased burden on the legal aid scheme would be unsupportable;

(2) it would encourage slander actions brought by plaintiffs against defendants from similar backgrounds so both parties would qualify for legal aid and the chances of recovering damages would be slight.

The effect of this restriction is to make defamation actions, if not a rich man's sport, then at least a rather exclusive area of legal battling. It is only proper that the court room should be the place of final resort, when the parties cannot agree to any settlement or compromise. The possession of personal capital to brief expensive counsel and extract, perhaps, a sizeable settlement from a newspaper because full trial costs are near prohibitive should not, however, be the prerogative of one particular segment of society. The man in the street is used as the notional guide as to whether words are defamatory. It seems strange that the law, through jury service, permits him to express his view of the meaning of words in respect of other people but effectively discourages him from bringing an action if the words are actually used about him.

The Committee recommend a change to allow for legal aid in defamation and injurious falsehood applications. The aid should be limited, at first, to obtaining a barrister's opinion of the law involved and, if this is favourable, a second opinion should be obtained about the merits of the case at the close of pleadings. Further action should depend on the second opinion. Linked with the proposal is a recommendation to change the costs involved in defamation actions where less than £1,000 is claimed as damages.

At the moment, the county courts cannot hear defamation actions unless, in rare situations, the High Court transfers such an action or both parties agree to a county court trial. Costs are lower in the county court, trial by jury is extremely rare and the court is normally geographically convenient to both parties (particularly in the case of a local newspaper and an aggrieved reader).

Significant is the following statement from the Committee:

"It has been suggested to us that neither circuit judges nor solicitors in the provinces have the necessary experience to deal with defamation proceedings. We doubt the validity of this contention

but, even if it has some force, we think it most desirable that exper-
tise in the law of defamation should be widened in legal professional circles."

The cost of providing legal aid for the less expensive county
court actions could be lower. The limitation of the initial
claim to under £1,000 would encourage realistic pre-trial settlements in appropriate cases.

The Committee also recommend a process to allow compli-
cated cases involving difficult points of law or requiring a
lengthy trial to be transferred to the High Court.

Summary of the Faulks Committee Report
on the Law of Defamation (Cmnd. 5909)

The following is a summary of some of the major changes or
clarifications recommended by the Faulks Committee. While
unlikely to be implemented speedily, the recommendations
themselves provide an undercurrent of possible change which
emphasises existing anomalies and which may have hidden
practical effects.

(1) There should be a statutory definition for defamation:
"Defamation shall consist of the publication to a third party of
matter which in all the circumstances would be likely to affect
a person adversely in the estimation of reasonable people
generally."

(2) The distinction between libel and slander in civil actions
should be abolished. The rules for libel should govern both
forms of action.

(3) The defence of justification should be renamed truth. A
defendant should be entitled to rely on the whole publication
in answer to a plaintiff suing on only part of it (to remove the
anomaly of *Plato Films* v. *Spiedel*): the defence should not fail
because the words are not proved to be wholly true if, in respect
of their truth, they do not materially injure the plaintiff's reputation.

(4) The defence of fair comment should be renamed comment. "Malice" should no longer be described as a factor
which may defeat the defence: instead, the defence should not

succeed if the plaintiff can prove the comment did not represent the defendant's genuine opinion. The requirement of quasi-justification in cases where improper or bad motives are imputed should be abolished.

(5) Fair, accurate and contemporaneous reports of court proceedings in the United Kingdom should be declared to have absolute privilege (because, at present, such reports only have "privilege" under the Law of Libel (Amendment) Act 1888).

(6) "Malice" in qualified privilege should be abolished and replaced with an allegation that the defendant was taking improper advantage of the occasion giving rise to the privilege. Qualified privilege should be extended to cover press conferences.

(7) Words transmitted live from Parliament should have absolute privilege. Pictures, and words transmitted otherwise, should have qualified privilege.

(8) Comment should not fail as a defence only because the publisher (as a defendant) has published something which is proved not to be the writer's genuine opinion: qualified privilege should not fail only because the publisher has published something which is proved to have been stated by the maker of the statement when taking improper advantage of the occasion which has privilege.

(9) Unintentional defamation, as a defence, should be adjusted so that:

(a) affidavits are unnecessary;

(b) disputes over offers of amends may be settled by the court;

(c) unaccepted offers do not amount to admissions of liability;

(d) the requirement that a publisher, who was not the author of the words complained of, must prove that the words were written by the actual author without malice should be abolished.

(10) Awards of punitive or exemplary damages in defamation actions should be abolished (thus, by an Act of Parliament, overruling *Broome* v. *Cassell*).

(11) Actions for defamation should survive against the estate of the deceased.

If a person dies after beginning a defamation action, his personal representative should be able to continue the action to recover both general and special damages.

For five years from the date of a person's death certain near relatives (wife, brother, sister, son, daughter, mother or father) should be able to sue for a declaration that the matter complained of was untrue, an injunction, and costs as the court may think fit but not for damages.

(12) Criminal libel should apply to broadcasting as well as to other matters in permanent form.

(13) Magistrates' courts should be able to try criminal libel cases with the consent of the defendant and fine up to £500 and/or imprison for up to nine months.

(14) Privilege and comment should be declared to be defences to criminal libel subject to rebuttal (on the criminal standard of proof) of improper advantage or false opinion.

(15) Libel actions should be brought within three years of the date of publication (not six years, as at present).

(16) County courts should be able to try defamation actions where the plaintiff claims damages not exceeding £1,000.

(17) Legal aid should be available for defamation actions. It should be limited, to begin with, to aid for counsel's opinion. If this opinion is favourable, a second opinion on the merits of the case should be obtained after the close of pleadings. Further aid should depend on this second opinion.

(18) Trial by jury in civil defamation actions should be at the discretion of the court. If a jury is permitted, its function should be limited to deciding whether the case is proved or not and not to the actual assessment of damages beyond indicating whether they should be substantial, moderate, nominal or contemptuous.

2 Rehabilitation of Offenders Act 1974

This Act came into force on July 1, 1975. It was the product of a Private Member's Bill based on a report by Justice called *Living it Down*. It has been estimated that the Act affects nearly a million people, from the motorist with a £25 fine for careless driving through to people who have been to prison (providing the sentence was for two and a half years or less). The Act has little to do with rehabilitation in the ordinary sense of the term.

From the Press point of view it should be understood at the outset that the Act does not prohibit revelation of criminal convictions, spent or otherwise, unless such information was obtained by fraud, dishonesty or bribery. Instead, the former "criminal" may bring a civil action for defamation if the conviction is spent and he is rehabilitated. He will only succeed if he can prove that the newspaper's dominant or overriding motive in referring to the spent conviction was to injure his reputation. This may be a heavy burden on such plaintiffs.

The Act creates a new class of persons who have greater rights, in this respect, than the non-criminal. The law of defamation has only been changed with reference to spent convictions. Allegations that X is an adulterer or that he is cruel to his wife and children, if they can be proved to be true, will still carry the defence of justification unchanged. Malice (spite or bad motive) on the part of the publisher will not destroy the defence of justification because there is no reference to a spent conviction.

The wording of the Act is not, with respect, a shining example of statutory clarity. There were a number of amendments during the passage of the Bill through Parliament. This accounts for some of the problems. The wording is complex and it would be a more than usually intelligent member of the public who could comprehend the effect of the Act without a great deal of study. The Home Office have published a guide to the Act, nearly twice as expensive as the Act itself, in an attempt to explain some of the general provisions.

The following sentences can never be rehabilitated. Reference may be made to them, however far back they occurred in a man's life.

(i) Life imprisonment.

(ii) Prison for a period over two and a half years.

(iii) Preventive detention or corrective training for more than two and a half years (neither form of sentence exists now).

(iv) Detention at Her Majesty's pleasure or for more than two and a half years passed under section 53 of the Children and Young Persons Act 1933 (used where juveniles are sentenced for grave crimes).

All other sentences may be rehabilitated. Sentences imposed on juveniles may have shorter rehabilitation periods as shown in the following table.

SENTENCE	ADULT R/H PERIOD	JUVENILE R/H PERIOD
Prison: between 6 months and 2½ years	10 years	5 years
Prison: not exceeding 6 months	7 years	3½ years
Dismissal from Her Majesty's Forces	7 years	3½ years
Fines	5 years	2½ years
Borstal	7 years	7 years
Detention: between 6 months and 2½ years	5 years	5 years
Detention: not exceeding 6 months or under a detention centre order	3 years	3 years
Absolute discharge	6 months	6 months

Conditional discharge, binding over, probation, care or supervision order	1 year from the date of conviction or order; *or* when the condition or order ceases to have effect, whichever is longer.	1 year
Hospital order (under Part 5 of the Mental Health Act 1959)	5 years from the date of conviction or two years from when the order ceased, whichever is longer.	5 years
Disqualification	The period of the disqualification.	

In every case, what matters is the stated length of the sentence and not the amount of time actually served in prison. A person sentenced to three years imprisonment will be released after two years with normal remission for good conduct. He will, however, be outside the terms of the Act and may be referred to as a convicted criminal at any time.

If sentences are imposed to run concurrently (at the same time) it is relatively straightforward to assess whether the 30 month maximum has been exceeded.

The Act states that, in relation to consecutive terms (one beginning where the other ceases), the total period is treated as a single term of imprisonment. Section 5 (9)(*b*) provides:

"consecutive terms of imprisonment or of detention . . . and terms which are wholly or partly concurrent (being terms of imprisonment or detention imposed in respect of offences of which a person was convicted in the same proceedings) shall be treated as a single term."

Problems within this area will only arise following a crown court trial. Magistrates, while they deal with 98 per cent. of all criminal work, can only sentence to a maximum of 12 months imprisonment for two or more offences. They cannot, therefore, impose sentences which exceed the 30 month maximum.

At the crown court, X is sentenced to 18 months for theft and 18 months for burglary.

If the sentences run concurrently, X may be rehabilitated after 10 years: if they run consecutively, they become a single term of three years and the convictions will never become spent.

A further anomaly appears from section 5 (9)(c): no account is taken of any subsequent variation, made by the court in dealing with an offender in respect of a suspended prison sentence, of the term originally imposed. So, if an accused is given a term of 18 months suspended for two years and, subsequently, the term is activated following a further offence but only for six months, the accused *still* faces a 10 year rehabilitation period and not a seven-year period.

Suspended sentences dealt with at the same time as later offences are not, however, to be treated in the reckoning-up period for the 30 month maximum. Section 1 (3) (b) states that "sentence" in respect of the Act excludes an order dealing with a person to activate a suspended term of imprisonment.

> X has been convicted of burglary and sentenced to a prison term of 18 months, suspended for two years. One year later he appears at the crown court and is sentenced to 18 months' imprisonment for theft. The suspended sentence is activated to run consecutively. X may rehabilitate himself during the next 10 years. He is not outside the terms of the Act even though the total sentence imposed amounts to three years.

If a number of offences are dealt with at the same time then the rehabilitation period is the one which runs for the longest period.

> X receives three months for assault, nine months for theft and two years for burglary.

(i) If the sentences are all to run concurrently, there is a 10 year rehabilitation period relating to all three offences.

(ii) If the first two sentences (three months and nine months) are to run concurrently but consecutive to the two year sentence then the period is beyond the scope of the Act because the total amounts to 33 months.

There is a re-activation provision in section 6(4). This extends the rehabilitation period for an earlier offence if there is a subsequent conviction. This will operate:

(i) if the subsequent conviction could have been tried on indictment; and

(ii) the subsequent sentence is within the 30 month maximum covered by the Act.

X receives three months' imprisonment for theft in January 1976. This would be rehabilitated, if no further offences were committed, after seven years (*i.e.* February 1983). In January 1981 he receives a nine months' imprisonment for handling. The rehabilitation period in respect of *both* offences now runs through to February 1991.

If the subsequent conviction had been for careless driving, resulting in a £25 fine, the theft rehabilitation period would have been unaffected (and achieved in 1983 for the theft). Careless driving is not an offence triable on indictment. However, if the subsequent offence had led to a conviction for more than 30 months, both that and the previous offence would be taken outside the Act and could never have become spent.

It should be clearly understood that the Act provides no protection to criminals during the period of rehabilitation. The criminal conviction does not become spent until the relevant rehabilitation period is completed. Only then, if malice can be proved against the publisher of the spent conviction, may the plaintiff former criminal have a defamation action.

Subject to what follows, a person who has become rehabilitated is treated for all purposes of law as someone who has not been charged with, prosecuted for, convicted of or sentenced for the offence which is spent. Crudely, a former criminal with a spent conviction is not a former criminal. Section 4 states this, subject to the exceptions in section 7 and section 8, quite clearly. But while the Act gives with one hand, the excepting sections claw back the bulk of any protection arising from a conviction having become spent.

If asked, in a job application form or for insurance purposes, whether the individual has previous convictions then the person with spent convictions may, if he chooses, answer negatively. Section 4(2)(*b*) provides that:

"the person questioned shall not be subjected to any liability or otherwise prejudiced in law by reason of any failure to acknowledge or disclose a spent conviction or any circumstances anciary to a spent conviction in his answer to the question."

The Act, however, did provide for the Home Secretary to make certain exceptions to this area. The excepted professions are listed in the Rehabilitation of Offenders Act 1974 (Exceptions) Order 1975, which came into force at the same time as the Act and which may receive additions from time to time.

The current list includes lawyers, policemen, probation officers, doctors, pharmacists, teachers and youth workers. Applicants for any of these professions or jobs must reveal convictions, spent or otherwise. Spent convictions may also be revealed in disciplinary proceedings against these people.

The major exception within the Act comes from section 7 (2):

> "Nothing . . . shall affect the determination of any issue, or prevent the admission or requirement of any evidence, relating to a person's previous convictions. . . ."
>   (a) "in any criminal proceedings before a court in Great Britain . . ."

This requirement, via section 7(3), may also take effect in any proceedings before a judicial authority (like the Disciplinary Tribunal of the Law Society). Here, there is a requirement that spent convictions should only be revealed if justice cannot be done without such convictions being admitted or required in evidence.

The foregoing makes it quite clear that criminal convictions which are spent may well be revealed in ordinary criminal proceedings. On June 30, 1975, the Lord Chief Justice, Lord Widgery, issued a Practice Direction for the courts under his jurisdiction (the Crown Court, the Divisional Court of the Queen's Bench Division and the Court of Appeal (Criminal Division)). This stated:

> "During the trial of a criminal charge reference to previous convictions (and therefore to spent convictions) may arise in a number of ways. The most common is when the character of the accused or a witness is sought to be attacked by reference to his criminal record. There are, of course, cases where previous convictions are relevant and admissible as, for instance, to prove system. . . . It is recommended that both court and counsel should give effect to the general intention of Parliament by never referring to a spent conviction when such reference can be reasonably avoided. If unnecessary references to spent convictions are eliminated much

will have been achieved.

After a verdict of guilty the court must be provided with a statement of the defendant's record for the purposes of sentence. The record supplied should contain all previous convictions, but those which are spent should, so far as is practicable, be marked as such.

No one should refer in open court to a spent conviction without the authority of the judge, which authority should not be given unless the interests of justice so require.

When passing sentence the judge should make no reference to a spent conviction unless it is necessary to do so for the purposes of explaining the sentence passed."

In Crown Court proceedings, where the accused is pleading not guilty, this practice direction sets out the basic form for bringing the spent conviction to the jury's notice. The jury have to judge the facts: they may be excluded at any stage while the judge decides, as a matter of law, whether they may hear certain facts. If the prosecution wish to introduce evidence of spent convictions (even against a witness) then they must make a submission on the point of law in the jury's absence and the judge must rule that the spent conviction is admissible to the jury on their return.

D pleads not guilty to a charge of rape. He is aged 40 and, when he was 29, he was sentenced to two years imprisonment for a rape offence but has had no further convictions. This earlier offence is, therefore, rehabilitated and the conviction is spent.

It may, however, be revealed to the jury at the judge's discretion under section 7 if:

(a) D's previous offence contained elements which were highly individual and these elements are present in the new allegation. The prosecution would, in effect, be arguing that D had a particular system which could only be revealed by reference to the spent conviction; or

(b) D has set up his own good character but, earlier in the case, has attacked the character of prosecution witnesses. He might have alleged that the police beat him up to obtain a "confession."

The judge has to decide, in either case, whether section 7 should apply as a matter of law. If the spent conviction is revealed to the jury by this process then newspaper reports may safely mention it (though not necessarily every detail of the

legal submission heard in the absence of the jury). If the judge
decides not to allow the spent conviction to be revealed then a
newspaper report of the legal submission would not carry absolute privilege (s.8 (6)) and would probably also be a contempt
of court.

With a trial on indictment, the situation is relatively clear
and straightforward. Where this aspect of the Act breaks down,
in principle, is in relation to criminal trials in the magistrates'
courts.

Magistrates have been asked to apply the Act within the
terms of the Lord Chief Justice's practice direction. But,
unlike the Crown Court situation, where there is a judge to
deal with the law and a jury to deal with fact, the magistrates
hearing a not guilty plea have both functions rolled into one.
They act as a jury during the evidence and, if they decide to convict, they become judges for the purpose of sentencing. If a
legal submission is made to them they have to decide whether,
as a matter of law, they can hear the evidence relating to spent
convictions as judges of fact. Their clerk may advise them on
points of law but they have to decide whether to accept his
advice.

The magistrates may rule that a spent conviction cannot be
presented to them in their jury capacity. It will be a naive
accused who is totally happy with this process. Reference in
newspaper reports to a spent conviction in the above situation
would not be covered by absolute privilege, so he has some protection. The Bench can reject what is true and newspapers,
wishing to retain the absolute privilege on the copy, would not
publish the details of the spent conviction.

The practice direction reveals one further point. Spent previous convictions remain on the accused's record. They are
almost highlighted because they are marked as spent. The
accused, whether facing a conviction in the Crown Court or at
the lower level, is not going to be completely convinced that
his sentencers have turned a blind eye of the marked spent
convictions.

Defamation and the Rehabilitation of Offenders Act 1974

Passing reference has been made to changes in the law of defamation, in particular to the defences of justification and absolute privilege. These changes are contained in section 8 of the Act.

The changes only operate where there is a reference to a spent conviction (s.8 (1)) after July 1, 1975 and not to references published before the Act came into force.

References to convictions during the period of rehabilitation incur no possible liability in the civil law of defamation. This section may only operate once the conviction has become spent. (s.8 (2)).

If the reference to the spent conviction was ruled inadmissible in judicial proceedings, yet the defendant publishes details of it, he is not entitled to the defence that the matter "constituted a fair and accurate report of judicial proceedings." This effectively rules out the defences of absolute and qualified privilege.

It is still open to the defendant to plead justification. While the conviction is spent, it is still a fact that it did exist at some stage.

However, via section 8 (5), the defendant cannot rely on the defence of justification if publication is proved to have been made with malice.

This means that the plaintiff will have to prove malice against the defendant to successfully destroy the defence of justification. As was suggested earlier, malice in this context may mean proof that the defendant's major motive in revealing the spent conviction was to injure the plaintiff's reputation.

Plaintiffs may find very few situations where such clear malice could be established. In any event the defences of fair comment and qualified privilege still exist. While these may be destroyed by proof of malice (which presumably has the same meaning as in the defence of justification), the defendant is not restricted in the matters he may establish to counter the allegation of malice.

It is suggested that a newspaper which, following an investigative inquiry, reveals that a former criminal with spent convictions is running a business which is, in itself, questionable and operating against the public interest would still have adequate defamation protection. The plaintiff could only succeed if he could prove that the newspaper was hounding him out of personal spite.

Criminal Penalties

The Act creates two new criminal offences.

(1) If a person with custody or access to court or police records reveals such information other than in the course of his job, he faces summary prosecution with a maximum penalty of a £200 fine.

This affects, among others, off-duty policemen, probation officers and court clerks. The latter category could commit an offence by revealing the result of a conviction to the Press who had been unable to attend particular criminal proceedings.

(2) Any person who obtains such information by fraud, dishonesty or bribery may be prosecuted summarily and faces a maximum fine of £400 and/or up to six months' imprisonment.

This provision is directed primarily at the excesses of certain private inquiry agents. It could catch the over-zealous reporter who, by offering a police contact several pints, is seeking to discover details about an individual's criminal convictions. It should be understood that it would not matter whether the convictions were spent or otherwise. The seeking of such information within the terms of the offence would be sufficient to set up the situation for a prosecution.

In conclusion, one final anomaly within the Act deserves mention. The provisions within the Act only apply "where an individual has been convicted" (s.1 (1)). If a person is charged with an offence but subsequently acquitted, he receives no protection from the Act because there is no sentence for him to rehabilitate. Special protection is only given to those who have actually been convicted.

It would be technically possible for a newspaper, in every reference it carried to that person acquitted, to state that several years previously he had been tried for murder but acquitted. The defence of justification would remain unaffected by the

Act no matter how malicious the newspaper was in its conduct. The individual would be unable to rehabilitate the suspicion which, in the case of an innocent person, leaves him with little redress except — in certain situations — a prosecution of the newspaper for criminal libel. He could take no action against those who, orally, insisted on referring to the matter.

3 Libel

Criminal Libel

Criminal libel, until 1976, remained a topic of academic rather than of immediate practical importance. While slander (defamation in a transitory or oral form) is not now, of itself, a crime, libel can lead to a criminal prosecution as well as a civil action for defamation.

Events in 1976 produced a situation which led to an examination of the role of criminal libel in a society rather different from that which developed the crime. An individual convicted of publishing a criminal libel may be sent to prison for up to two years and/or fined. There is no limit on the amount which may be imposed as a fine.

History

Criminal libel appears, by an historical irony, to have developed from the spoken rather than the written word. King Alfred, wishing to discourage "rumouring" against the State, gave offenders the option of loosing their tongues or, if they so elected, their heads. "Rumouring" in the thirteenth century was obviously by word of mouth (slander) yet, by the late seventeenth century, slander had ceased to be a common law crime. Before this occurred, however, the idea that defamatory words could be criminal because their publication might cause a breach of the peace, had become an established principle: even thirteenth century local English courts were dealing with slander as both a crime and a tort.

Once the principle was extended to libels, it was not difficult to keep the crime alive. The State had an obvious interest in preserving the peace of the realm. One limitation, voiced in 1888 by Lord Coleridge, was that "an indictment for libel is only justified when it affects the public as an attempt to disturb the peace."

Then, in 1936, came the case of *R.* v. *Wicks* which, if correctly decided, determined that the tendency in the words to provoke a breach of the peace no longer had to be proved. A breach of the peace is apparently presumed as a legal inference in those libels in which the words are clearly defamatory.

C had been arrested and charged with forgery, following a complaint by the Sun Life Insurance Company of Canada. G was the company's solicitor. Wicks, who had unsuccessfully taken action against the company in the past, wrote to C describing G as a man of "depraved moral character, even more so than" another man described as G's "criminal associate." At Wicks' trial, the Recorder rejected a submission that there was no case to go before the jury because there was no evidence that the libel was likely to result in a breach of the peace. Wicks was convicted and sentenced to 12 months' imprisonment. The Court of Criminal Appeal, in a judgment delivered by Mr Justice du Parcq, dismissed the appeal with the observation that the libel in question did not have to be proved to have been "unusually" likely to cause a breach of the peace.

Criminal libel proceedings should not be instituted for trivial cases and juries may be directed by judges to acquit in such cases. When the libel is serious, however, it is no defence for the libeller to show that the person he defames is unlikely to commit a breach of the peace (because of the *Wicks* decision) though it is a defence to show that the libel was published on a privileged occasion.

When Sir James Goldsmith began his private prosecution of *Private Eye* in 1976 for an alleged criminal libel (discussed in detail below), defence counsel, at committal proceedings, established from Sir James himself that a breach of the peace was unlikely. It was clear that, had the case gone to trial, the *Wicks* decision would have been thoroughly questioned.

Differences Between Civil and Criminal Libel

Because the offence grew out of a tendency to cause a breach of the peace, there are four major differences between criminal and civil libel.

(1) A civil action requires the parties to be alive. Civil libel of the dead is (at present) an impossibility and is not actionable.

If, however, relatives can show that the object of the publication was to bring contempt and scandal on relatives of the deceased, then a criminal libel prosecution will lie on additional proof that there is a risk of a breach of the peace.

It should be noted that a libel on a dead person *may* contain an innuendo which reflects on a living person, creating the grounds for a civil action. Madam Sukarno, the wife of the former president of Indonesia, had an action settled in her favour without full trial because a book, mentioning her dead husband's past, made reference to a proliferation of mistresses. She claimed this suggested she was an unsatisfactory wife.

(2) If the purpose of the libel is to excite hatred against any class or section of society, this may lead to a criminal libel prosecution. The authority is rather ancient (*R. v. Osbourne* (1732)) and proceedings might more properly be taken under the Race Relations Act 1976.

(3) Civil libel requires publication to a third party; a criminal libel may be prosecuted even though the material is only published to the person libelled (*e.g.* in a letter).

(4) Truth (with the limited erosions of the Rehabilitation of Offenders Act 1974) is a complete answer in a civil action. Only if the plaintiff can prove that there has been a malicious publication of a spent criminal conviction would it fail. The Libel Act 1843 created a statutory defence to a charge of criminal libel. Until then, proof of the truth of the libel was no defence because publication of the truth could still lead to a breach of the peace. It is from the pre-1843 law that the enigmatic cliché "the greater the truth, the greater the libel" gained support. One commentator in 1792 noted: "For libelling against a common strumpet is as great an offence as against an honest woman and perhaps more dangerous to the breach of the peace for, as the woman said, she would never grieve to be told of her red nose if she had not one indeed."

Since 1843 there is a defence in a criminal libel action if:
(a) the truth of the facts stated is proved; and
(b) publication was for the public benefit.

From the passing of the Libel Act, English law has contained the following peculiar anomaly. If you can prove that what you said was true you can never be made to pay damages but you may, in certain cases, be sent to prison (if there is no public benefit in the revelation of the truth).

This is because, when the 1843 legislation was in Bill form, the House of Commons deleted the "public benefit" requirement for truth as a defence if pleaded in civil actions. It remained a component of the criminal libel defence. When the Bill returned to the House of Lords, it was August and, with the harvest approaching, no revision was made.

Mr Paul Sieghart traced the history of the anomaly and commented (*The Times*, May 3, 1976): "It is to historical accidents such as these that we owe the illogicality of some of our laws, but once they have been in force for a few generations they acquire the sanctity of age, and today's libel lawyers are apt to vaunt the great principle of English law that no one can be made to pay damages for printing the truth — as if being locked up were any better."

Penalties and Procedure

The penalties are embodied in the Libel Act 1843. If the prosecution can prove that the accused knew the libel was untrue, the maximum penalty is two years' imprisonment; if knowledge of falsity cannot be proved then the maximum penalty is one year's imprisonment. As already mentioned, there is no limit to the fine which may be imposed in addition to imprisonment on conviction.

A person who is seriously libelled either takes criminal libel proceedings himself or invites the police or the D.P.P. to take over the case.

Section 17 of the Criminal Law Act 1977 abolishes the summary procedure of section 5 of the Newspaper Libel and Registration Act 1887. The old procedure had allowed newspapers to agree to summary trial of a criminal libel charge if the matter was trivial and they intended to plead guilty: the maximum fine was £500.

The Law of Libel Amendment Act 1888 provides that no criminal prosecution may be begun against any proprietor, publisher, editor or any person responsible for publication of a newspaper without the permission of a judge in chambers (*i.e.* a High Court judge).

While radio and television broadcasts are declared actionable in the law of libel rather than slander, by section 1 of the
Defamation Act 1952, this only relates to civil actions. If the
publication complained of came from an unscripted broadcast, then no criminal libel proceedings could be taken. The
Faulks Committee recommend a change in the law so that
criminal libel proceedings could be brought against broadcasting organisations.

The Faulks Committee considered the statistics for criminal
libel prosecutions to see whether the offence was a major
source of prosecution. The figures revealed:

	CONSIDERED FOR PROSECUTION		PROSECUTED
1950-1954	81	averages for the	4
1955-1959	66	years in question	2
1960-1964	32		2
1965	27		1
1966	41		1
1967	14		-
1968	29		3
1969	9		1
1970	10		2
1971	13		1
1972	8		2
1973	19		1

These figures are for England and Wales. In Scotland, criminal libel is not recognised as a matter for prosecution.

During the years 1956-1975, the Central Criminal Court
(Old Bailey) tried two such cases. In both, the defendant was
convicted and sent to prison.

A "typical" prosecution (in 1976) involved the following
facts:

X had an affair with a woman, Y. The affair was terminated by Y.
To take revenge, X daubed allegations about Y on walls in the
town where they both lived, suggesting she was immoral and a

prostitute. Y became depressed and suicidal as a result of this campaign and X was successfully prosecuted for criminal libel and for causing criminal damage.

The Faulks Committee considered whether the law should be changed and criminal libel abolished. "The fact that there are very few prosecutions for libel does not mean, in itself, that the offence should be abolished. The law which protects some people, if only a few, from injury should not be discarded unless there is something better to put in its place," they state.

Five categories are identified where, they feel, criminal libel provides a necessary remedy:

(1) Where there is a persistent flow of libellous letters, the injured party should have the right to stop this bombardment by using the criminal law (and the tort of nuisance probably does not cover this situation);

(2) Libels on the Sovereign or a member of the Royal Family;

(3) Libels by people without any money to pay damages (or costs);

(4) Libels on people who have no money to bring a civil action. At the moment legal aid is not available for defamation actions in the civil courts. The committee want legal aid to be available. They point out, however, that even if this happens "such aid frequently leaves quite a sizeable sum of money to be found . . . and some people could not afford the expense. Moreover, there are many people over the legal aid limit on whom the expense of a libel action would be a grave burden";

(5) Libels on people who in the distant past have committed some crime or who have otherwise misbehaved themselves. (The Rehabilitation of Offenders Act 1974 provides a degree of protection but the expense of a civil action would still be a critical factor).

"In some cases of libel the defamatory matter may be gross and persistent and the conduct of the defendant very bad indeed. If criminal libel is abolished such a man might escape too easily, particularly if our recommendations for the abolition of punitive damages are accepted. A libellous attack on a man's reputation may be as much a matter of public concern as an attack on his body," they state.

Goldsmith v. Pressdram Ltd. (1976)

Mention was made earlier that a judge in chambers must give leave before a criminal libel prosecution is brought against a newspaper. *Goldsmith* v. *Pressdram Ltd* is an exploration of when a judge will give such permission.

The brief facts are as follows:

> *Private Eye*, on December 12, 1975, published an article headed *"All's well that ends Elwes."* This suggested that:
>
> (a) there was a conspiracy among friends of the missing Lord Lucan to obstruct the course of justice and aid the fugitive Earl;
>
> (b) Mr James Goldsmith, a City financier, was the powerful leader of the conspirators;
>
> (c) Mr Goldsmith compelled Mr Dominic Elwes to go and see Lady Lucan in hospital to find out what she had told the police; and
>
> (d) Mr Goldsmith pressured Mr Greville Howard into evading giving evidence at the inquest on the death of the Lucan's children's nanny, Miss Sandra Rivett.
>
> (e) The article also suggested that the conspirators ganged up on Elwes later, banned him from clubs and restaurants and increased pressures on him until ultimately he committed suicide.

Mr. Justice Wien granted permission for the criminal libel prosecution to be brought. He said he was satisfied that there was a prima facie case. He said he was an advocate of the freedom of the Press but that did not mean the Press had a licence to publish scandalous or scurrilous matter wholly without foundation.

That the allegations complained of were without foundation, was to be seen from a letter of April 5, 1976, sent by *Private Eye* to Mr Goldsmith's solicitors, stating that *Private Eye* were satisfied that there was no truth in their allegations and that they accepted that they were mistaken and withdrew and apologised for the allegations. That was a private apology which had not reached the attention of the public in any shape or form and was an admission of a very serious libel made on the character of Mr Goldsmith.

The public interest required the institution of criminal proceedings. Mr Goldsmith was entitled to come to the court and say it was not a question of damages, but that it was a case where a judge should exercise his discretion and permit criminal proceedings to be launched, the judge concluded.

This decision created something of a vogue for criminal libel. Two weeks after it was delivered, solicitors acting for Mr Jeremy Thorpe, former leader of the Liberal Party, warned *Private Eye* that criminal libel proceedings would be started if the magazine continued to suggest that Mr Thorpe had in some way been connected with the killing of a dog belonging to a man who claimed to have had a homosexual relationship with Mr Thorpe.

A major problem, which became apparent after Mr. Justice Wien's decision to permit Mr Goldsmith to prosecute, was that there was no procedure for *Private Eye* to appeal against the decision. It was also quickly realised that, if criminal libel became a popular form of action, it could be used to silence the Press. While a newspaper can insure itself against damages in civil libel actions, the possibility of losing an editor for up to two years is not so welcome. This latter risk, however, is nothing new: an editor who deliberately published material which could prejudice a person's fair trial could be sent to prison for a lengthy period for contempt of court.

The battle in the Old Bailey between Sir James and the satirical magazine never took place. A week before the criminal libel trial was due to begin, the parties reached a settlement.

The magazine carried an apology, which also appeared in the *Evening Standard*, and contributed some £30,000 towards Sir James's estimated £75,000 costs (the contribution to be spread over a 10-year period).

Lord Shawcross, a former Attorney-General and chairman of the Press Council, questioned the continued existence of criminal libel and its use as a weapon in personal vendettas between private individuals (*The Times*, May 26, 1977).

The Attorney-General, Mr. Sam Silkin Q.C. replied: "Whilst there is much to be said for the view that the private citizen who is libelled, however persistently, has ample remedies by way of damages and injunction in the civil courts, many will wonder whether these civil rights are adequate to deal

with the immense power to injure the public interest which
modern methods of communication make available." He
added that Parliament had to decide what role criminal libel
should play and that ". . . it would be wrong for an Attorney-
General, in advance of legislation, to instruct the Director (of
Public Prosecutions) to take the prosecution over, unless matters of public interest so plainly outweighed private interests
that no other reasonable course could be considered."

It only remains for Parliament to find the time to examine
this and other areas of law which relate to freedom of speech.

The Other Libels: Obscenity, Blasphemy and Sedition

The topic of obscenity has a clear relevance to the law of publications. Matters under the headings of blasphemy and sedition
had appeared to drift, in practical terms, into the mists of the
ages responsible for developing these crimes. Any complac-
ency felt in the mid 1970s about archaic crimes relating to
publication, should have been dispelled by Sir James Goldsmith's resort to the law of criminal libel. It was, however, a
surprise to see the resurrection of the crime of blasphemous
libel late in 1976 in the prosecution of *Gay News* for the publication of a poem and cartoon relating to Christ initiated, in the
name of the Crown, by Mrs. Mary Whitehouse.

Obscene libel

Obscenity originated as an ecclesiastical offence but, in *Curl's*
case (1727), the common law recognised obscene libel as a mis-
demeanour. The Obscene Publications Acts 1959 and 1964
now contain the relevant law.

By section 1 (1) of the Obscene Publications Act 1959, matter
is obscene if:

"... its effect ... is, if taken as a whole, such as to tend to deprave
and corrupt persons who are likely, having regard to all the relevant circumstances, to read, see or hear the matter. ..."

This definition is more narrow than the common meaning of

the word "obscene" as anything filthy, lewd or disgusting. The restricted meaning was emphasised in *R*. v. *Anderson, Neville and Dennis* (1972): convictions under the 1959 Act were quashed on appeal in relation to the *Oz* School Kids' issue because the judge had allowed the jury to think that "obscene" meant anything which was repulsive, filthy, loathsome or lewd.

Matter may be any of these things but, if it does not have a tendency to deprave and corrupt, it is not obscene. Indeed, if the matter is so revolting that it would put people off the activity described or portrayed, it cannot be obscene.

Depravity and corruption are not to be viewed in sexual terms only. In *Calder (John) Publications Ltd.* v. *Powell* (1965), a book stressing the favourable effects of drug-taking (*Cain's Book*) was held within the scope of statutory obscene libel. Matter which advocates or portrays violence or conduct beyond the accepted norms of behaviour may be held to be obscene.

In *D.P.P.* v. *Whyte* (1972) the House of Lords went a step further and destroyed the notion that publication to those who were already depraved or corrupted could not lead to an offence being committed.

> A husband and wife sold "hard core" pornography. Their customers were held by the magistrates to be middle-aged men already depraved and corrupted and the informations against the sellers were dismissed. The prosecution appealed by way of case stated to the Divisional Court, unsuccessfully, and then to the House of Lords on a point of law of general public importance. The House of Lords directed the justices to convict because, among other things, the proposition that people who were already depraved and corrupted could not be further corrupted was a fallacy. The law existed to prevent further and deeper corruption.

It is an offence for a person to:

(i) publish an obscene article, whether it is for gain or not (s.2 (1) of the Obscene Publications Act 1959); or

(ii) "have" an obscene article for publication for gain, whether this is for his benefit or for the benefit of another (s.2 (1) as amended by s.1 (1) of the Obscene Publications Act 1964).

Publication, within the Acts, takes place if:

(i) there is any distribution, circulation, sale, hire, giving or lending of the material; or

(ii) in the case of recording or films, there is any playing or showing of the material.

This second category specifically did not apply to the public showing of films (via s.1 (3) (*b*) of the Obscene Publications Act 1959). The reason for this was explained and explored by Lord Denning in the following case:

> *R.* v. *G.L.C., ex p. Blackburn* (1976): Mr. Raymond Blackburn was attempting to prevent the G.L.C. from allegedly acting *ultra vires* (beyond their powers) by delegating their powers of censorship to the British Board of Film Censors and allowing indecent films to be shown. The G.L.C.'s test was whether films had a tendency to deprave or corrupt. The Court of Appeal held the G.L.C.'s test should be changed to one of indecency.

Lord Denning, who had taken part in the debate in the House of Lords on the 1959 Act, said that four exceptions had been built in to the Private Member's Bill. Stage plays, the cinema, television and broadcasting were specifically excluded from section 1 (3). He said:

> "It was because they could be left to the common law and the existing means of censorship. No doubt those reasons seemed sufficient in 1959. But they are no longer valid today. During the last two or three years pornographic films have been imported from Sweden, I believe, in large numbers and no doubt at much expense. They have been exhibited in cinemas in London to the shame of its decent citizens. The existing censorship has proved totally ineffective to stop it. . . . A film called *More about the Language of Love* was refused a certificate by the British Board of Film Censors, but the exhibitors appealed to the G.L.C. The G.L.C. granted consent to its being shown. It was shown at a public cinema. The redoubtable Mr. Blackburn brought it to the notice of Sir Robert Mark, the Commissioner of Police. A prosecution was brought on the ground that it offended against common law. The owners and managers were charged with showing a film that was grossly indecent. The jury found them guilty. The judge fined the two companies £500 a piece and the manager £50.
>
> Why did the G.L.C. grant their consent to the showing of that film — which was found by the jury to be grossly indecent — and which was, therefore unlawful? The answer is because they have been applying the wrong test. They have applied the test of 'tend-

ency to deprave or corrupt' under the 1959 Act, instead of the test of 'indecency' under the common law."

However, section 53 of the Criminal Law Act 1977 changed this situation. Films are brought within the scope of the Act, but prosecutions require the consent of the Director of Public Prosecutions.

Section 4 of the 1959 Act sets out the defence of "public good."

(1) There can be no conviction if it is proved that the article in question is justified as being for the public good on the grounds that it is in the interests of science, literature, art or learning, or of other objects of general concern;

(2) the opinion of experts about the literary, artistic, scientific or other merits of the article may be used in proceedings under the Act to establish this defence.

The section 4 defence of public good is extended to cover films and soundtracks by section 53 of the Criminal Law Act 1977. In relation to films, however, "other objects of general concern" is specifically omitted.

The sequence is that the jury should consider whether the material is obscene and then, if they decide it is, should consider whether the section 4 defence applies.

In *R.* v. *Jordan* (1976), the House of Lords rejected a particular line of approach and argument which had developed under section 4;

A bookseller had been convicted under the 1959 Act. There was no argument that the material possessed any literary, scientific or artistic merit but section 4 was sought to defend publication under the general heading of being "other objects of general concern." The accused wanted to call expert evidence that the pornographic material before the court had some psychotherapeutic value for particular individuals (*i.e.* frustrated heterosexuals, homosexuals and for people with perversions) and that access to the material meant they could relieve their sexual tension. This, the argument would have continued, benefited society by providing these people with a safety valve, saving them from psychological disorders and diverting them from anti-social and possibly criminal acts against the public.

The House of Lords held that this evidence was correctly ruled inadmissible.

Lord Wilberforce put the matter quite concisely:

> "Section 4 has been diverted from its proper purpose, and indeed abused, when it has been used to enable evidence to be given that pornographic material may be for the public good as being therapeutic to some of the people."

Viscount Dilhorne said:

> "In view of the wide range of hard pornographic material to which his evidence (would have) related, it is difficult to visualise any obscene publication to which his evidence would not apply, in which case if . . . the jury came to the conclusion that . . . publication of the material was justified as being for the public good in the interests of an object of general concern, there could be no conviction no matter how obscene the material might be."

The common law offence of obscene libel has not been completely destroyed. Section 2 (4) of the 1959 Act states that a person publishing an obscene article shall not be prosecuted for the common law offence "consisting only of the publication of any matter contained or embodied in the article where it is of the essence of the offence that the matter is obscene."

As the common law crime of conspiracy to publish an obscene libel appears to be outside the scope of this section, the common law is not dead. The Act envisages straightforward publication prosecutions being brought under the statutory provisions, but does not abolish more subtle lines of attack.

Certain fringe publications face the danger of a prosecution for conspiracy to corrupt public morals or conspiracy to outrage public decency. Conspiracy, in brief, is an agreement between two or more persons to effect some "unlawful" purpose and, in relation to public mischief, covers a vast and ill-defined area of acts or attempts which might prejudice the community.

In *Shaw* v. *D.P.P.* (1962): the House of Lords held that the publisher of the *Ladies Directory* had conspired to corrupt public morals. The directory advertised the names and addresses of prostitutes with, in some cases, photographs and details of the particular perversions which they were willing to practice.

In *Knuller* v. *D.P.P.* (1972): the House of Lords held that an agreement to publish advertisements to enable homosexuals to meet and commit homosexual acts between adult males in private was a conspiracy to corrupt public morals despite the fact that, since the Sexual Offences Act 1967, s.1, such conduct is no longer a crime. In this case, the House of Lords also held that there was the common law offence of outraging public decency: it was therefore an offence to conspire to commit this crime as well.

Blasphemous Libel

This is a common law offence committed if the matter published vilifies the Christian religion, the Bible, the Book of Common Prayer or the existence of God. The offence owes its existence to judicial support for the idea that the public importance of the Christian religion is so great that no one is allowed to deny its truth in scurrilous terms.

In *Bowman* v. *Secular Society Ltd.* (1917), the House of Lords held that a company formed to promote the secularisation of the State was not unlawful even though one of its objects was to deny Christianity. This case relates more to company law and the lawfulness of particular ventures. Lord Sumner, in that case, made the following observations:

> "In the present day reasonable men do not apprehend the dissolution or the downfall of society because religion is publicly assailed by methods not scandalous. . . . The question of whether a given opinion is a danger to society is a question of the times and is a question of fact. . . . I desire to say . . . there is nothing in the general rules as to blasphemy and irreligion, as known to the law, which prevents us from varying their application to the particular circumstances of our time in accordance with that experience."

In the most recent blasphemy case prior to *R. v. Gay News*, a conviction was upheld following a direction from Avory J. that the publication had to be found to be calculated to cause a breach of the peace.

> In *R. v. Gott* (1922), he told the jury: "What you have to ask yourselves is whether . . . these matters which are published in these two pamphlets are, in your opinion, indecent and offensive attacks on Christianity or the Scriptures or sacred persons or objects, calculated to outrage the feelings of the general body of the community and so lead, possibly — not inevitably, but so lead, possibly, to a

breach of the peace.

You must ask yourselves if a person of strong religious feelings had stopped to read this pamphlet whether his instinct might not have been to go up to the man who was selling it and give him a thrashing or, at all events, to use such language to him that a breach of the peace might be likely to be occasioned, because that would be quite sufficient to satisfy this definition. . . ."

The similarity between this type of direction and elements within the law of criminal libel may be apparent.

It seems that only the Christian religion is protected, so that scurrilous attacks on the Jewish or Moslem or Buddhist faiths would be outside the law of blasphemy.

There have been several unsuccessful attempts to abolish blasphemous libel and, while prosecutions have been rare (four in the 120 years until 1976) the law in this area will undoubtedly receive further scrutiny with the latest prosecution.

In December 1976, Bristow J. gave Mrs. Mary Whitehouse permission to prosecute *Gay News* and its editor, Mr. Denis Lemon. The judge also issued a voluntary Bill of Indictment, which had the effect of taking the matter to the Central Criminal Court for trial without the need for the normal committal proceedings. (See Appendix A for the trial result and further developments.)

The procedure for a voluntary Bill of Indictment, which is an alternative to normal committal proceedings, is rather special. The proceedings are never heard in open court. The applicant presents written material plus a draft indictment to a High Court judge and an affidavit stating the reasons for the application. The judge gives his decision in writing and he need not actually have anyone attending before him. He can, however, call for the applicant or proposed witnesses to attend if he so wishes. The application can neither be made nor heard in open court.

Seditious Libel

Dicey, in his *Law of the Constitution* (1885), stated: "The law . . . sanctions criticism on public affairs which is bona fide intended to recommend the reform of existing institutions by legal methods. But any one will see at once that the legal definition of a seditious libel might easily be so used as to check a great deal of what is ordinarily considered allowable discussion, and would if rigidly enforced be inconsistent with prevailing forms of political agitation."

Sedition is basically one step away from treason. It was described by Sir James Fitzjames Stephen late in the nineteenth century as:

"... an intention to bring into hatred or contempt, or to incite disaffection against the person of, Her Majesty, her heirs or successors, or the government and constitution of the United Kingdom, as by law established, or either House of Parliament, or the administration of justice, or to excite Her Majesty's subjects to attempt, otherwise than by lawful means, the alteration of any matter in Church or State by law established, or to raise discontent or disaffection amongst Her Majesty's subjects, or to promote feelings of ill-will and hostility between different classes of such subjects."

At least 13 different activities or actions could be seditious within this description, something of an omnibus offence. The narrative for the defences is no less interesting.

"An intention to shew that Her Majesty has been misled or mistaken in her measures, or to point out errors or defects in the government or constitution as by law established, with a view to their reformation, or to excite Her Majesty's subjects to attempt by lawful means the alteration of any matter in Church or State by law established, or to point out, in order to their removal, matters which are producing, or have a tendency to produce, feelings or hatred and ill-will between classes of Her Majesty's subjects, is not a seditious intention."

The current law would appear to involve the following ingredients:

(i) A deliberate intention to achieve a seditious object by violence.

(ii) A tendency in the words used to incite public disorder.

In R. v. Aldred (1909) Coleridge J. directed the jury in the following terms and this statement appears, fairly, to represent the twentieth century attitude to the offence:

"You are entitled to look at all the circumstances surrounding the publication with a view to seeing whether the language used is calculated to produce the results imputed; that is to say that you are entitled to look at the audience addressed, because language which would be innocuous, practically speaking, if used to an assembly of professors or divines might produce a different result if used before an excited audience of young and uneducated men. You are entitled to take into account the state of public feeling. Of course there are times when a spark will explode a magazine. . . . A prosecution for seditious libel is somewhat of a rarity. It is a weapon that is not often taken down from the armoury in which is hangs, but it is a necessary accompaniment to every civilised government. . . . A man may lawfully express his opinion on any public matter, however distasteful, however repugnant to others, if of course he avoids defamatory matter or if he avoids anything that can be characterised either as blasphemous or as an obscene libel. Matters of State, matters of policy, matters even of morals — all these are open to him. He may state his opinion freely, he may buttress it by arguments, he may try to persuade others to share his views. Courts and juries are not the judges in such matters. For instance, if he thinks that either a despotism or an oligarchy, or a republic, or even no government at all is the best way of conducting business affairs, he is at perfect liberty to say so. . . . He may warn the executive of the day against taking a particular course. . . . He may seek to show that rebellions, insurrections, outrages, assassinations and such like are the natural, the deplorable, the inevitable outcome of the policy which he is combatting. All of that is allowed because it is innocuous, but on the other hand if he makes use of language calculated to advocate or to incite others to public disorders, to wit, rebellions, insurrections, assassinations, outrages, or any physical force or violence of any kind, then whatever his motives, whatever his intentions, there would be evidence on which a jury might, on which I think a jury ought, to decide that he is guilty of a seditious publication."

More than a century has passed since there was a successful prosecution of a newspaper edition for sedition. In *R.* v. *Caunt* (1947), a provincial newspaper ran a strongly-worded leading article attacking British Jewry. This was at a time when anti-Jewish feeling was high because of atrocities committed against British troops in Palestine prior to the birth of the Israeli state.

The article in the *Morecambe and Heysham Visitor*, stated

in particular:

> "If British Jewry is suffering from the righteous wrath of British citizens, then they have only themselves to blame for their passive inactivity. Violence may be the only way to bring them to the sense of their responsibility to the country in which they live."

Mr. Justice Birkett told the jury that Caunt could be convicted if they were satisfied that the article had been written with the intention of stirring up hostility between Jews and non-Jews. If, having heard the evidence, they felt there was room for more than one view about Caunt's intention and were in doubt about which actually operated, he should be acquitted. He said:

> "You will recollect how valuable a blessing the liberty of the Press is to all of us, and sure I am that that liberty will meet no injury — suffer no diminution at your hands."

The jury acquitted. While seditious libel may not be one of the most active areas of Press law, it is a component of the law relating to free speech.

4 Injurious Falsehoods and the Trade Descriptions Act

In addition to defamation, which seeks to remedy injuries to a person's reputation, there is the additional tort of injurious falsehood which divides into three categories:

(1) slander of title — falsely suggesting that someone does not own property;

(2) slander of goods — falsely attacking the quality of a person's goods; and

(3) malicious falsehood — falsely suggesting, for instance, that a person has died, retired from his trade or profession or has ceased to trade.

For this area of law to operate, it is up to the plaintiff to prove:

(a) that the defendant was actuated by express malice;

(b) that the statement was false; and

(c) either

(i) the falsehood was calculated to cause financial loss and was in a permanent form

or (ii) the falsehood was calculated to cause damage in respect of his office, trade, profession or calling.

With injurious falsehoods there is no wrong to the person's reputation. What is critical, and it is up to the plaintiff to prove this, is that there has been a malicious publication of a false statement about his trading interests or activities.

In defamation, the plaintiff need only prove that there has been publication of words referring to him which lower him. The burden then falls on the defendant to prove a valid defence (*i.e.* privilege or fair comment).

X, a famous film star, is reported to have joined a religious sect which shuns publicity and opposes accumulation of wealth. Sect members work anonymously within society, attempting to ease suffering and hardship and to spread compassion. X's general reputation will not have been lowered in the eyes of right-thinking members of society. The report, if untrue, might lose him book-ings and lead to an action for malicious falsehood.

X, if he wishes to succeed in an action for malicious falsehood, will have to prove very much more in his portion of the case than in a defamation action.

There are elements in the *Savalas* v. *Associated Newspapers Ltd.* (1976) case, mentioned already under "Defamation," which perhaps emphasise the relative difficulty of malicious falsehood actions when set against defamation claims.

The *Daily Mail* copy referred to Mr. Savalas as someone who could not cope with super-stardom because his night-life led him to forget his lines on a film set and keep his co-star, Mr. James Mason, waiting. Mr. Savalas gave evidence that a producer visited him because it looked as if he had suffered from a personality change and a Hollywood columnist came out to see "if the applause had blown Telly out of proportion and if he does have a Dr. Jekyll and Mr. Hyde personality." He said that Universal Studios had cancelled a big budget film, *Nick the Greek,* in which he was to have starred. He told the court: "I would not be surprised if that was something to do with the *Daily Mail* article. Studios nowadays will not risk money on irresponsible artists, however successful they may be."

While Mr. Savalas recovered £34,000 damages for libel, if he had sued for malicious falsehood he would have had to prove that the article was published out of some dishonest or improper motive on the part of the *Daily Mail* and that it was calculated to cause him damage. His loss of the part in Universal's film might have had to be proved rather than left as the subject of supposition. That he chose the easier route to recover damages is offered as no criticism.

If the reports about X joining a religious sect had come from occasions attracting absolute or qualified privilege, a newspaper would have a complete defence as it would if what it stated was true. What is less clear is the position of reports arising from non-privileged situations. If the report came from X's manager (who knew it was untrue and who was acting maliciously, perhaps because he had just been dismissed), would the manager's malice "infect" the newspaper's publication of the falsehood?

It is suggested that the correct approach is as follows:

(1) the manager can be sued for malicious falsehood;

(2) the newspaper could also be sued if X could prove that their publication had been malicious in express terms rather than merely "infected" terms: perhaps the newspaper should have made a direct check with X for confirmation and comment or, perhaps, the manager's statement was issued in terms indicating that X would not be prepared to comment on the matter at all. Certainly the newspaper would be liable if they were aware of the falsity of the statement but, in the absence of X proving this, it is submitted that they should not be liable unless there were additional elements showing they were, at least, recekless rather than careless.

The dangers of this tort can be consideraly diminished by the simple expedient of checking details with the subject of the material statement.

Slander to goods, in this age of consumer-consciousness, is an area of potential danger. Care should be taken that comparative tests of products are correctly interpreted.

Trade Descriptions Act 1968

If a trader makes a false or misleading statement about the goods or services he is offering, he is liable to a £400 summary fine or, if tried on indictment, an unlimited fine and up to two years' imprisonment. The Trading Standards departments of local authorities have the responsibility of enforcing the Act and, if a false or misleading trade description is contained in a newspaper or magazine advertisement, the editor and publisher may also be liable.

It is this publishers' liability which will be examined, because the bulk of the Act (and other legislation like the Trade Descriptions Act 1972, the Fair Trading Act 1973 and the Consumer Credit Act 1974) relates to liability at the supplier's or manufacturer's end.

From the Press point of view:

(1) Where the offence has been committed by an individual because of the act or default of another person, then that other person may be charged with and convicted of the offence whether or not action is taken against the "innocent" party (s.23).

(2) A publisher of an advertisement who can prove:

(a) his business is to publish or arrange for the publication of advertisements;

(b) he received the advertisement in the normal course of business; and

(c) he had no reason to suspect that the publication could amount to an offence,

can use the defence in these terms set out in section 25.

The offence only relates to matter in advertising copy, so descriptions of goods and services in editorial copy are outside the terms of the Act. The editor and writer are not liable even though the description was false or misleading. But, if the original information came from a handout, then the person responsible for issuing the handout may be liable.

An advertising supplement falls within the terms of the Act. Copy written by a journalist for this, containing a false or misleading statement, could lead to a prosecution. He may have a defence via section 24 of the Act if he can prove:

(a) that the offence was due to a mistake or reliance on information supplied to him or to the act or default of another person, an accident or some other cause beyond his control; and

(b) that he took all reasonable precautions and care to avoid committing the offence.

Under the Consumer Credit Act 1974, certain offences may be committed in connection with the publication of advertisements for the provision of credit services (ss.44-45). A newspaper is protected in publications by a defence identical to that in (2) above.

5 Contempt and the Phillimore Committee

The law of contempt is as important to the Press as the law of defamation. The critical difference is that contempt is generally a criminal matter as far as the Press are concerned; defamation, apart from criminal libel, relates to the civil law. Contempt is a common law offence for which (with certain exceptions) the punishment is a fine and/or imprisonment: there is currently no maximum on what a court may impose with either penalty. Actions for defamation begin with the more stately process of the issuing of a writ and may at worst only result in a sum of money being awarded to the successful plaintiff. The defendant in the normal defamation action does not face prison or a punitive fine.

The importance of these two areas was further emphasised by reports which appeared within four months of each other. The Faulks Committee, examining defamation, reported in March 1975; three months before saw the publication of the Phillimore Committee report on contempt. Work started on both in June 1971.

The Press, itself, has been testing certain frontiers. The *Sunday Times* was responsible for the first contempt case directly affecting the Press to appear before the House of Lords (in 1973). Further developments following this case ocurred in 1977. Since that time, there have been numerous problems in this area: issues within the demise of the architect Mr. John Poulson, the revelation of witnesses' names in a blackmail trial and the refusal of a reporter to reveal his source of information are but a few.

It is to be hoped that Parliament will correct many of the criticisms levelled at the current law of contempt as speedily as possible. It was argued during the American "Watergate" revelations that the existing English law of contempt would not permit such disclosures.

The law has to strike a balance between allowing individuals a fair trial and permitting the Press to reveal situations which might otherwise rest without correction. Too often, however, the law in this area has protected the judicial machine rather than those who seek to use the machine. For this reason and because of uncertainties, which will be explored, some fairly radical change is imperative.

The law of contempt has developed over the centuries to give the courts sanctions to act on conduct which might obstruct, prejudice or distort the administration of justice.

The law recognises two categories of contempt and it is the second which will be dealt with in detail because it is this aspect which really affects the Press. Contempt may be civil or criminal. The Press abide by direct court orders and the significance of civil contempt is, therefore, reduced.

Civil Contempt

This occurs when a party disobeys an order of the court either negatively or positively. The court may order a defendant in a civil case to pay damages (e.g. in a defamation action) or to quit premises: refusal to comply with the order is in the negative form. The court may, in other cases, order someone not to do a particular thing. It might be in the form of an injunction not to publish a particular article, not to pester an individual or not to engage in a particular enterprise within a certain area. Refusal to comply with this type of order is contempt in a positive form.

In 1975, a journalist was committed to prison because he publicised details about a pop festival. The High Court had issued an injunction to restrain the holding of the festival (*Att.-Gen.* v. *Dwyer and Rawle* (1975)).

It is the power to punish for disobedience which distinguishes the Queen's Courts from unofficial tribunals. If the Press Council were to order the publication of an adjudication and a newspaper failed to comply, there is no direct sanction: the Press Council does not form part of the Queen's Courts.

The old civil sanction used to be imprisonment until the contemnor agreed to be obedient. Everything rested on the contemnor and he could be released within one week or stay in prison indefinitely; it all depended on his stubbornness. When an individual can be imprisoned, the system may just work. The courts have come to accept that, in civil cases, when they are dealing with corporate bodies like companies or trade unions, this is not feasible. As a result, in 1972, fines totalling £185,000 were imposed on the Transport and General Worker's Union by the National Industrial Relations Court (as it then was). This was the minimum penalty which the court felt able to issue in the circumstances. Non-payment of this fine led to the sequestration (taking over by the court) of assets within the Union totalling the required amount.

In any event, there is no trial by jury. The judge deals with the matter himself.

Because of some of the problems in this area the Phillimore Committee recommend that the distinction between "civil" and "criminal" contempt be abolished. They also recommend that *sine die* committals (imprisonment until the contempt is "purged") be abolished and that proof of contempt should have the overall criminal standard of "beyond reasonable doubt."

In 1976, Mr. Robert Relf spent over six weeks in prison for refusing to take down a sign outside his house declaring he would sell the property only to an English family, which contravened the Race Relations Act 1965. The case posed a number of problems. The committal, by a county court judge, was until the contempt was purged by the removal of the sign. Relf countered by making it clear that he would not remove the sign and staging a hunger strike. The Official Solicitor, who watches over all contempt cases, monitored events and Relf was eventually released effectively because of the danger to his health. The case highlighted the flaws of *sine die* committals.

Criminal Contempt

Criminal contempt can be classified according to three general types of conduct:

(1) publishing matter which may prejudice a pending trial;
(2) "scandalising" the court; or
(3) interfering with judicial proceedings or refusing to

reveal sources of information to a competent court or tribunal.

The procedure for contempts is highly individual. Over the years, it has come to be accepted that this subject is within the direct and independent jurisdiction of the courts. The judges, therefore, have wide powers of investigation and punishment: there is no jury to assess matters of fact and the procedure is summary in nature.

For contempts committed "in the face of the court" the judge is prosecutor, chief witness, jury and then judge. This omnibus function rather erodes the objectivity normally associated with English criminal law.

At the High Court-crown court level and above ("courts of record") the judges' power to act is unrestricted. The county court is classed as an inferior court of record and there are certain restrictions, as there are in the lowest courts (*i.e.* magistrates' and coroners' courts). The superior courts of record, like the High Court, have not been fettered by Parliament beyond the establishment of an appeals procedure.

Under section 157 of the County Courts Act 1959, county courts have power to impose a fine of £20 or 30 days' imprisonment for contempts in the face of the court. The Phillimore Committee recommend that these powers be increased to a fine of £150 or up to three months' imprisonment.

An important case on the edge of this area in relation to court proceedings occurred in 1975. Section 84 of the County Courts Act 1959 (as amended) states that if a person refuses or neglects, without sufficient cause, to produce a document, he is liable to be fined up to £50. It should be emphasised that the issue before the court in this case was not straightforward contempt but that of the basic jurisdiction of the county court and the Supreme Court.

Senior v. *Holdsworth* (1975): a pop festival in 1974 held in Windsor Great Park was broken up by the police. I.T.N. news film recorded some of the incidents. Senior, one of the organisers of the festival, issued a summons to I.T.N. to produce "all film and video taken of the break up" in what proved to be a successful action against the police for assault. I.T.N. were prepared (and did) shows the film which had been transmitted but objected to producing all the film. They argued that what remained untransmitted might be misleading, that reporting teams might face violence in future situations and that all that was relevant was the transmitted film. Because of their refusal to show all of the film to the county court judge in the case, they were fined £50 for disobedience. The fine was set aside by the Court of Appeal because the summons was much too wide in its terms: it was oppressive to require the whole of the film to be shown when only one small incident was involved.

The Court of Appeal emphasised, however, that there was jurisdiction to compel a broadcasting authority to produce untransmitted film in civil or criminal proceedings, but that the court should only require this where it is relevant, as well as proper and necessary, for the course of justice.

The verbatim notes of a reporter covering an incident would fall within this ruling and would be subject to the same requirements for production. It might be argued, however, that subjective impressions recorded by the reporter would not provide the recorded visual scene in the same way as news film.

Magistrates have no powers, save binding over to keep the peace and outright exclusion, to use the law of contempt to punish disruptive conduct in court. For disobedience to court orders, they can fine £1 a day (up to a total of £20) or commit in custody for up to two months. Witnesses who refuse to appear before them may be committed in custody for up to seven days. Other conduct amounting to an alleged contempt could be referred to the Attorney-General and ultimately considered by the Divisional Court of the Queen's Bench.

The Phillimore Committee recommend that magistrates' courts should be able to deal with contempts in the same way as they can deal with recalcitrant witnesses (up to seven days' imprisonment) with the alternative of a fine of up to £20.

(1) Prejudicing fair trial

From the Press point of view, the areas of concern here are:
    (a) pre-trial interviews;
    (b) pre-trial information;
    (c) prejudicing the due administration of justice (while it may involve (a) and (b)) covers other conduct.

Despite some of the examples which follow, the dangers are often caused by inadvertence or misunderstanding rather than by deliberately prejudicial conduct.

An initial point which must be considered is a statutory provision which, in fairness, was brought in to give the Press some limited protection in an area of law riddled with uncertainties and traps for the unwary.

Section 11 (1) of the Administration of Justice Act 1960 provides a defence of innocent publication to a charge of contempt as follows:

"A person shall not be guilty of contempt of court on the ground that he had published matter calculated to interfere with the course of justice in connection with any proceedings pending or imminent at the time of publication if at that time (having taken all reasonable care) he did not know and had no reason to suspect that proceedings were pending . . . or imminent. . . ."

There are two requirements for this defence to succeed:

(1) all reasonable care must have been taken to check the situation; and

(2) there must have been no knowledge that proceedings were pending or imminent.

This section resulted from the case of *R.* v. *Odhams Press Ltd.* (1957), where the *People* were found guilty of a contempt in respect of an article headlined "Arrest this beast!" The person referred to in the article had, unknown to the newspaper, been arrested and was awaiting trial on charges similar to those detailed in the article. The proprietors were fined £1,000 and the editor and reporter £500 each for what the court regarded as a circulation-boosting exercise.

Unfortunately, the key phrase in this section, "pending or imminent," is not further defined. In the House of Lords, the Lord Chancellor, Viscount Kilmuir, stated, in debate on the Bill, that proceedings were imminent when no one has been charged but arrest is expected hourly. This statement has no force of law. On the basis of the wording of the section, it has been held, in Northern Ireland, that it is a contempt to publish information about a man suspected of an offence but not yet arrested or charged (*R.* v. *Beaverbrook Newspapers Ltd.* (1962)).

In this case the defendants were fined £5,000, their Manchester editor £750 and their London editor £500. (The *Daily Mail*,

for a more trivial infringement on the same facts, was fined
£500.)

The total confusion about the effect of this section led the
Phillimore Committee to recommend not its abolition, but
rather a complete change in the relevant time period when contempts may be committed in relation to criminal cases.

The major alteration, discussed later, is that interviews or
information, before a person is arrested and charged, should
not automatically constitute contempts.

If and when this recommendation becomes effective
through legislation, the relevance of the section 11 defence
would diminish. It cannot be emphasised too strongly that,
until legislation puts the proposal into effect, section 11
remains the only safeguard and one of very limited application.

(a) *Pre-trial interviews.* After an incident which may, eventually, lead to criminal or civil proceedings the news reports are
necessarily based on eye-witness accounts. The "grilling" on
television of a person involved (or potentially involved) in a
court case may seem to take the form of a cross-examination in
court and may affect or distort the evidence he might give at the
trial.

> *R.* v. *Savundranayagan and Walker* (1968): When the Fire, Auto
> and Marine Insurance Company, controlled by the late Dr.
> Savundra, collapsed there was considerable public interest and con-
> cern. David Frost, on a television programme, secured an interview
> with Savundra when it was obvious that he was about to be
> arrested and charged with gross fraud. The interview, which was
> also published verbatim in the *Sunday Times,* established Savund-
> ra's guilt. A later appeal by him and his associate on the grounds
> that their trials had been prejudiced by this interview was unsuc-
> cessful. The Court of Appeal pointed out that he had willingly
> agreed to the interview and any prejudice which arose was of his
> own making. The programme and newspaper were, however, criti-
> cised for their conduct.

This case, however, does highlight one problem. Witnesses (or
accused persons) may commit themselves to one version of the
story in advance and be scared, or unable, to change that version to the truth.

The Phillimore Committee commented: ". . . it is only right to say that, responsibly conducted, they [Press interviews] may make a useful contribution to public information."

Crimes are a regular feature of news reports and, if police efforts are successful, a trial is a subsequent probability. Crime reports can often contain detail, completely unforeseeable and trivial at the time, which is hotly contested at the eventual trial.

"In order to compile a report it is usually necessary to interview witnesses, who may later be witnesses at the trial. A reporter may be able to obtain a very full account of what occurred, and be in a position to publish a considerable amount of what would later become evidence at the trial. There are particular dangers where the circumstances of a crime seem to lay suspicion upon a particular person. The law of libel may afford some protection, but not against publication of a true account of the suspect's past, which could be highly prejudicial."

This comment by the Phillimore Committee was promptly brought into focus by the Press coverage of the case of Cambridge rapist, Cook, in 1975. When a suspect was arrested, Press reports were accompanied by photographs of the accused man at remand proceedings, interviews with the man's wife concerning his past and his family life and other detail which, it is submitted, went beyond the bounds not only of the existing law, but also of the changes proposed by the Phillimore Committee.

Since this case, certain sections of the Press have acted as if the Phillimore Committee's recommendations are actually the law.

This was evident in the coverage given to the hunt for the "Black Panther" (Donald Neilson). An arrest can scarcely be more imminent than when the police have the suspects trapped in a seige situation. In the "Spaghetti House" restaurant seige in Knightsbridge in 1975, the Press and media revealed details of the criminal convictions of some of the men inside, prior to their capitulation. When Mr. Ross McWhirter was killed outside his home, there was an unequivocal link between this event, a bombing incident in London and members of the I.R.A. involved in the Balcombe Street seige, before the suspects gave themselves up for arrest in the glare of television lights and cameras.

Such coverage probably prejudices the proposals for change more than encouraging reform but the Attorney-General has, on these matters, taken no action.

On the matter of photographs, the Phillimore Committee demonstrated an appreciation of some of the difficulties facing editors. Identification is often a crucial issue in criminal trials, however cut and dried this may seem before the hearings begin. Photographs may seriously prejudice the issue and witnesses may be unable to swear that they have been unaided by pre-trial pictures. This situation may be as damaging to the prosecution as to the accused person. On the other hand, photographs of wanted men are often published at the request of the police either in true or photofit form. It should be clearly understood that, at the moment, the editor, who consents to publish such pictures, does so at his own risk. There is no defence to contempt that publication was in the public interest and in good faith, from material supplied by the police.

The Phillimore Committee recommend that the defence of "public benefit" should not be introduced into the law of contempt. Some members of the committee were attracted by it initially because it would remove technical contempts and ensure much greater freedom from liability for publications designed to help the police catch criminals. Most publications, however, take place before the wanted man is charged (and this period should be contempt-free: see below) so the extra change is not so necessary. The committee want to introduce greater certainty into the law of contempt so that the Press know exactly where they stand. They conclude: "To decide whether, in respect of a particular matter, a defence of public benefit could be successfully advanced would on the contrary be extremely difficult. Public benefit is notoriously difficult to define: the creation of a defence on that basis would introduce a fresh area of uncertainty into the law."

To sum up, eyewitness accounts of incidents and even photographs of the incident may be used by any prejudicial detail must be left out. This is a matter of fact for each case as it presents itself and caution rather than carefree optimism are recommended.

(b) *Pre-trial information*. Much of what has been discussed under pre-trial interviews applies equally to this section and the basic recommendations are the same. Certain recent cases and examples, however, are more conveniently explained under this category.

In 1949, the editor of the *Daily Mirror* was imprisoned for three months and the paper fined £10,000 for a suggestion that Haigh, the acid-bath murderer, had committed offences in addition to those for which he was awaiting trial. Haigh, himself, was not mentioned by name in the copy, it should be noted: the type of crime hardly required this. There was a warning within this case to the directors of the *Daily Mirror* that if, for the purposes of increasing their circulation, their paper should in future attempt such a contempt they, too, might find themselves punished individually.

The leading case in this area arose from the Thalidomide tragedy and the forthright presentation of certain aspects by *The Sunday Times*.

Att.-Gen. v. *Times Newspapers Ltd.* (1973): *The Sunday Times*, in 1972, had published a long article criticising the law relating to the liability of drug companies and, in particular, Distillers Ltd. who manufactured thalidomide.

The first article stated: "the thalidomide children shame Distillers . . . the law is not always the same as justice. There are times when to insist on the letter of the law is as exposed to criticism as infringement of another's legal rights. The figure in the proposed settlement is £3.25 million spread over 10 years. This does not shine as a beacon against pre-tax profits last year of £64.8 million and company assets worth £421 million. Without in any way surrendering on negligence, Distillers could and should think again."

This article was held to fall outside the law of contempt eventually, but Distillers were sufficiently upset to refer it to the Attorney-General so that the contempt issue could be considered by the courts.

A second article, to show that Distillers had not exercised due care in checking that the drug was safe, was written and sent by *The Sunday Times* to the Attorney-General so that it could receive adjudication at the same time as the first article.

Proceedings were begun for an injunction to prevent its publication. The Divisional Court ruled that the draft article was a con-

tempt because Distillers were being subjected to pressure which
created a serious risk that they would be denied justice as their freedom of action in the pending case was being affected.

The Court of Appeal (Lord Denning in particular) lifted the
injunction because they felt the article was comment on a matter of
outstanding public interest which did not prejudice litigation
which had been dormant for several years.

The House of Lords agreed the first article was not a contempt
but re-imposed the injunction on the second because:

(1) it was a contempt to publish an article expressing an opinion
when this could give rise to a "real risk" that the fair trial of the
action would be prejudiced; and

(2) it was a contempt to use improper pressure to induce a litigant to settle a case on terms to which he did not agree.

The different routes taken by their Lordships to reach their
unanimous decision show variety and breadth if not stunning
clarity. As this was the first contempt case relating to the Press
to reach the House of Lords, perhaps too much was expected.

The judgments are not going to be explored in detail
because of subsequent recommendations from the Phillimore
Committee. The "real risk" formula, developed by Lord Reid
in this case, has had definite practical application in some
cases considered later.

On the "real risk" formula, he said:

"There is no contempt if the possibility of influence is remote. If
there is some but only a small likelihood, that may influence the
court to refrain from inflicting any punishment. If there is a serious risk some action may be necessary. And I think that the particular comment cannot be considered in isolation when considering
its probable effect. If others are to be free and are likely to make similar comments, that must be taken into account. . . .

If people are led to think that it is easy to find the truth disrespect
for the processes of the law could follow and, if mass media are
allowed to judge, unpopular people and unpopular causes will
fare very badly. . . . I do not think that the freedom of the Press
would suffer, and I think that the law would be clearer and easier to
apply in practice if it is made a general rule that it is not permissible to prejudge issues in pending cases. . . .

There is no magic in the issue of a writ or in a charge being made
against an accused person. Comment on a case which is imminent
may be as objectionable as comment after it has begun. And a 'gagging' writ ought to have no effect. But I must add to prevent any

misunderstanding that comment where a case is under appeal is a very different matter. For one thing it is scarcely possible to imagine a case where comment could influence judges in the Court of Appeal or noble and learned Lords in this House. And it would be wrong and contrary to existing practice to limit proper criticism of judgments already given but under appeal."

The thalidomide injunction was partially lifted in 1976 and as a result of developments when the case was taken to Strasbourg, the second article appeared, in full, in the summer of 1977.

The prejudicing of the fair trial of this action could only have come about if, as seems to have been accepted by the House of Lords, judges in the High Court would have been influenced by the contents of the article. The case was a civil matter, which would have been tried in the Queen's Bench Division without a jury. The victims of the thalidomide tragedy would have been the plaintiffs and Distillers the defendants. The trial judge would have had before him, at the trial, the plaintiff's allegations and the defence denials in the form of written pleadings between the parties. He would have heard evidence in support of these pleadings.

Lord Salmon told the Phillimore Committee that he thought this type of contempt was completely irrelevant in civil proceedings, where the case would be tried by a judge on his own:

"I think the law of libel takes care of anything you may say about a civil case, and if a judge is going to be affected by what is written or said he is not fit to be a judge."

The Phillimore Committee recommend that, in relation to civil proceedings, contempts should only be possible when the case has been set down for trial. This is the technical stage when pleadings between the parties have ceased and they wish the case to enter the court lists for determination. The time between a case being set down for trial and actually being tried is generally between six and nine months for High Court actions and a lesser period for county court actions. These periods can, of course, be greater but the Press would have the advantage of knowing that, after a particular date, this type of contempt would have to be avoided.

The thalidomide case was an exceptional one. The brunt of pre-trial prejudice usually occurs in criminal cases where juries are involved if the accused pleads not guilty to the offence. About 2 per cent. of all criminal cases are tried by jury but these are, of course, the one which generally attract Press interest.

The extent to which juries may be influenced by pre-trial information is hard to ascertain. Juries, and the methods by which they reach their eventual decisions, remain an unchartable area of English law. It could be that they are not nearly as susceptible to influence as the courts fear. At the first *Kray* trial, a number of defendants were convicted of murder. In addition to the court reports, a number of newspapers carried detailed feature articles about the background and activities of the Kray brothers and their associates. There was then a second trial, on further murder charges: the jury acquitted the defendants. The jury which acquitted Miss Janie Jones of blackmail charges (see later: *R.* v. *Socialist Worker and Foot* (1974)) must have been aware that she had been convicted a short time before on other charges which received a great deal of publicity.

Perhaps the most outstanding example of pre-trial information and interviewing comes from the Lord Lucan saga.

The relevant facts for consideration are:

A man entered the Belgravia home of the seventh Earl of Lucan and battered to death the nanny to Lord Lucan's children. At about the same time, in the same house, Lady Lucan was attacked and struck four or five times on the head. Lord and Lady Lucan were estranged and, from initial reports, it was evident that Lord Lucan was the suspect.

Press reports mentioned the fact that the couple were estranged, the fact that Lord Lucan had visited his brother-in-law about two hours after the incident in a distressed and dishevelled state, that his car had been found at Newhaven with bloodstains and that he was thought by the police to have with him two antique firearms. Pictures were published of the suspect and details given of his past life. A warrant was then issued for his arrest. Subsequent coverage by the Press re-iterated some of the above details. An inquest was held into the death of the nanny, Mrs. Sandra Rivett. At the inquest, Lady Lucan said her attacker was her husband. "He thrust three gloved fingers down my throat . . . during the course of the fight he attempted to strangle me from the front and gouge my eyes out. I was on the ground."

It was also revealed at the inquest that bloodstains in the car found at Newhaven matched the groups of both the nanny and Lady Lucan.

The jury decided that Lord Lucan had murdered the nanny and the Coroner issued a warrant for his arrest and trial at the Old Baily.

There are a number of issues raised by this case:

(1) The prejudicial information published before the police issued a warrant for Lord Lucan's arrest;

(2) The prejudicial information published after the police issued a warrant for his arrest but before the inquest evidence was heard;

(3) The prejudicial information arising from the inquest and subsequent issue of the Coroner's Warrant for Lord Lucan's arrest.

On the first point, there is the defence within section 11 (1) of the Administration of Justice Act 1960. On the second, there appears to have been a transgression of the strict law of contempt in certain coverage. These two areas could be irrelevant if the Phillimore Committee recommendations become the law. On the third point, the law is unclear but the committee's recommendations would put such reports of judicial proceedings inside the law and make them defensible (though Coroners' juries have lost the power to name an individual for murder since section 56 of the Criminal Law Act 1977).

The issues raised by this case, legal and ethical, deserve some consideration. The trial of Lord Lucan, if he is eventually found alive, has apparently been prejudiced. Evidence of identification is bound to be crucial yet pictures have been published of him. Certain reports *prior* to the Coroner's inquest referred to the "murdered" nanny. Murder is something that a man may actually be charged with or a verdict which the jury may return. Neither had occurred until a Coroner's jury, in Lucan's absence, named him. It is permissible to describe the method of killing — stabbing, strangling, shooting or battering — in relation to the victim, but to suggest that a person has murdered another, pre-supposes that a jury at the criminal trial will return such a verdict. The reporter should understand that his function in criminal matters is basically to inform and not, despite unofficial police remarks, to act as a juryman. Murder requires a number of ingredients and, even in what appears to be the most clear-cut case, the jury may either return or be directed to return a verdict of manslaughter for various reasons. There is a fundamental difference between reporting, as a fact, that a murder hunt is in progress and stating that the police are treating the matter as one of murder (which is their opinion and not necessarily that of the jury). Any "hunt" is for a man suspected of a crime: unless and until the police are given the right by law to convert suspicions into proven fact by a mere statement of their belief (at which stage the criminal courts will no longer have any purpose) this is the law. The pre-arrest prejudicial detail will be discussed along with the problem of reports of legal proceedings, not necessarily criminal, which reveal criminal conduct or suggestions of such conduct.

The lack of prosecutions for contempt should not be taken as an indication that such prosecutions could not be brought by the Attorney-General in the future on this case or on other similar cases. In such matters, time does not run against the Crown and it is, fortunately, no defence to say that others have transgressed, therefore, this transgression is justified.

Colouring and slanting of copy to effect "trial" by the Press, is one certain method of ensuring that current uncertainties within the law of contempt become definite restrictions, rather than enacted provisions which would benefit the Press.

To remove the current uncertainty about when interviews and information become potential contempts in criminal cases, the Phillimore Committeee have produced their most far-reaching proposal. In their own words: "We have come to the conclusion that the right point in England and Wales is the moment when the suspected man is charged or a summons served." In short, only information after this point should be a potential contempt.

In London, where the time periods are greatest, it takes about 22 weeks between a man being committed for trial by magistrates and his coming before a jury. The time period before the committal depends on the complexity of the case. The Press should know from which point contempts in this area may occur. The current period is when a warrant for the accused's arrest is pending or imminent because, before this time, newspapers have the section 11 defence. The problem is that warrants are usually issued in private and even the actual arrest may not be immediately announced in public: the Press, consequently, are at risk without fault under the present law. The committee note: "Moreoever, if the wanted man was never found publication would be restricted, at least in theory, as long as the warrant for his arrest still existed." The *Lucan* case adds ironic relevance to this comment.

If the recommendation is accepted, Press comment would be possible until a person is charged. This means that the individual must actually have been apprehended (something which the Press will be aware of through general police contacts) and the formality of a charge completed. Interviews and information before this time would be permissible, within the parameters of the other recommendations of the committee. This suggestion would aid certainty in this area of the law and deserves enactment as soon as possible.

There is one danger, however. It would be open to the police, in certain cases, to delay arresting an individual until prejudicial details about background facts had been leaked to the Press. This tactic, while theoretical, would make subsequent conviction more certain. Press convenience should not lead to the endangering of individual rights which the Press should seek to uphold.

The third issue raised by the *Lucan* case is the position of judicial proceedings before a person is arrested and charged with an offence. Until 1974, it was thought that a fair and accurate report of legal proceedings published in good faith could not constitute a contempt: in January of that year, the Poulson scandal broke in full. Mr. Justice Waller, at the trial of Poulson and his co-accused Pottinger, ruled that certain items of evidence should not be published because there was a risk of prejudicing other criminal proceedings relating to the collapse of the Poulson empire. A case from 1821 (*R. v. Clement*) which concerned the Cato Street conspiracy, was quoted as authority for the ruling.

The second *Kray* trial has already been mentioned. In that case, in 1969, Mr. Justice Lawton said:

"I can see no reason why a newspaper should not report what happens in court, even though there may be other charges pending. The reporting of trials which take place in open court is an important part of the functions of a newspaper, and it would not be in the public interest, in my judgment, if newspapers desisted from reporting trials, and from reporting verdicts and sentences in those trials, merely because there was some indictment still to be dealt with. What is more, the mere fact that a newspaper has reported a trial and a verdict which was adverse to a person subsequently accused ought not in the ordinary way to produce a case of probable bias amongst jurors empanelled in a later case. I have enough confidence in my fellow-countrymen to think that they have got newspapers sized up ... and they are capable in normal circumstances of looking at a matter fairly and without prejudice even though they have to disregard what they may have read in a newspaper."

The *Poulson* and *Kray* rulings conflict. The former is the most recent statement. It places an unnecessarily heavy burden on court reporters. It is not unusual for evidence to emerge during the course of a trial which could damage the trial of other people, whether witnesses before the court or completely unconnected with the proceedings. If the Press had to check every person mentioned, to see whether criminal or civil proceedings were pending against them, copy might never appear from court cases.

The same problem applies to the public examination in bankruptcy proceedings and to coroner's inquests. If criminal conduct is revealed during the course of these proceedings, and other criminal proceedings follow, then the accused's ultimate trial has been prejudiced, yet the Press are seeking to report judicial proceedings in good faith.

The Phillimore Committee felt strongly that proceedings in open court should not be liable to be treated as issues for contempt in reports. They recommend that there should be a statutory defence for contempt proceedings, providing the defendant could show that *publication was a fair and accurate report of legal proceedings in open court, published contemporaneously and in good faith.*

This defence incorporates the defamation concept of absolute privilege into the law of contempt: the requirements are similar, but the protection for the former is in civil law while the latter relates to criminal law. The duality does serve to emphasise the close relationship, as far as the Press is concerned, between these two areas of law.

The committee point out that certain evidence is heard in criminal cases in the absence of the jury but still in open court (*e.g.* arguments about whether alleged confessions or previous convictions should be revealed to the jury as admissible evidence). Such argument may not be reported unless the judge summarises it when the jury returns: in this case, his summary is used. The whole purpose of excluding the jury is that they should not hear certain facts unless and until the judge rules them admissible. The Press are permitted to remain in court during these submissions but, if the judge ruled the issue inadmissible and the court copy contained details of the argument, the whole purpose of excluding the jury would have been defeated. Such evidence, if revealed, would still be a contempt.

The requirement of good faith would bar the above defence from someone publishing a report maliciously and with the deliberate intention of causing prejudice. The committee make a further comment:

> "The recent publication of the names of two victims of alleged blackmail in a case being tried at the Old Bailey, however, suggests that the traditional co-operation of the Press can no longer be relied on. We incline to the view that the important question of what the Press may publish concerning proceedings in open court should no longer be left to judicial requests (which may be disregarded) nor to judicial directions (which, if given, may have doubtful legal authority) but that legislation . . . should provide for these specific circumstances in which a court shall be empowered to prohibit, in the public interest, the publication of names or of other matters arising at the trial."

The result of the case, referred to above, is discussed under the next heading. The recommendation is of some importance because it would cover matters where the court wished the identities of witnesses in other cases to remain undisclosed.

A number of cases in 1976 highlighted, in a practical fashion, points already made. 1976, in fact, proved to be something of a watershed year for the law of contempt because it saw the common law tests being applied dynamically and, from the Press point of view, constructively.

The *Evening Standard*, in their first edition of October 27, 1975, had used a picture of Mr. Peter Hain, formerly a prominent Young Liberal. He had just been arrested for an alleged robbery. The picture was used with the headline "HAIN: He's No Bank Robber" and a caption explained that he was due to appear on an identity parade the following day suspected of a bank robbery. In 1976, Mr. Hain was acquitted and, in November, the Attorney-General brought the *Evening Standard* before the Divisional Court where the paper admitted its contempt and was fined £1,000 for this pre-trial matter.

The case was somewhat novel for two reasons. Firstly, the pre-trial prejudice related to favourable rather than unfavourable matter. This was no less of a contempt. The Lord Chief Justice, Lord Widgery, pointed out that an identify parade was the only method available for deciding whether a witness could identify a suspect.

He said that:

"In order that the identity parade should be worth the ground it stood on, it must be totally fair and none of the witnesses approaching the line should be given any kind of indication that one particular individual should be preferred to another as the choice of suspect. In the present case the witnesses could easily have gone to the identification parade with copies of the *Evening Standard* sticking out of their pockets. That did not happen but it might have happened. The court must have that very much in mind."

Secondly, action was taken against the newspaper and not against the editor (who was, at the time of the publication, in China). While the editor normally bears complete responsibility for matter published, this procedure permitted the court to consider only punishing the newspaper rather than the absent Mr. Charles Wintour.

The *Evening Standard* admitted the offence but the court considered four points, put forward by counsel for the newspaper; in setting the fine:

(1) the nature of the contempt;
(2) how the contempt had happened (*i.e.* was it deliberate or was it a mistake?);
(3) the degree of distribution; and
(4) the effect on the administration of justice.

Lord Widgery also made the following comments:

"In every newspaper office there should be some precaution taken
to prevent a mistake like the one in the present case from happen-
ing again. One had to accept the fact that a well-known newspaper
office on a particular day made an elementary mistake which
ought to have been covered by proper systems and checks. ...
Another factor in assessing the penalty was that it would be a great
pity if the courts allowed newspapers to think that the cost of their
legal department was unjustified. The penalty should be a figure
not totally insignificant to an organisation of the size of the *Evening Standard*. ..."

The second significant contempt case (or series of cases)
related to Sir James Goldsmith's battles with *Private Eye*. The
criminal libel aspect of this saga is dealt with separately but
the chronology of certain events is of significance in the matter
of contempt.

(1) On May 21, 1976, members of *Private Eye* gave undertak-
ings not to refer to Sir James or his solicitor, Mr. Eric Levine,
prior to a hearing of an application for a formal injunction in
those terms.

(2) On July 16, 1976, Mr. Justice Donaldson refused to issue
the injunction in terms which would stop *Private Eye* saying
anything lawful about Sir James or Mr. Levine. The injunction was issued, however, limited to publishing matter which
amounted to a contempt of court (which, it was stressed, did
not require an injunction). What Sir James effectively
achieved here was a judicial "public warning" to *Private Eye*.

(3) On August 10, 1976, Sir James applied to the High Court
setting out breaches of the May 21 undertaking. He asked for
two members of *Private Eye* to be imprisoned and the assets of
the magazine and its distributor sequestered (taken over by the
court). Mr. Justice Goff held that the breaches of the undertak-
ings did amount to a serious attack on Sir James but, rather
than imprisonment and sequestration, he ordered the defendants to be fined £250 each.

(4) On August 20, 1976, *Private Eye* published an article
headed "The Erasing of Lazarus." This was partly a summary
of the legal actions taken by Sir James against them up to that
date but highlighted the fact that two prominent men had committed apparent professional suicide. They were Mr. Leslie

Lazarus Paisner, a solicitor, and Mr. John Addey, a public relations man, who had apparently changed their stories to *Private Eye* after seeing Sir James or his solicitor, Mr. Levine.

(5) On October 29, 1976, the Divisional Court turned down an application by Sir James to have Mr. Richard Ingrams, the editor of *Private Eye*, committed to prison and the magazine's assets sequestered for publishing "The Erasing of Lazarus." The Lord Chief Justice, sitting with Mr. Justice Eveleigh and Mr. Justice Peter Pain, listened to argument that the piece on August 20 was a contempt because it prejudiced the fair trial of five sets of proceedings. Sir James's counsel said the article suggested that Mr. Paisner and Mr. Addey had been "got at" and that Sir James was the person responsible.

Lord Widgery, considered the effect of the judgments in *The Sunday Times'* thalidomide case and said that everything came back to a single, basic question of whether there was a real risk of the fair and proper trial of some pending proceedings. He put himself in the place of a jury and asked whether he was satisfied beyond reasonable doubt of facts which gave rise to a real risk of an effect on fair and proper trial in future proceedings. His answer was that he was not so satisfied.

The Divisional Court refused leave to appeal to the House of Lords against their decision.

(6) On December 9, 1976, the Appeals Committee of the House of Lords (Lords Diplock, Kilbrandon and Edmund-Davies) turned down Sir James's appeal against the Divisional Court's refusal to allow an appeal to the House of Lords. Mr. Lewis Hawser Q.C., for Sir James, argued that the Divisional Court had taken too narrow a view of the case. *Private Eye's* counsel, Mr. James Comyn, Q.C., was not even called on to reply to this.

The stages in this convoluted battle have revealed two points of significance. The first is that resumés of legal in-fighting in terms of a review of court proceedings are definitely permissible providing they do not set out to prejudice fair trial of the eventual action or actions. Provocative, if obvious, questions may rest in the copy but only if they clearly reflect what has been raised in the preliminary legal proceedings. The second point is offered by way of comment. It is that an individual, who complains that his trial of certain actions is being prejudiced, can appear to create exactly the kind of pre-trial prejudice he objects to in another by over-using the public forum of the courts, with attendant publicity.

The third significant contempt action saw a nearly immediate application of the case mentioned above (*R.* v. *Ingrams, ex p. Goldsmith* (1976)).

In *Blackburn* v. *British Broadcasting Corporation* (1976), Mr. Raymond Blackburn failed to get the Divisional Court to commit the B.B.C. and Mr. James Ferman (now Secretary to the British Board of Film Censors) for contempt. There had been a broadcast debate on censorship from the B.B.C.'s Plymouth studios in July 1975. Mr. Ferman, then secretary designate to the B.B.F.C., had referred to pending criminal proceedings instituted by Mr. Blackburn in London against a cinema and the B.B.F.C. in relation to the showing of *The Language of Love*, a Swedish film. Mr. Ferman had said: "The context of the film was seriously educational and could do nothing but good in the board's opinion and in my opinion."

Mr. Blackburn claimed these words amounted to a trial by television of the very issue which the magistrate at Bow Street would have to rule on, in deciding whether or not to commit the defendants for trial and, by the same token, the issue a crown court jury might have to consider. The B.B.C. claimed support from the "real risk" formula but Mr. Blackburn argued that it did not apply to this type of case.

Mr. Justice Park, delivering the major judgment, said:

> "the matter complained of consisted of spoken words in the middle of a general discussion about film censorship in the south-west of England, those words being immediately followed by an expression of Mr. Ferman's opinion that the courts should be the final arbiter. . . . It was very unlikely that Mr. Ferman's words would have been heard by, or if heard, recollected by anyone liable to serve as a juror at the Central Criminal Court at some unknown date in the future. There was no real risk that the fair trial of Mr. Blackburn's proceedings might have been prejudiced."

The Divisional Court's solid and consistent interpretation of the "real risk" formula has at least clarified matters to a point. The *Goldsmith* and *Blackburn* contempt actions demonstrate the fact that individuals can bring alleged contempts to the

attention of the High Court, using the *ex parte* procedure. Mr.
Comyn had suggested, in the *Goldsmith* case, that this could
present a possibility of harassment because, in his view, the correct person to act as the "prosecutor" was the Attorney-General (who had declined to act in the *Goldsmith* matter). This
point may receive further consideration in any future attempts
by Parliament to rationalise the law of contempt.

The final case of importance related to the identification of a
16-year-old girl ward of court by the *Daily Telegraph* and the
Slough Evening Mail.

In *Re F. (A Minor) (Publication of Information)* (1976), the
Court of Appeal explored section 12 (1) of the Administration
of Justice Act 1960, which relates to information about wards
of court, and the effect of the defence of innocent publication
in section 11 of that Act.

When F was 15 and still at school, she formed a relationship with a
28-year-old man with a criminal record and a history of drug use.
He had sexual intercourse with her, knowing she was only 15, and
gave her drugs. Her parents discovered the association and tried to
terminate it but F ran away from home. She was made a temporary
ward of court and, ultimately, a ward until she was 18 under the
control of the Official Solicitor. F. was placed in a hostel run by the
local council and a social worker submitted a report to the Official
Solicitor suggesting that the man be allowed to visit the girl at the
hostel under supervision to prevent the girl taking more devious
means to see him if contact was totally denied.

F's parents were disturbed by this report, particularly as they had
heard of another 15-year-old girl in care who was said to have
worked as a prostitute. They decided to contact the *Daily Telegraph*. A reporter was shown a number of relevant papers and
thought that wardship proceedings had terminated when F. was
put into care. The reporter asked the father whether any legal proceedings were in progress and received a negative reply. The director of the local council's social services was also contacted.

The *Daily Telegraph* then published a piece headed: "Jailed
lover 'should visit hostel girl, 16'." It continued: "The parents of a
16-year-old school-girl, who was placed in a council hostel to stop
her associating with a criminal, are fighting a social worker's
recommendation that she should be allowed to meet the man, who
is now in prison. . . ."

The *Slough Evening Mail* picked up the story, checked its factual accuracy, rang the Official Solicitor and was told that that official was the guardian *ad litem* but no more. They were not told that the girl was a ward of court. They, therefore, ran a similar article.

The Official Solicitor then took action against the two newspapers and they were held in contempt by Mr. Justice Tudor Evans for a contravention of section 12 (1) of the Administration of Justice Act 1960. As the newspapers had apologised he made no order except that they should pay the costs.

The section runs: "The publication of information relating to proceedings before any court sitting in private" (*i.e.* in camera or in chambers) "shall not of itself be contempt of court except in the following cases, (a) where the proceedings relate to the wardship or adoption of an infant. . . ."

The two newspapers appealed against this judgment. In particular, the judge's ruling that "the publication of information is absolutely prohibited . . . it was the intention of Parliament to make the mere publication of information a contempt of court."

Lord Denning M.R. examined the matter carefully. He noted that the judge had ruled there was an exception to this absolute offence when the court itself asks a newspaper to publish information say, for instance, to trace a missing ward. He said:

"If this construction be correct, it means that Parliament has created an entirely new offence, not known to the law before. Just see what it means. Suppose a newspaper says of a ward of court: 'She has just won a scholarship to Oxford' or 'she has got into bad company and is taking drugs,' the newspaper would be guilty of contempt of court even though it did not know she was a ward of court and had no knowledge of any wardship proceedings, and took all reasonable care to find out. The existence of wardship does not give the ward a privilege over and above other young people who are not wards. It does not give her exemption from comment on her activities, be they favourable or adverse, be they helpful to her or injurious. The remedy for defamatory remarks about a ward is the law of libel, not contempt of court.

I go simply by this. If Parliament seeks to create a new offence, it must do so in plain words. All the more so if it creates an absolute offence — of which a person may be found guilty, even though he had no guilty knowledge or intent and took all reasonable care. So far from section 12 using plain words to create a new offence, it says, as clearly as can be, that it does not create any new offence at all. Section 12 (4) says in terms:

'Nothing in this section shall be construed as implying that any publication is punishable as contempt of court which would not be so punishable apart from this section.'

Apart from this, there are two places in section 12 where Parliament expressly refers to the existing law, and tells the judges to look into and go by it. . . ."

Both papers had checked as far as possible and no one had told them that F. was actually a ward of court. They also felt that the matter was of such public interest that it should be brought to the public's attention unless it was clearly forbidden by law.

Lord Denning concluded: "That was a legitimate view to take. . . . In the circumstances, I do not think there was any guilty knowledge or intent on their part such as to warrant that they were in contempt of court.

He pointed out that the judge's view that section 11 (the defence of innocent publication) related only to publications which prejudice a fair trial, and not to the publication of proceedings in private, was not necessarily the correct interpretation. On this point, however, he was in a minority and Lord Justices Scarman and Geoffrey Lane agreed with the High Court judge that section 11 was not worded in such a way as to provide protection in this type of case.

The three judges did agree to allow the appeal on the scope of section 12. They added a further point, for advice. It is not a contempt to publish information about a ward of court which does not relate to wardship proceedings heard in closed court. Once wardship proceedings are over, publicity is permissible.

While problems relating to wards of court may not figure prominently in a reporter's day-to-day work, this case demonstrates a common-sense approach applied to a difficult and previously untested area of statute law. The reader might be forgiven for wondering why, if the Official Solicitor was initially reticent with the information, he brought an action on confusion he had caused.

Section 12 relates to more than wardship or adoption of an infant. It also protects proceedings relating to guardianship, maintenance and upbringing of infants and rights of access to infants (matters normally taken in chambers). Section 12 (1) (d) makes it a contempt to publish details of evidence heard in camera in relation to a secret process, discovery or invention which is in issue in the proceedings. Section 12 (1) (*e*) has a similar effect if the court, having power to do so, expressly forbids publication of all information relating to the proceedings, or all information of the description which is published.

When a court sits in private, it is either "in camera" or "in chambers." When part of the trial proper is in private, the hearing is "in camera." When preliminary or side issues are dealt with privately, this occurs "in chambers."

If evidence is taken "in camera" it would be a potential contempt for a newspaper to speculate about its substance. In *R*. v. *Prager* (1971), an Official Secrets Act case, Lord Widgery stated: "It is just as damaging if information of that kind can leak out as to have representatives of the Press present and taking their notes at the time."

(c) *Prejudicing the due administration of justice.* While a journalist will always be aware of his duty to be objective, there are very few publications which can be considered objective in the final analysis. The presentation of a particular set of facts will inevitably be subjective: no two reporters would write a piece of copy in exactly the same way.

The following case resulted from a situation where a politically-committed journalist looked at a set of facts, decided there was a conflict and wrote an article which the court found to be a criminal contempt of court.

The law's view of objectivity and an individual journalist's view may differ: it is the legal machine rather than the individual which sets the standard of objectivity. This proposition is unexceptionable.

R. v. *Socialist Worker and Paul Foot* (1974): Foot, as editor of the *Socialist Worker*, published an article headed "Y, oh Lord, oh why . . . ." which revealed the identities of prosecution witnesses at a blackmail trial. The judge at that trial, Mr. Justice King-Hamilton, had said, before the jury were in court, "May I say that if, by accident, any counsel happens to mention the name of a witness other than by letter I hope, but I have *no jurisdiction over the Press,* I hope they will not mention the name if it slips out accidentally."

Foot appreciated that the judge had the power to keep the witnesses anonymous in the proceedings in the court room. The judge stated that he felt he had no jurisdiction over the Press for publica-

tions outside the court and consequently he made his request. Foot
revealed the names of these witnesses for two specific reasons:

    (1) he regarded the judge's direction as a simple request; and

    (2) a victim in a rape case at Norwich Crown Court *had* been
named despite a similar direction and pictures of the woman used
in the national Press.

    Foot argued that the blackmail victims had been willing partici-
pants in the events which led to the alleged crime, whereas the rape
victim had not consented to anything. He felt it was inequitable
that the blackmail witnesses should be shielded because they were
prominent city businessmen but the latter should be named
because she was a dancer with the "Black and White Minstrels."

    The Divisional Court ruled that Foot and the paper were both in
contempt and fined each £250.

    The Lord Chief Justice, Lord Widgery, specified two con-
tempts. By publishing the names of the witnesses in defiance
of the judge's direction they were committing the sort of flagrant affront to the authority of the court that amounted to contempt. Further, they were in contempt because it was quite
evident that if witnesses in blackmail proceedings were not ade-
quately protected, the readiness of others to come forward in
other cases could be affected.

    The Attorney-General, Mr. Sam Silkin Q.C., who presented
the application for committal, admitted that there was no evidence that any direct harm had been caused by the publication.
He admitted that there was no legal authority which bore
directly on the case. He accepted that the judge did not
expressly forbid publication outside the court.

    It may seem strange that Lord Widgery was able to find that
Foot's conduct was in defiance of the judge's direction. As previously mentioned, the wording of section 12 (1) (*e*) of the
Administration of Justice Act 1960 permits a court, if it has
power to do so, to prohibit publication of all, or of particular
information in the proceedings. But Mr. Justice King-Hamilton's actual words suggest he was not making such a direction.
Lord Widgery appears to have ignored this. He used the case of
Att.-Gen v. *Butterworth* (1963) as his foundation. This case
held that it was a contempt to victimise a witness after court
proceedings had finished. He did not accept the analogy
between ineffective requests to protect the identities of rape victims and requests for anonymity for blackmail witnesses. For

the former, only Parliament could act to change the law: (and has: Sexual Offences (Amendment) Act 1976): the courts, themselves, could act to protect blackmail witnesses.

The fines were imposed, he added, because Foot had acted recklessly and no word of apology had come from him. The defendants were also ordered to pay the costs of the action.

English law operates a presumption of innocence and a man who denies an offence can hardly assert his innocence in one breath whilst, in another, apologising for something he believed to be correct.

It is respectfully submitted that there is a great deal of difference between finding that Foot had committed a contempt in an area of law which, as the Attorney-General admitted, was unclear and the imposition of fines and costs on top of this finding.

Lord Widgery's second ground for contempt seems sensible and in the public interest, but it broke new ground using old machinery. The judgment is specifically limited to blackmail cases. The "defiance" point is less clear and satisfactory and may have introduced confusion about the practical differences between requests and directions.

(2) Scandalising the court

This archaic description prohibits:
(a) scurrilous abuse of a judge as a judge, or of a court and
(b) attacks on the integrity or impartiality of a judge or court.

The object is to protect the administration of justice and preserve public confidence in the judiciary. The quality of judges throughout the centuries has not been uniform and this heading preserved, in legal form, the cliché "ignorance is bliss."

At the end of the last century, one Lord of Appeal expressed the view that this form of contempt was obsolete: a case then arose the following year. The former National Industrial Relations Court (N.I.R.C.) and its president, Sir John Donaldson, suffered a barrage of criticism during the early 1970s which, in former times, would have been made the subject of contempt proceedings under this head. One publication stated as a fact that the judge had conferred in private with one party and advised him about the next step to take. This was untrue and a gross contempt but no contempt proceedings were taken.

The Lord Chief Justice, Lord Widgery, has stated that "judges' backs have got to be a good deal broader than they were thought to be years ago." The courts seem now to be satisfied to leave to public opinion attacks or comments which are derogatory or "scandalous."

The strict law is, however, that to attribute a particular decision to the personal weakness of a judge is to suggest he is incapable of administering impartial justice. An allegation of incompetence or even serious infirmity, mental or physical, which clouded his judgment, would amount to a contempt.

> *R*. v. *New Statesman* (1928): Dr. Marie Stopes, the birth control reformer, had had advertisements stopped in a particular paper. She wrote to the proprietor alleging this was because the editor had conceded to pressure. The editor sued her for libel. Commenting on the libel action, the *New Statesman* remarked: "an individual owning to such views as those of Dr. Stopes cannot apparently hope for a fair hearing in a court presided over by Mr. Justice Avory . . . and there are so many Avorys." Three fellow judges held that this remark was a contempt, implying partiality

It is, however, permissible to discuss the merits of a legal decision on the ground that it was contrary to good law or the public good. Lord Reid emphasised this in the passage already quoted from *Att.-Gen* v. *Times Newspapers Ltd.* The criticism should be kept to the legal merits of the case. Responsible criticism following a trial is safe provided that it is responsible criticism.

In 1936, Lord Atkin stated:

> "But whether the authority and position of an individual judge, or the due administration of justice, is concerned, no wrong is committed by any member of the public who exercises the ordinary right of criticising, in good faith, in private or public, the public act done in the seat of justice. The path of criticism is a public way: the wrong-headed are permitted to err therein: provided that members of the public abstain from imputing improper motives to those taking part in the administration of justice, and are genuinely exercising a right of criticism, and not acting in malice or attempting to impair the administration of justice, they are

immune. Justice is not a cloistered virtue: she must be allowed to suffer the scrutiny and respectful, even though outspoken, comments of ordinary men."

In 1968, Mr. Quintin Hogg (now Lord Hailsham, a former Lord Chancellor, entitled to deliver judgments in the House of Lords) inaccurately criticised court decisions on gambling, when he wrote an article in *Punch*. The Court of Appeal held he was not guilty of a contempt because "no criticism of a judgment, however, vigorous, can amount to a contempt of court providing it keeps within the limits of reasonable courtesy and good faith."

Comments during 1970, and then later in 1976, about judgments and sentences, from Mr. Justice Melford Stevenson have been, at times, acutely critical but no proceedings have been taken.

The Phillimore Committee considered, at one stage, whether scandalising the court should be subject to penal sanctions at all. Judges have the law of defamation in extreme cases, should they choose to take action short of the quasi-criminal process. But the committee felt that the administration of justice (rather than judges individually) still required protection.

Their ultimate recommendation is that the remedy should not be part of the law of contempt but should be a separate criminal offence defined by statute. The offence would be committed by publication, in whatever form, of matter imputing improper or corrupt judicial conduct with the intention of impairing confidence in the administration of justice. Prosecution should only be possible at the instance of the Attorney-General.

The defence would be required to satisfy two conditions:
(1) that the allegations were true; and
(2) that publication was for the public benefit.

This defence would equate to the requirements of the defence in criminal libel, where truth alone is insufficient but where truth plus publication for the public benefit is sufficient for the defence to succeed.

The committee does, however, point out that they feel the correct course, in cases where there is evidence of judicial corruption or lack of impartiality, is to send a report to the Lord

Chancellor (who has overall responsibility for the administration of justice in England).

Following a case of 1975, where a circuit judge imposed a suspended sentence for rape offences on an offender, advice was given to Mr. Jack Ashley, M.P., that the Lord Chancellor had power to remove a circuit judge from office on the ground of incapacity or misbehaviour. For judges above this rank, the procedure appears to be by address and motion of both Houses of Parliament.

Mr. Ashley, who had been campaigning for some action as a result of the case, wrote to the Lord Chancellor (Lord Elwyn-Jones): "Consequently I do not propose to press my motion for the resignation or removal of Mr. Christmas Humphreys since the decision now clearly lies in your hands. . . . I do not seek to damage the judge nor, indeed, to re-open the case which he has tried. But I am attempting to avert the consequences of his deplorable judgment, which has allowed freedom to a man who admitted raping two women at knife-point."

The Lord Chancellor also controls the conduct of judicial personnel such as magistrates.

(3) *Interfering with judicial proceedings and refusal to reveal sources of information*

(a) *Interfering with judicial proceedings.* Contempt under this heading can mean deliberate interruption of the court case or more subtle interference. Welsh Language demonstrators shouted at a High Court judge in 1970 during one hearing and found themselves imprisoned for up to three months (although the sentences were suspended on appeal).

A plan to introduce nitrous oxide (laughing gas) during a Crown Court trial of a pornography case led to the next case.

Balogh v. *Crown Court of St. Albans* (1974): there was a trial at St. Albans concerning pornographic films and books. Balogh was assisting a firm of solicitors appearing for the defence. He became bored with the case and devised a plan to introduce laughing gas through the ventilation system so that it would emerge in the court room in which the case was being heard just above the row for counsel. He tried a dummy run and found that he would have to get out on to the roof of the building via Court No. 1 (next to his court room). He stole a cylinder of nitrous oxide from a local hospital and put it in a case on a seat in Court No. 1 in the public gallery. The police had seen him do the dummy run and thought a bomb might be in the case. After he had left the case they arrested him and he told them frankly what he had intended to do.

Mr. Justice Melford Stevenson was the presiding judge in Court No. 1 and the whole incident was reported to him. The judge was not amused. Balogh was brought before him and did not aid matters by pointing out that it was the next-door court he had intended to subvert. Balogh asked for legal representation but was told, in effect, that as he was arguing with Mr. Justice Melford Stevenson, he could continue, but without any legal assistance. The judge sentenced him to six months imprisonment for attempting the contempt. Balogh then replied: "You are a humourless automaton. Why don't you self-destruct?"

After 11 days in prison, Balogh appealed and the Court of Appeal set aside the prison sentence.

The following remarks by the Master of the Rolls, Lord Denning, are of interest:

"... a judge should act of his own motion only when it is urgent and imperative to act immediately. In all other cases, he should not take it on himself to move. He should leave it to the Attorney-General or to the party aggrieved to make a motion in accordance with the rules in R.S.C. Order 52 ... he should not appear to be both prosecutor and judge, for that is a role which does not become him well.

... it was not a case for summary punishment. There was not sufficient urgency to warrant it. Nor was it imperative. (The appellant) was already in custody on a charge of stealing. The judge would have done well to have remanded him in custody and invited counsel to represent him. ...

Contempt of court is a criminal offence which is governed by the principles applicable to criminal offences generally. In particular by the difference between an attempt to commit an offence and an act preparatory to it ...

... was Mr. Balogh guilty of the offence of contempt of court? ... No proceedings were disturbed. No trial was upset. Nothing untoward took place. No gas was released. A lot more had to be done by Mr. Balogh. (Even if he had released the gas) it is very doubtful whether it would have had any effect at all. ... Mr. Balogh had the criminal intent to disrupt the court but that is not enough. He was guilty of stealing the cylinder but no more. On this short ground, we think the judge was in error.''

What Lord Denning was emphasising was, that for a criminal offence to be proved (or an attempt at such an offence) the guilty act (the *actus reus*) must be accompanied by a guilty mind (*mens rea*): it is no crime to want to commit an offence; there must be acts along with this which show almost that the accused could not have avoided committing the full offence. Balogh had a number of things to do before even an attempt was committed. He had to return to the case, take it up on to the roof, open it, open the gas cylinder and introduce the gas into the ventilation system. During any of these stages he might have changed his mind and abandoned the plan. No criminal offence had been committed or attempted in relation to contempt.

The Court of Appeal judgment instanced two contempt cases where this judge acted summarily, but correctly. In *R. v. Lydeard* (1966), he held that an employer, who threatened to dismiss an employee if the latter served on a jury, was guilty of a contempt. In *Lecointe* v. *Courts' Administrator of the Central Criminal Court* (1973), he held that a person who had distributed leaflets in the public gallery of the Old Bailey inciting people to picket the court, even though the judge had not seen this incident, was in contempt.

As will be discussed later, the Phillimore Committee recommend changes to prevent judges acting hastily and without due consideration of the law in such contempt cases.

In 1950, the United Kingdom signed the European Convention on Human Rights. Article 6 of this Convention lays down certain safeguards for people accused of criminal offences. It provides:

> 1. In the determination of his civil rights and obligations or of any criminal charge against him, everyone is entitled to a fair and public hearing within a reasonable time by an independent and impartial tribunal established by law. Judgment shall be pronounced publicly but the Press and public may be excluded from all or part of the trial in the interest of morals, public order or national security in a democratic society, where the interests of juveniles or the protection of the private life of the parties so require, or to the extent strictly necessary in the opinion of the

court in special circumstances where publicity would prejudice the interests of justice.

2. Everyone charged with a criminal offence shall be presumed innocent until proved guilty according to law.

3. Everyone charged with a criminal offence has the following minimum rights:

(a) to be informed promptly, in a language which he understands and in detail, of the nature and cause of the accusations against him;

(b) to have adequate time and facilities for the preparation of his defence;

(c) to defend himself in person or through legal assistance of his own choosing or, if he has not sufficient means to pay for legal assistance, to be given it free when the interests of justice so require;

(d) to examine or have examined witnesses against him and to obtain the attendance and examination of witnesses on his behalf under the same conditions as witnesses against him;

(e) to have the free assistance of an interpreter if he cannot understand or speak the language used in court.

Cases like *Balogh's* show breaches of Article 6 (3) (*b*) and (*c*) when the contempt occurs in the face of the court and yet, in over 25 years, nothing has been done to remedy the situation.

The Phillimore Committee recommend that, as a matter of principle, contempt jurisdiction should only be invoked where:

(a) the offending act does not fall within the definition of any other offence; or

(b) where urgency or practical necessity require that the matter be dealt with summarily.

They further recommend:

(1) that all defendants in contempt proceedings should be entitled to legal representation and, if necessary, granted legal aid on an emergency basis to secure this;

(2) that in all cases where more than a small fine is considered appropriate, there should be a "cooling off" period between the determination of the issue of contempt and the imposition of the penalty; and

(3) if the court considers imposing a prison sentence there should be power to remand in custody during the "cooling off" period. Magistrates' courts would only be able to remand

in custody for a 24-hour period. The contemnor should be entitled to be heard in mitigation of sentence and have legal representation and, if necessary, legal aid for this as if he had denied the contempt.

The Phillimore Committee emphasises that in serious cases, when the offence (if proved) would attract severe penalties, the practice should always be to leave the matter to the slower process of ordinary criminal law unless urgency predominates.

(b) *Refusal to reveal sources of information.* There has been a long-standing conflict between the courts and the professions about the disclosure of sources of information. Certain categories can claim immunity from detailed questioning. Lawyers have a general duty not to mislead courts but they can refuse to answer questions relating to matters told to them by their clients in confidence. This is known as legal privilege. The Crown, in certain situations, can resist requests for detailed information on the ground of general public policy.

Doctors, priests and journalists cannot, however, claim any privilege recognised by law to refuse to answer questions without being in contempt of court. A doctor may be compelled to break his Hippocratic oath, a priest his vow of confessional confidentiality and a journalist to break the ethical confidence afforded to all his sources of information. Failure to comply can mean imprisonment or a fine.

The battle has been rather one-sided. The courts judge what is relevant and necessary. To allow this decision to rest on the individual, would be to deny the purpose of the courts and set the individual as the sole judge of relevance. This would be a negation of the purpose of law.

There are occasions when the journalist's professional duty never to reveal his sources will conflict with the courts' power to compel an aswer. If no answer is forthcoming, the court may punish the journalist (or doctor or priest) for contempt.

The major battle on this, from the Press point of view, occurred before a Tribunal of Inquiry set up by Parliament in the early 1960s to investigate offences committed by John Vassall, an Admiralty employee, who was convicted of passing secrets to the Russians. The Press comment alleged he was a known homosexual and therefore open to blackmail.

The Tribunals of Inquiry (Evidence) Act 1921, s.1 (2) (*b*), states that any person, who is a witness at a tribunal and who refuses to answer any question which may legally be required, may be sent to the High Court. The High Court (if they decide the question is relevant and admissible) may look into the refusal to answer and, on continued silence, punish the person as if he had been guilty of contempt.

Att.-Gen. v. *Mulholland and Foster* (1963): a *Daily Mail* reporter, Mulholland, was interviewed by the Tribunal of Inquiry and asked to state his sources for the following pieces of copy: "Colleagues of his in the Admiralty called Vassall 'Auntie' to his face. . . . a girl typist in the Admiralty office where he worked had decided that no £15-a-week clerk could possibly live the way he did honestly. . . . it was the sponsorship of two high-ranking officials which led to Vassall avoiding the strictest part of the Admiralty's security vetting.'

He refused to reveal his sources for this information and went to prison for six months for contempt

Lord Denning said: "The judge . . . will not direct him to answer unless it is not only relevant but also a proper and indeed necessary question in the course of justice to be put and answered. . . . I hold that so far as Mulholland is concerned, these questions were both relevant and necessary to the inquiry which the tribunal had in hand."

The most recent case concerns a Scottish reporter who refused to reveal his source of information at a trial. Gordon Airs, the chief reporter of the *Daily Record* (the *Mirror's* Scottish sister) was fined £500 in June 1975, for failing to identify one of the defendants in the *Tartan Army* trial.

The questions asked of him were competent and relevant but the court took a lenient view and only imposed a fine. The judges accepted that he acted "with what he considered honourable professional motives and did all in his power to be released from an undertaking he had given to one of the defendants." Lord Emslie said: "Let us, however, sound a note of clear warning. Now that all possible causes of misapprehension have been dispelled any witness, including any journalist witness, who declines to answer any competent and relevant question in court must realise that he will be in contempt and be liable to incur severe punishment." The Lord Justice-

Clerk, Lord Wheatley, commented that Airs' work as an investigative journalist contained an element of seeking to secure a scoop, thus increasing the newspaper's circulation. It was, therefore, a highly commercial enterprise.

The Phillimore Committee avoid the topic completely with the following statement:

> "We have not pursued this because the question when and whether there should be a privilege of refusal to answer is part of the law of evidence, not the law of contempt. The law of contempt is concerned with the consequences of defying an order of the court (for example refusing to answer a question) rather than the rules as to the circumstances in which the witness should have a privilege to refuse to answer. . . . the representations we received have not led us to form a different view."

It must be accepted by all journalists, national or provincial, that their ethic on this point conflicts with the law. The refusal to reveal sources is not a matter of heroics: it is part of a job which, in many instances, puts the reporter between two entrenched factions. A reporter's responsibility is to the law: his duty is to his source. If he dislikes the consequences of this, he should consider a less onerous profession.

Gagging Writs

One tactic which had considerable vogue among those subjected to Press comment or investigation was the issuing of a writ alleging libel followed by the warning that any further revelations or investigation, as the matter was *sub judice* would constitute a contempt of court. As the writ was evidence of a potential action, further comment or facts could prejudice the potential proceedings which might come to trial

Lord Reid, in the *Distillers* case, stated, quite clearly, that he thought gagging writs should have no effect and the next case effectively terminated the tactic.

In *Wallersteiner* v. *Moir* (1974), there was a dispute between a shareholder in a company and Dr. Kurt Wallersteiner, who controlled the company. The shareholder, Mr. Moir, accused Dr. Wallersteiner of fraud and breach of trust in a circular to other shareholders. The plaintiff sued for libel. Having issued the writ, he tried hard to stop any investigation into his past actions or conduct.

In the Court of Appeal, Lord Denning described the tactics in this way:

"When Mr. Moir proposed to raise questions at a general meeting of the company, Dr. Wallersteiner tried to stop him. He could not, of course, rely on the law of defamation. Statements made by a shareholder at a meeting of a public company are clearly privileged. So is a newspaper report of them. . . . This court will never restrain the use of words on a privileged occasion. Nor will it grant an injunction when the defendant says that he intends to justify them or that they are fair comment on a matter of public interest. . . . Baulked in the law of defamation, Dr. Wallersteiner turned to the law of contempt of court. On several occasions when Mr. Moir or anyone sought to put a point, which was awkward for Dr. Wallersteiner, he used a simple way out: 'The matter is *sub judice*,' he said, 'My lawyers advise me that if it is discussed, you and I will be in contempt of court.' This way of escape was so plausible that on one occasion a judge in chambers . . . whilst refusing an injunction for libel, nevertheless gave a warning to Mr. Moir not to commit a contempt of court: saying that, if he did, he would deprive him of the costs. Emboldened by this success, Dr. Wallersteiner, time and again, at the meetings of the company used the abracadabra: 'This is *sub judice*.' He used it so as to avoid any discussion, not only on matters concerned in the litigation, but other matters also. He invoked, not only the English litigation, but also litigation in Germany, in the Bahamas, and elsewhere. . . .

I know that it is commonly supposed that once a writ is issued, it puts a stop to discussion. If anyone wishes to canvass the matter in the press or in public, it cannot be permitted. It is said to be 'sub judice.' I venture to suggest that it is a complete misconception. The sooner it is corrected, the better. If it is a matter of public interest, it can be discussed at large without fear of thereby being in contempt of court. Criticisms can continue to be made and can be repeated. Fair comment does not prejudice a fair trial. . . . The law says — and says emphatically — that the issue of a writ is not to be used so as to be a muzzle to prevent discussion. . . . Matters of public interest should be, and are, open to discussion, notwithstanding the issue of a writ."

Procedure and Appeals

It will have become apparent that various courts have the power to act on issues of contempt. In the *Balogh* case, a High Court judge sitting in the crown court dealt with the apparent contempt in the face of the court himself. In the *Foot* case, a different High Court judge referred the matter to the Attorney-General, who took it for determination to the Divisional Court of the Queen's Bench.

The basic rule is that the Divisional Court has supervisory jurisdiction over this whole area but that individual judges in the superior courts may deal with matters before them as they occur.

Contempt proceedings may be instituted after a complaint by an individual (as the *Distillers* case shows). The Attorney-General takes action when he feels the matter is not trivial. If he declines to take action, the individual can take the matter to the Divisional Court himself (*Goldsmith* v. *Ingrams* and *Blackburn* v. *B.B.C.*) although there were proposals prior to the 1960 Administration of Justice Act that such proceedings should only be taken by the Attorney-General or the Director of Public Prosecutions.

The basic routes for appeal, which have only existed since 1960s, are outlined below. The diagram is something of an over-simplification in relation to civil contempts.

If the contempt is committed before a court-martial, the appeal is to the Courts-Martial Appeals Court (similar, in composition to the Court of Appeal, Criminal Division) and, ultimately, to the House of Lords.

If magistrates were given the power to punish for contempt, the line of appeal would be, on a point of law, to the Divisional Court or, by way of a complete rehearing on the facts, to the crown court sitting as an appeal court.

Summary of the Phillimore Committee Report on
Contempt of Court: Cmnd. 5794

(1) Anything which is intended to pervert or obstruct the

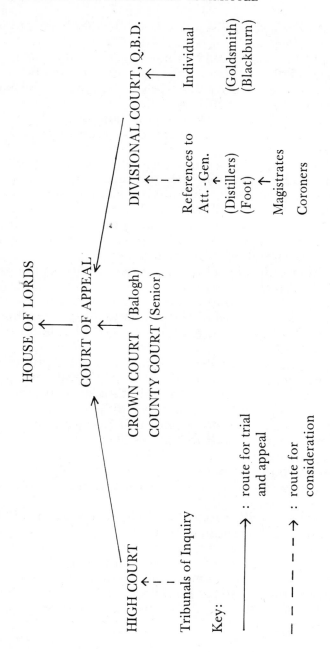

HOUSE OF LORDS

COURT OF APPEAL

DIVISIONAL COURT, Q.B.D. ← Individual

(Goldsmith)
(Blackburn)

References to
Att.-Gen.

(Distillers)
(Foot)

Magistrates

Coroners

CROWN COURT (Balogh)
COUNTY COURT (Senior)

HIGH COURT

Tribunals of Inquiry

Key:

———— : route for trial
and appeal

– – – → : route for
consideration

course of justice should be contempt but only if the proceedings have started and not been finally finished.

(2) A publication would be contemptuous if it created a risk of serious prejudice (intentionally or unintentionally).

(3) Publication means any speech, writing or broadcast addressed to the public at large.

(4) A publication would be contemptuous only if it created a risk that the course of justice would be seriously impeded or prejudiced.

(a) In criminal proceedings this rule would only operate when an accused person is charged or summonsed.

(b) In civil proceedings the rule would only apply when the case was actually *listed for trial.*

(5) It would be a defence to an allegation of contempt that publication was a fair and accurate report of legal proceedings in open court published contemporaneously and in good faith. This would give clear statutory cover to, among other matters, bankruptcy hearings which indicated possible criminal proceedings to follow and to proceedings at coroners' inquests. The defence would be similar to the civil defamation defence of absolute privilege envisaged by the Faulks Committee.

(6) It would be a defence to show that publication formed part of legitimate discussion on matters of general public interest and that is only incidentally and unintentionally created a risk of serious prejudice to the proceedings.

(7) There should be no defence that publication is for the public benefit (*i.e.* minus the factors above).

(8) "Scandalising" the court should cease to be part of the law of contempt. It should become an indictable offence to defame a judge in such a way as to bring the administration of justice into disrepute.

The defence to this proposed new offence is identical to the existing defence to criminal libel:

(a) that the allegations were true; and

(b) that publication was for the public benefit.

(9) For contempts committed in the face of the court (*i.e.* *Balogh* v. *Crown Court of St. Albans*):

(a) the judge should allow the accused proper defence facilities;

(b) the accused should be allowed legal aid for his defence;

(c) before any substantial penalty is imposed, the judge should adjourn for a "cooling off' period;

(d) if the contempt amounts to a criminal offence, the judge should consider referring it to the prosecuting authorities to be dealt with as an ordinary criminal offence (*c.f. Att.-Gen.* v. *Socialist Worker and Foot*). This process should occur unless there are good reasons for departing from it.

(10) In the crown court and above, the power to fine should remain unlimited but imprisonment for contempt should be limited to a maximum of two years.

(11) In magistrates' courts, justices powers for contempt in the face of the court should be a fine of up to £20 or seven days' imprisonment. More serious cases should be certified for trial in the High Court.

(12) In the county court, for contempt in the face of the court, penalties should be increased to a fine of up to £150 or up to three months' imprisonment.

6 Privacy

In 1972, the Younger Committee presented a major report on privacy. While Sir Harold Wilson was Prime Minister, there were occasions when legislation to create a new tort of invasion of privacy seemed likely. In March 1976, a new approach became evident.

Speaking to the Liverpool Press Club, Mr. Wilson (as he then was) announced there would be a Green Paper for discussion of issues raised by the Phillimore, Faulks and Younger Committee reports. He said:

> "In the Government's view, changes in the law of contempt and defamation which would, in the interests of the Press and the public, increase the right of the Press and broadcasting authorities to comment on issues of public concern must be balanced by voluntary measures, agreed with the Press, to guarantee the individual citizen and his family an effective right to privacy."

The Green Paper is still awaited. There seems, at the outset, to be an unsatisfactory mixing between "voluntary measures" and "effective rights." If an effective right is infringed, then some sanction should operate. An individual member of the public may feel that censure from the Press Council of the infringer is an inadequate and ineffective voluntary measure.

A summary of the Younger Committee findings in relation to the Press and broadcasting authorities follows.

The Committee found that the bulk of complaints received in evidence related to Press and broadcasting activity. There were two major grounds of complaint:

(1) objectionable means of getting information; and
(2) publicity given to "personal" information.

Teachers and doctors complained about Press treatment of pupils and patients.

> "the nub of many of the complaints against newspaper publicity is the identification of private persons involved in news' stories. It

134

may be that people prominent in public life also object to publication of their private activities but we have received no complaints of this; it is, however, an important issue to have in mind in considering the problem of the right balance between privacy and the public interest. The complaints we have received, from people not in public life, all concern the coupling of identities with news' publicity. The news concerned accidents, organ transplants, proceedings for minor criminal offences in the lower courts, offenders on probation or parole, court proceedings involving domestic matters, notably divorce cases, disputes over guardianship of children, wills, and unusual forms of religious practices."

There were complaints of entry and interview by deception, pestering and harassing, publication of private trivia in an embarrassing fashion and criticism of unusual but lawful activity. Such publicity damaged the individual out of proportion to any general benefit derived from the publicity.

Only 1 per cent. of those interviewed in a public survey conducted for the committee, even after prompting, complained that their privacy had been invaded by newspaper reports. Publication of details of wills and identification of individuals acquitted in summary criminal proceedings were two sources of critical response.

The Press told the committee that there were times when newspaper conduct over-stepped the mark and maintained that the Press Council was the best body to deal with such incidents. Press evidence was that the existing remedies in defamation and breach of confidence provided adequate protection for genuine cases. The Committee said:

"Some Press representatives told us that the ethical conduct of individual journalists is improving, partly as a result of better training. . . . Perhaps the Press evidence to us can best be summed up in the words of one leading spokesman, who asked whether the shortcomings of some newspapers and some reporters from time to time were, in sum, so outrageous that the very principle of freedom of speech needed to be subordinated to a general right of privacy."

Existing Protection

There is protection in the civil law of defamation if false defamatory information is published and this spills over into the area of injurious falsehoods.

If the information is true, there are five possible areas in which a remedy may be sought:

(1) If the information was obtained in confidence, there may be an action for damages and/or an injunction for the tort of breach of confidence. The scope of this tort is still developing. In *Argyll* v. *Argyll* (1967), the Duke of Argyll was prevented by an injunction from revealing to a newspaper details of marital confidences he was told by the Duchess, and the newspaper was similarly prevented from publishing such details.

One problem in this area is the use, by a newspaper, of material they do not know has been obtained in breach of confidence. The attitude seems to be that, when they are informed there has been a breach of confidence, then an injunction may be obtained against the Press.

Central to this area, from the Press point of view, is the defence argument to a breach of confidence action that disclosure of the information is in the public interest. In *Initial Services* v. *Putterill* (1968), Lord Denning M.R. coined the phrase that there is "no confidence in iniquity" and made several other points of consequence. He refused to limit the defence to cases where the confidential information related to crimes or civil wrongs, but thought that it extended to plans for such activity. He said: "The disclosure must, I should think, be to one who has a proper interest to receive the information. Thus it would be proper to disclose a crime to the police; or a breach of the Restrictive Trade Practices Act to the registrar. There may be cases where the misdeed is of such a character that the public interest may demand, or at least excuse, publication on a broader field, even to the Press."

While the law is in its infancy, in terms of defences in this area, the area is of critical importance to the Press. The committee postulated:

> "Suppose a newspaper comes into possession of information, which it knows to be confidential and obtained surreptitiously by the newspaper's informant, that a particular firm is about to discharge 10,000 employees. It approaches the firm who will neither confirm nor deny the report but immediately proceeds to apply for an injunction to prevent publication of the information. Perhaps

the newspaper would have a defence, but it cannot be asserted with certainty."

Such situations, while not commonplace, are far from unknown. Local authority agenda, marked "confidential" are frequently circulated to the Press: items which they do not receive may still be circulated to members who wish to inform the Press and public in the public interest. While it may be open to the local authority to try for an injunction (in anticipation of an actual leak) or damages, the practical situation seems to be that no one knows exactly what the legal position is. It is possible that Lord Denning's dicta would be applied and crystallised: the scarcity of authority on this area indicates at least a tacit acceptance of this defence even if it has not become totally clear.

> In *Fraser* v. *Evans* (1969), F. had submitted a report to the Greek Government on ways of brushing up its image in the United Kingdom. *The Sunday Times* obtained a copy of this report from sources in Greece. F. failed to obtain an injunction preventing publication. The newspaper had not breached F.'s confidence but had obtained the material after he had submitted the report.

Allied to this area is the implied contractual obligation on an employee not to disclose, during or after employment, confidential information received during the course of employment. An injunction may be obtained to prevent disclosure or damages may be obtained if there has been such a disclosure causing financial loss. If an employee is induced to disclose such information, perhaps by a newspaper, there may be tort liability providing the newspaper was aware of the employee's contractual obligation. The committee cite the example of a doctor's receptionist being induced by a reporter to reveal confidential details of the doctor's private life, of which she obtained knowledge in the course of her work. If publication has taken place, the doctor might obtain damages against the newspaper for the actual and possible loss suffered by his practice.

A recent case has drawn together some of the uncertain strands in this area and clarified the situation. It is, however, an interlocutory (preliminary) matter: this is no great weakness because the very nature of this area of law means that these preliminary matters often set the standards which come to govern other incidents.

In *Woodward* v. *Hutchins* (1977), the Court of Appeal decided that pop singers who courted publicity were not entitled to an interlocutory injunction, prior to trial of an action for alleged breach of confidence, to prevent their former Press Relations agent publishing articles in the *Daily Mirror* about the other side of their lives.

The singers, Tom Jones (Woodward), Englebert Humperdink (Arnold Dorsey) and Gilbert O'Sullivan had employed the defendant as their Public Relations agent and he had left on amicable terms. While employed, he had signed a document stating that he would keep some matters secret and not "make any statement or give any interview or pass any information to any third party, whether for reward or otherwise, touching or concerning either (his) employment with the company or touching or concerning any principal . . ." during his employment or at any time afterwards.

He said he had signed the document but that it had later been torn up and the managing director of the company (M.A.M. Ltd.) had kept the pieces.

The series of revelations begun in the *Daily Mirror* were publicised "Tom Jones and Marji. The Truth! Starts today; the most explosive show business story of the decade. The Family, by Chris Hutchins, the man on the inside."

The plaintiffs wanted to prevent further articles and had issued writs alleging libel, breach of contract and breach of confidence.

Lord Denning, lifting an interim injunction imposed by a single High Court judge, said:

"On the libel action, the *Daily Mirror* and Mr. Hutchins indicated that they proposed to justify all that had been written, on the ground that it was true. Therefore, it was clear that no injunction would be granted to restrain a publication for a libel, for, on all the authorities the public interest, in knowing the truth, outweighed the interest of the plaintiff, who said he was being libelled. . . .

No doubt in some employments, there was an obligation of confidence clearly present such that, if a former servant disclosed confidential information obtained in the course of his employment, the court would quite properly restrain him. But the present case was different: there was no doubt whatever that the pop group sought publicity, which would create a favourable image among those who supported their performances; and Mr. Hutchins had been engaged to produce or help produce that favourable image to the public.

If a group like the present sought publicity which was to their advantage, they could not complain if a servant or employee was persuaded that there was another side to that image, for it was in the public interest that it should be made known.

At all events, there were limits to the cause of action for breach of confidence. When a group like the present sought publicity, the court should not grant an injunction, restraining publication of the material said to show the other side of the picture, so that the public could know both sides of the matter. Therefore, on the ground of breach of confidential information, the court should not go to the length of granting an injunction."

He pointed out that it would be difficult for the newspaper and the writer to know the extent of the injunction. He concluded:

"In cases like the present, as also in a libel action, the public interest was that the truth should out, if it be the truth; if it was not the truth, there was the cause of action for damages in libel, and damages would be exceedingly heavy if what was said was not true.

If the libel action failed on the ground that what was said was true, it seemed unlikely that there would be much in the way of damages on the ground of breach of confidence."

Lord Justice Lawton agreed that the libel aspect of the claim should resolve most of the issues. Lord Justice Bridge commented that, those who sought publicity of every kind on their private lives, so long as it showed them in the best light, could not complain when publicity showed them in an unfavourable light.

A technical point which has some relevance is that, in interlocutory proceedings, the matter is decided on the balance of convenience. At full trial of civil matters, issues are decided on the balance of probabilities. The convenience of the freedom of the Press in preliminary matters should not be confused with the heavier burden of proof at trial proper.

This case is of interest because it appears to have prevented another by-pass technique similar to the "gagging" writ in contempt. The senior courts have been emphasising, during this decade, that tactical use of preliminary procedural points to stifle the Press is not going to be condoned. The Press appears to be prepared to accept the responsibility which runs with this: heavy damages at full trial, if what was stated was either without real substance or an adequate defence (or settlement prior to such a trial).

A leader in *The Times* following the "Watergate" issue in America pointed to the fact that our law of contempt could have prevented such revelations. Lord Denning, in the case above, commented that if the law on confidence in the United States was as the High Court judge thought, Mr. Richard Nixon might have been able to save his career.

(2) even though the material is true, the current state of the law of criminal libel appears to allow a prosecution in cases where publication of the facts could not be shown to have any public benefit (see the section entitled "Criminal Libel" and *Goldsmith* v. *Pressdram* (1976)).

(3) In Scotland, an action for *convicium* might lie. The elements are that the plaintiff has suffered some kind of loss because of malicious publication of material which made the plaintiff appear ridiculous or a fool, which held him up to hatred or which attributed unpopular opinions to him.

(4) Certain statutes prohibit the publication of information, despite its truth. In this area, there are penalties for transgressions:

(a) Criminal Justice Act 1967, s.3: reporting restrictions at committal proceedings.

(b) Children and Young Persons Acts 1933, 1963 and 1969: restrictions on identification of accused and witnesses in juvenile court proceedings.

(c) Judicial Proceedings (Regulation of Reports) Act 1926, s.1 (1) (c) and identical provisions in the Magistrates Courts Act 1952, s.58: restrictions on detail which may be reported in matrimonial or domestic proceedings.

(d) The Sexual Offences (Amendment) Act 1976: penalises the unauthorised disclosure of the female complainant's identity and prevents unauthorised revelation of the identity of the accused.

(5) The provisions of section 8 of the Rehabilitation of Offenders Act 1974 which would permit a person with a "spent" criminal conviction to sue in defamation if he could prove that the true details had been published maliciously by the newspaper.

The Press Council

Any person objecting to a particular Press action can complain to the Press Council, which was set up in 1953. After an application to the secretary of the Council, setting out the nature of the complaint, there is a reference to the editor of the relevant newspaper giving him an opportunity to act and correct the complaint. If the editor takes no such action, he then receives from the secretary an account of the complaint plus any supporting evidence and is invited to give an oral or written reply.

The Complaints Committee of the Press Council meets every month. In certain cases the complainant may be required to give up his right to sue the newspaper if he wishes the Council to adjudicate on the matter. This is to prevent the Council being used as a tactical means of discovering the strength of a newspaper's defence prior to a defamation action.

From 1953 to 1970, the Press Council dealt with 65 complaints about invasions of privacy. Of these, 37 were upheld and 28 rejected (giving an annual ratio of two upheld: one and a half dismissed).

The only current sanction within the Council's power is censure but a newspaper cannot be forced to publish a critical adjudication relating to itself. There have been at least five occasions on which newspapers have not published such adjudications. In evidence to the Younger Committee, some Press representatives felt the Council should be able to direct that a critical adjudication should receive equal space and treatment as had the offending piece of copy.

The Younger Committee stated: "We do not . . . see how the Council can expect to command public confidence in its ability to take account of the reactions of the public unless it has at least an equal membership of persons who are qualified to speak for the public at large."

They recommended:

(1) half the membership should be drawn from outside the Press and that the composition of the Council should emphasise its independence of the Press, its varied experience of public life and its standing with the general public; and

(2) publication of critical adjudications should receive the

same prominence as the offending copy; and

(3) the Council should codify its adjudications on privacy for working journalists and keep this material up to date.

[Since this recommendation, Press Council membership has altered so that half the members of the Complaints Committee are lay members.]

There was consideration of the distinction between something being "of" public interest and material published "in" the public interest but the Committee was not prepared to lay down inflexible rules in this area.

The Committee felt that privacy was sufficiently protected within the existing laws of trespass, breach of confidence and defamation (civil and criminal). They did, however, recommend a new tort of disclosure or other use of information "unlawfully acquired." "Although it is possible to steal a document which contains information, the information itself, not being either tangible or intangible property, is not capable of being stolen within the terms of the Theft Act 1968. It follows, that anyone who comes into possession of 'stolen' information even with knowledge of its origin, is not guilty of a criminal offence if he discloses it or if he uses it for profit," they note.

In respect of this new tort, they recommended defences to cover situations where disclosure of the information was in the public interest or on a privileged occasion. (See also Appendix B: Royal Commission on the Press, 1977.)

In 1975 and 1976, there were prosecutions of journalists for allegedly "handling" stolen information. One case related to possession of identity documents of a man who had been kidnapped, the other to possession of a police photograph of an individual. Both prosecutions resulted in acquittals but, had there have been convictions, the injured parties might, if the new tort existed, have taken action. Section 11 of the Civil Evidence Act 1968 allows proof of the criminal conviction to be used in related civil proceedings.

It could be argued that, as the prosecutions have been singularly unsuccessful, the civil law should provide some intermediate remedy. Given the suggested defences of publication in the public interest and privilege, a balance would have been struck. However, such an action would be yet one more tactical weapon in the armoury for those wishing to stifle public opinion.

The Law Commission (Working Paper 58) also examined the area of confidence. The Working Paper suggested that a duty of confidence should be owed by a person who knows or ought to know that information has reached him directly or indirectly through another person who received it in confidence. The injured party should have a right to recover damages for wrongful disclosure if it caused him distress (and would be likely to cause distress to a reasonable person).

As a link between this topic and the next chapter, the problems raised by the publication of extracts from the Crossman Diaries deserve some attention.

In *Att.-Gen.* v. *Jonathan Cape Ltd. and Times Newspapers Ltd.* (1975), Mr. Richard Crossman, a Cabinet Minister in the Labour Government of 1964-1970, kept a detailed diary. He prepared this with a view to publication after his death. Extracts were serialised in *The Sunday Times* when he died. The Attorney-General tried to obtain injunctions against the publishers of the diaries and the newspaper, claiming that the material was confidential and that there should be no disclosure in the public interest because of the principle of Cabinet secrecy.

Lord Widgery, the Lord Chief Justice, refused to impose the injunctions and decided the following points:

(1) The court could stop publication of public secrets with an injunction.

(2) Revelation of Cabinet secrets would be prevented if it could be shown that publication:

(a) would be a breach of confidence;

(b) would be against the public interest because it would upset the principle of collective Cabinet responsibility;

(c) and that these principles over-rode any other considerations.

(3) The confidential nature of the material diminished with time and the court would only act if it could be shown that non-disclosure was still relevant.

(4) Publication of the first volume of the *Diaries*, relating to matters which occurred nearly 10 years before, did not upset the existence of the doctrine of joint Cabinet responsibility.

(5) Advice given by civil servants to Government ministers was not confidential for all time.

(6) There were, therefore, no grounds for stopping publication.

Lord Widgery's closing words in the judgment are revealing:

"It may, of course, be intensely difficult in a particular case, to say at what point the material loses its confidential character, on the ground that publication will no longer undermine the doctrine of joint cabinet responsibility. It is this difficulty, which prompts some to argue that cabinet discussions should retain their confidential character for a longer and arbitrary period such as 30 years, or even for all time, but this seems to me excessively restrictive. The court should intervene only in the clearest of cases where the continuing confidentiality of the material can be demonstrated. In less clear cases, and this, in my view, is certainly one, reliance must be placed on the good sense and good taste of the minister or ex-minister concerned.

In the present case there is nothing in Mr. Crossman's work to suggest that he did not support the doctrine of joint cabinet responsibility. The question for the court is whether it is shown that publication might now damage the doctrine, notwithstanding that much of the action is up to 10 years old and three general elections have been held meanwhile.

So far as the Attorney-General relies in his argument on the disclosure of individual ministerial opinions, he has not satisfied me that publication would in any way inhibit free and open discussion in cabinet hereafter."

One concluding point on privacy. There is no law against taking a photograph: the act of doing this cannot turn into trespass if there was no trespassing. This was the result of an action brought by Lord Bernstein against an aerial photography company which took pictures of his house and land.

In *Bernstein* v. *Skyview Ltd.* (1977), he claimed that his privacy had been invaded and the space above his land trespassed upon when the defendant firm took pictures of his country house. The judge held that the aircraft had not been proved to have overflown his land and the mere taking of a picture did not render them trespassers.

7   Official Secrets Acts and The "D" Notice System

During the early part of 1976, it appeared that the Labour Government was prepared to make changes in the Official Secrets Act legislation but it has since become clear that, due to legislative priorities and civil service disquiet about the effect of liberalisation, such changes are unlikely to be made in the immediate future.

A journalist might, initially, be forgiven for wondering why he should be concerned with legislation which, ostensibly, seeks to prevent State secrets falling into the hands of unfriendly powers. The reason is that the drafting of the Official Secrets Acts has created a series of potential offences which have little or nothing to do with spying. On various occasions, there have been prosecutions under the Acts which, one supposes, could never have been contemplated when the legislation was actually enacted.

This topic will be dealt with in some considerable detail. No claim is made that the issues form part of what a reporter would have to consider in the day-to-day running of events. However, a lack of awareness of the scope and application of the Acts and the influence of the "D" notice system can lead to two dangers. Either the journalist transgresses the law in ignorance and may face a prosecution or he may be persuaded that a matter is the subject of Official Secrets Acts restrictions when it is not.

Two examples may serve to illustrate the practical effect of these dangers. In 1932, a journalist on the *Daily Mail* gave a small sum of money to a clerk at Somerset House for details about the wills of three rich men before the information was officially released. The clerk lost his job and received a six week prison sentence; the journalist received a two month sentence. In 1950, Chapman Pincher, the defence correspondent of the *Daily Express,* was investigating a story about the building of large atomic reactors. The concrete had been incorrectly

poured and the walls were porous to radio-activity. The chief
civil servant in the relevant ministry warned the then editor
that, if the story was printed, a prosecution under the Official
Secrets Acts would follow. A year later, when the walls had
been repaired at vast cost, the ban was lifted. "The civil servant
concerned later told me, with some hilarity, that we could
never have been prosecuted. He was astonished that the paper
had given in so easily," Pincher subsequently revealed.

The first Act appeared in 1889, covering spying and
breaches of official trust. It became an offence for a Crown servant or Government contractor to communicate official information "corruptly or contrary to his official duty" to anyone if
this was against the state or public interest.

Leaking of official information continued and, in 1911, the
major Act came into being. The Bill passed all its stages in a
single afternoon. It sought to provide greater protection
against leakages of any kind of official information. The information did not need to be connected with defence or national
security.

In a letter to *The Times* in 1920, a former Conservative Attorney-General (Sir Lionel Heald) commented that section 2 of
this Act is so restrictive that it "makes it a crime, without any
possibility of defence, to report the number of cups of tea con-
sumed per week in a Government department or the details of
a new carpet in a Minister's room."

In 1920, with Mr. Lloyd George's administration troubled
by Press disclosures, came an additional Official Secrets Act.
There was considerable Press opposition to section 6 in particular. This gave power to require information in connection
with offences under the Acts and the Press realised this could
be used to force journalists to reveal their sources of information.

This section is discussed more fully later but, in response to
these criticisms, the then Attorney-General (Sir Gordon
Hewart) declared the provisions had nothing to do with anything but spies. Odd, then, that *Lewis* v. *Cattle* (1938) saw the
conviction of a Manchester journalist for failing to reveal the
source of a statement that a particular person was wanted by
the police on a comparatively minor charge.

In the same year Mr. Duncan Sandys questioned the

adequacy of London's anti-aircraft defences, in parliamentary proceedings. He then told Parliament that he had been approached by the Attorney-General and threatened with a prosecution under section 6 unless he revealed the source of the information. The House of Commons Committee of Privileges ruled that any such harrassment of a Member of Parliament constituted a breach of parliamentary privilege (here, the privilege of free speech).

There were changes made in 1939, to narrow section 6 offences to the area of spying. Then, in 1962, six members of the Committee of 100 (C.N.D.) were sent to prison after a sit-down at an airfield had led to a prosecution under section 1 of the 1911 Act. The House of Lords held their conduct amounted to sabotage and extended the effect of section 1 beyond spying.

The Acts in Detail

Section 1 of the 1911 Act covers spying and prohibits the making of any sketch, model or note that could be useful to any enemy or communicating such information to an enemy. It is up to the accused to show that his activities were really for an innocent purpose.

Section 2 relates to the unauthorised communication of official information:

(1) if any person having in his possession or control ... information ... which has been entrusted in confidence to him by any person holding office under [the Crown] or which he has obtained ... owing to his position as a person who holds or has held office under [the Crown] ...
(a) communicates the ... information to any person, other than a person to whom he is authorised ...

Should this be the case, then, on conviction, there is a maximum two year prison sentence.

This relates to officials passing on information. The real danger from the Press point of view comes from section 2 (2):

"If any person receives any ... information, knowing, or having reasonable ground to believe, at the time when he receives it, that the ... information is communicated to him in contravention of this Act ..." then he faces the same penalty as above unless he can prove that the communication of the information "was contrary to his desire."

All information that a Crown servant learns in the course of his work is "official", regardless of its nature or importance. The poster, reproduced on p. 149 emphasises this.

This poster, published by H.M.S.O., is for display in Government offices, factories engaged in defence contracts and the like.

As the poster is a Crown publication, if it had been given to the author by a Crown servant who was not authorised to communicate it, that person would have committed an offence. The author and any person receiving it, "knowing or having reasonable grounds at the time he receives it" for believing that the Act is being contravened, could go to prison for up to two years. Readers would have the defence that the information was communicated to them contrary to their desires.

"Authorisation" is nowhere defined in the Act. Ministers, effectively, are self-authorising, and senior civil servants have considerable personal discretion in deciding what they decide to make public (or remain silent about). The deliberate leaking of Social Security information to the magazine *New Society* in 1976, while definitely unauthorised, could have led to prosecutions under section 2 (1) and (2). One of the problems, at the moment, is that the Acts are so discredited that in situations like this, with a definite public interest in the disclosures, they are almost unworkable.

The Franks Committee, which reported on section 2 of the Act in 1972, concluded: "Section 2 is rarely activated in the courtroom, but it is seen by many as having a pervasive influence on the work and behaviour of hundreds of thousands of people."

No prosecution may be brought under the Acts without the consent of the Attorney-General. This is sometimes offered as evidence that the Acts cannot be misused, but this is scarcely tenable (either historically or theoretically). If a particular Government wanted X prosecuted, but the Attorney-General felt unwilling to proceed, then a more "sympathetic" Attorney-General could be appointed. In any event, his position is parti-

THE OFFICIAL SECRETS ACTS

AFFECT YOU...

YOU MUST NOT TALK ABOUT or pass on information about your work unless you are authorised to do so.

YOU MUST NOT KEEP or copy any drawing or document unless it is your job to do so.

YOU MUST TAKE CARE not to lose any drawings or other documents.

YOU MUST HAND THEM BACK when they are finished with or asked for.

Penalties for infringing the Acts may be heavy

cularly unenviable. He represents the public interest; he has to decide whether to prosecute on purely legal grounds and he is a member of the government whose interests may be at stake. *The Sunday Telegraph,* in 1971, commented: "Even a saint should not be faced with such temptations, and saints are probably as rare among Attorney-Generals as among the rest of us."

Professor Hugh Thomas, in 1968, commented: "If every occasion when this Act is broken were to be the subject of proceedings in court, a tenth of the working population might find themselves in jail."

The Sunday Telegraph Trial 1971

The real impetus for changing section 2 of the 1911 Act came from the prosecution of *The Sunday Telegraph* in 1971 and the spectacular failure to secure a conviction.

The *Sunday Telegraph* had published a report by Colonel R.E. Scott, defence advisor to the British High Commission in Lagos. A retired General had showed the report to Mr. Jonathan Aitken, who had photocopied the report before returning it. It related to the Biafran war and criticised the poor leadership and tremendous waste displayed by Nigerian officers. It concluded, however, that the Nigerian forces would overcome the Biafran "rebels." The report also revealed that the Prime Minister (the then Mr. Harold Wilson) and his Foreign Secretary (the then Mr. George Brown) had misled the public about the extent of British army support provided to Nigeria.

Before printing the report, the paper had checked with the secretary of the "D" notice committee, Admiral Norman Denning. They were informed that, since the document did not relate to British forces or British defences, "D" notices were not concerned. The report was already circulating among Biafran circles in London and no effort was made by any minister to contact the paper or request non-publication.

At the trial it was established that the Scott report contained no military secrets and the defendants contended that every single fact was public knowledge. The prosecution claimed that the story had severely endangered diplomatic relations with Nigeria.

After a 17 day trial, the jury, after two hours, returned a "not guilty" verdict. The trial judge, Mr. Justice Caulfield, summed up to the jury that the prosecution argument, that anyone who revealed information from an official source, acted unlawfully was *not* the law (though it almost certainly was). He commented, inviting an acquittal:

> "One recognises that an opinion-forming medium like the press must not be muzzled. The warning bark is necessary to help maintain a free society. If the Press is muzzled you may think it becomes no more than a tenant of the political power. . .
>
> The 1911 Act achieves its 60th birthday on August 22nd this year.
>
> This case, if it does nothing more, may well alert those who govern us at least to consider whether or not section 2 of this Act has reached retirement age and should be pensioned off.
>
> And whether it should be replaced by a section that will enable men like Colonel Cairns, Mr. Aitken, Mr. Roberts and other editors to determine without difficulty whether a communication by anyone of them of a certain piece of information, originating from an official source and not concerned in the slightest with national security, are going to be put in peril of being enclosed in a dock facing a criminal charge.
>
> You may find it easy to conclude not only that the Crown has failed to prove its case but, on the contrary, that Colonel Cairns has satisfied you that he was authorised to do what he did. But that is a question of fact exclusively for you. . .
>
> There is no censorship in this country; there is no duty in law for an editor or his newspaper to go running to Whitehall to get permission to print articles or news. Indeed, it would be absurd for a government office to have the power to dictate to an editor what he should or should not publish.
>
> It may well be that, during the course of this case, you, members of the jury, have said to yourselves: 'We cannot see the wood for the trees' but are there any trees at all? You might well think it was all a barren waste.
>
> The case for the prosecution has been put on the basis that anyone handling a document from an official source and marked 'confidential' was breaking the law. I hope I have been able to show you that this is not breaking the law."

Despite this case, which indicates a certain stubborn commonsense, the Acts remain broadly worded and a threat, in that they inhibit the Press from doing things which may be quite legitimate.

Section 6 of the Official Secrets Act 1920

While the terms of this section are stated to relate to section 1 of
the 1911 Act (spying), it has already been shown that the scope
of section 1 has been extended by the House of Lords.

Section 6 of the 1920 Act runs:

> (1) "Where a chief officer of police is satisfied that there is reason-
> able ground for suspecting that an offence under section one [of
> the 1911 Act] has been committed and for believing that any person
> is able to furnish information as to the offence or suspected
> offence, he may apply to a Secretary of State for permission to exer-
> cise the powers conferred [by the Secretary of State] and, if such per-
> mission is granted, he may authorise a superintendent of police, or
> any police officer not below the rank of inspector, to require the
> person believed to be able to furnish information to give any infor-
> mation in his power relating to the offence or suspected offence . . .
> and if a person . . . fails to comply with any such requirement or
> knowingly gives false information. . . ." he faces up to two years'
> imprisonment if tried on indictment or, if tried summarily, up to
> three months' imprisonment, or up to a £50 fine.

This section allows detailed questioning about sources and
failure to answer carries a potentially heavy penalty. It is reinforced by an additional power, in cases of emergency, for the
chief officer of police to act without obtaining permission (subject, only, to a requirement that he later tells the Secretary of
State what has happened).

Section 9 of the 1911 Act permits search warrants to be issued
without, necessarily, the authority of a magistrate in cases of
emergency. The warrant allows the police to enter, search and
seize anything, which seems to be reasonably relevant to any
offence under the Act (*i.e.* papers or information coming
under section 2 of the Act as well).

Conclusion

In November 1976, the Home Secretary, Mr. Merlyn Rees,
promised a revision of section 2 of the Official Secrets Act 1911.
Such revision had been part of the Labour Party manifesto.

Asked how the current law would operate in the interim, he replied:

> "While the exercise of the Act is a matter for the Attorney-General, no doubt it will be open to him to take into account the Government's intention to introduce legislation in considering whether to bring proceedings under section 2. For that reason alone, it was vital that this statement should be made."

The importance, which can be attached to this statement, became apparent in February 1977, barely three months later, when two journalists, Crispin Aubrey and Duncan Campbell, and a former Signals Corps N.C.O., John Berry, were arrested under section 2 of the 1911 Act.

The three had been connected with the campaign to prevent the deportation of two American journalists, Mark Hosenball and Philip Agee.

The Home Secretary's statement in the House of Commons had no force of law. The Attorney-General, while a member of the Government, stressed, in a dispute over the intention of Post Office workers to "black" mail to South Africa in January 1977, that he is a law unto himself.

Even if the Home Secretary's statement had not been eroded by events, the Press cannot be sure what the eventual law will contain.

The 1911 and 1920 Acts cover a wide and ill-defined area. They can operate to restrict information which the public should have access to: they may be used against the Press. Journalists may be required to reveal their sources of information on pain of imprisonment.

Reform in this area should take place as a matter of legislative priority so that unnecessary inhibitions are removed from the Press. The prospect of reform, unfortunately, can be used as a carrot to secure Press co-operation on sensitive political issues of the day. Certain cynics have noted that there is a relationship between the imminence of elections and promises of reform. Doubtless they are mistaken because the issue is much too broad and much too important for this kind of *badinage*.

From the Press view-point, these two points remain for consideration:

(1) over six years have passed since *The Sunday Telegraph*

trial and section 2 has still not been pensioned off;

(2) police officers, as they take an oath of allegiance to the Crown, are subject to the Acts and information from them comes within the terms of the Acts.

The "D" Notice System

Prosecutions, under section 2 of the 1911 Act against newspapers, run to a figure of four during the years 1911-1972 (on the available information). One reason for this limited number of prosecutions is, undoubtedly, the Attorney-General's discretionary power to authorise proceedings. A further important factor is the existence of the "D" notice system.

This system relies on memoranda issued to the media, requesting a ban on publication of certain subjects connected with national security.

"D" notices are issued by the Defence, Press and Broadcasting Committee, composed of five Government and 11 Press and broadcasting representatives. It was originally formed in 1912, operating a voluntary censorship system. In 1939, it was superseded by a censorship department and, in 1945, was reformed. Very little was known of this committee until 1961 but since then, particularly in 1967, more information about this committee has become available.

Chapman Pincher recounts that, when he joined the *Daily Express* in 1946, the then editor, Arthur Christiansen, would never allow him to mention the "D" notice system. "At first I thought that this was because the mere existence of the system was secret. In fact, Chris told me that it was because he was ashamed to let his readers know that he was a willing party to any form of censorship."

A "D" notice does not relate directly to the Official Secrets Act. The notices are voluntary and have no legal authority but there is always the possibility of an Official Secrets Act prosecution in the background, should material be printed which contravenes the Acts. As Pincher has noted, "only the British would call the system voluntary."

A notice can only be issued on the authority of the committee. In an emergency, the government may ask the committee to issue a special "D" notice but such notice can only be issued with the approval of at least three of the Press-Broadcasting members and must later be reviewed by the full committee.

The notices are distributed in loose-leaf form marked "Private and Confidential" and identify areas of danger and sensitivity. Most of the guidance relates to technical and strategic information and suggests ways in which material may, if mentioned, be discussed. There is a regular review of matters subject to "D" notices and items are taken off the list as soon as possible.

The "D" notices are accepted as confidential communications. Every editor of national or provincial prominence receives two copies, one for himself and one for the news editor's file.

Deliberate breaches of the notices are unusual and those which do occur are normally mistakes rather than deliberate publication. Breach of a "D" notice by one newspaper puts competitors in a difficult position, almost compelling them to follow suit.

The Press-Broadcasting representatives require definite proof of a need for secrecy before approving a particular notice. If a Government department wants a "D" notice issued, a draft is sent to the secretary of the committee who, from experience, advises on the form most likely to be acceptable to the Press.

The notices, in effect, provide some flexible middle ground between a strict application of the Official Secrets Acts and a written code. They indicate what may or may not be safely published at any particular time (theoretically). Apart from occasional complaints about the system being used for departmental convenience, newspapers, until 1967, were relatively content with the system.

Then, in that year, Pincher revealed that security authorities regularly screened all wireless and cable communications going out of the country. The Prime Minister (then Mr. Wilson) claimed in Parliament that this was sensationalised, inaccurate and a clear breach of two "D" notices. Pincher argued that, while non-publication was requested, he had been told that "D" notices did not apply to this information.

Lord Francis-Williams provided some interesting background material on this issue.

> "Instead of having a word with the editor, which would have been
> the proper course, he (George Brown, the Foreign Secretary)
> decided to approach Sir Max Aitken, chairman of Beaverbrook
> Newspapers Ltd., the owners of the *Daily Express*, with whom he
> had a slight acquaintance. Sir Max was at a dinner at the Garrick
> Club at the time. However, he was finally reached with a message
> at 10.15 in the evening and took the Foreign Secretary's call in the
> porter's box in the hall of the Club. Thereupon, since he had never
> heard of the story and Mr. Brown did not like to describe it in any
> detail on a public telephone, there followed a conversation of farci-
> cal incomprehensibility in which Sir Max could not understand
> what Mr. Brown was talking about and Mr. Brown jumped to the
> conclusion that since their conversation, if confused, had been
> polite and friendly, all was well."

The affair led to a Committee of three Privy Councillors being
appointed under Lord Radcliffe (chairman of the Vassall Tribunal). This eventually reported that the decision to publish
was not taken "with a deliberate intention of evading or defy-
ing the 'D' notice procedure" and that the *Daily Express* story
was "not inaccurate in any sense that could expose it to hostile
criticism on that score" (*i.e.* inaccuracy).

The Prime Minister, on the same day that this report was
published, issued a White Paper rejecting these findings. His
views were ultimately accepted in Parliament after a long
battle.

The Fleet Street view is that the effect of this affair was to
engender a degree of cynicism about the whole system. With
the delay in proposals to reform or change section 2 of the Official Secrets Act 1911, this cynicism is hardly diminishing.

PART 2

THE COURTS AND REPORTING RESTRICTIONS

1 The Legal Profession, Law Officers and Legal Aid

Lawyers can choose to practise in either of the two branches of the legal profession in England and Wales. There are solicitors (some 28,000) and barristers (numbering about 3,500). The reasons for the division of the profession are rooted in the mid-fourteenth century when professional advocacy began to evolve. Barristers were recognised as advocates by the Common law courts; preparatory work was conducted by attorneys. Solicitors appeared in the mid-fifteenth century, connected with the old Court of Chancery. By the mid-nineteenth century, attorneys and solicitors had united to form what is now the Law Society: practitioners were called solicitors, and barristers continued as expert advocates. The barristers' Inns of Court had refused, after the sixteenth century, to admit attorneys or solicitors to membership.

The following is a brief examination of the current differences between the two branches.

Solicitors

These are controlled by the Law Society, given special discretionary powers by Parliament (see Disciplinary Bodies). Solicitors may practise in partnership, to share the profits, losses and overheads. They may appear as advocates before magistrates' courts, county courts, certain crown courts, some tribunals, the coroners' courts and in bankruptcy matters before the High Court. The bulk of their work, however, is not concerned with court appearances and may not include any litigation (legal battles) at all. While they do prepare documents and statements of a client's case to form a "brief" to be sent to a barrister, they also draft wills, supervise trusts and settlements, administer estates and deal with conveyancing (the legal side of buying or selling property). It is these latter activities which produce a practice's working income.

159

Court appearances generally cost a practice money in terms
of what could be earned using that time on other work.

There is a contract between a solicitor and his client: solicitors may sue for their fees and be sued themselves. Solicitors are
instructed by the public directly.

Because solicitors, when qualified to practise, are entered on
the Rolls of the Supreme Court, the court retains power over
these officers of the court. The court may force a solicitor to
pay damages and costs caused by his negligence, or punish a
solicitor for contempt in failing to obey an order. *Weston* v.
Court Administrator of the Central Criminal Court (1976), is
an example of a solicitor successfully appealing against a finding of contempt and an order to pay the costs of his refusal to
attend court in a case because there were valid reasons.

Barristers

These are controlled by the Inn of Court to which they belong.
These are four Inns: Lincoln's, the Inner Temple, the Middle
Temple and Gray's. Originally these were medieval living
quarters. The Inns, in 1966, set up the Senate of the Four Inns
of Court to deal with disciplinary matters (see Disciplinary
Bodies). It is the barrister's Inn which "calls" him to the Bar.

In every Inn there are three ranks:

(1) *Benchers:* the governors, who are judges or senior members of the Bar, with absolute control over the admission and
call of students;

(2) *Barristers;* and

(3) *Students:* before call, the student must "dine" eight legal
terms in his Inn (usually three meals each term), pass his Bar
Finals and pay the necessary admission fees. Before he can practise, he must serve 12 months pupillage with a senior member
of the Bar (who may not be a Queen's Counsel).

Barristers (known as "counsel" in the singular and plural)
may appear in any court. In addition to basic advocacy, many
spend time on paper work, drafting pleadings, divorce petitions, settlements and giving written opinions.

There is no contract between a barrister and his lay client.
The money a barrister receives is by way of an *honorarium* and

he cannot sue for his fees. On the other hand, a barrister cannot be sued for professional negligence. The justification for this immunity is that:

(a) there could be perpetual argument about the result of a case, and a series of re-trials, if the conduct of the barrister could be constantly challenged by the dissatisfied party;

(b) there is a general professional duty not to mislead the court;

(c) a barrister cannot pick and choose his clients. He must, except in very limited circumstances, take every brief presented to him; and

(d) he must retain his independence and cannot be constantly looking over his shoulder, worrying about whether the lay client will bring an action against him.

Barristers can, generally, only act when instructed by solicitors and may not receive instructions from lay clients direct. They may not tout for business among solicitors and may never practise within any kind of partnership situation. Each member of the Bar is, in effect, completely independent and individual.

Experienced barristers may apply to the Lord Chancellor to "take silk" (become Queen's Counsel). Appointment is by the Queen, on the Lord Chancellor's recommendation. The old rule, that a Q.C. could only appear if a junior (ordinary) barrister was also briefed, was abolished in 1977. Because of the increased costs of briefing a Queen's Counsel, it is a decision of some importance for an experienced barrister to apply to take silk since he may find that he has priced himself out of the market.

Law Officers

One feature of English law is the intermingling of what is apparently political with what is judicial. Journalists should be aware of the basic functions and relative status of the law officers and some of the senior judicial appointments. The law officers change (as their tenure is political) on a change of government.

(A) *Political appointments*

Lord Chancellor. He is the ultimate head of the judiciary
and the chief judge in England. He is chairman of the Judicial
Committee of the Privy Council (the Law Lords in their advisory capacity). He advises the Crown on all High Court
appointments, circuit judgeships and Recorders and appoints
Justices of the Peace. He keeps the Great Seal, which represents the Crown's signature, and he is the Speaker of the House
of Lords. As Speaker (unlike his House of Commons counter-
part) he may vote and take part in debates but he has no casting
vote. In his judicial capacity he is in charge of the Lords of
Appeal in Ordinary (the Law Lords) hearing appeals on
points of law of general public importance. The Lord Chancellor is a Cabinet Minister.

His position emphasises that there is no separation of powers within the British Constitution. While other countries
avoid mixing the judicial, the legislative and the executive
powers (*i.e.* the Supreme Court, Congress and the President's
administration in the United States), the Lord Chancellor in
England is involved in all three branches.

The Attorney-General. By convention, he is not usually a
member of the Cabinet, although he is usually a member of the
House of Commons. His job is to represent the Crown in civil
matters and prosecute in important criminal cases. He is head
of the English Bar and points of professional practice are
referred to him. He advises the government on legal matters
and the courts on matters of parliamentary privilege. Part of
his job is to protect the public interest and he can begin proceedings to protect the public. If, for instance, he feels that a
contempt has been committed by a newspaper publishing
details which might prejudice a person's fair trial, he could
take action (see *Att.-Gen.* v. *Times Newspapers* (1973)). The
barrister who holds this office may not, while in office, engage
in private practice. He can prevent prosecutions by entering a
nolle prosecui (do not proceed) and his consent is required, on
occasions, for certain criminal prosecutions.

Solicitor-General. Ranks directly under the Attorney-General and, despite his title, is also a barrister. Effectively he acts
as the Attorney-General's deputy: anything which the senior is

required to do may be done, in addition, by the Solicitor-General. He, too, is normally a member of the House of Commons and may not engage in private practice while in office.

Director of Public Prosecutions. This post is not, in fact, a political appointment but the Director, appointed by the Home Secretary, works under the supervision of the Attorney-General. He must be a barrister or solicitor of at least 10 years' standing. He must prosecute through his own staff or Treasury Counsel (practising barristers nominated on a special list by the Attorney-General to receive briefs from the D.P.P.) if the offence is punishable by death, in manslaughter and where a statute requires him to conduct or consent to a prosecution.

While the D.P.P.'s office is, effectively, a civil service department there have been recent suggestions that it should provide the focal point for a national system of prosecutors similar to the District Attorney in America or the Procurator Fiscal in Scotland.

Current responsibilities include:

(i) giving advice, on his own initiative or on request, to clerks, magistrates, chief officers of police and others in criminal proceedings;

(ii) taking over proceedings from the police or a private prosecutor where the case is important or difficult; and

(iii) appearing for the Crown on appeals to the Court of Appeal.

(B) *Judicial appointments*

Details of the range of normal judicial appointments may be found in the chapters on the "Criminal Process" and the "Civil Courts." Covered at this stage, are the judicial heads of department. It should be remembered that the Lord Chancellor is overall head of the judicial system.

Master of the Rolls. Head of the Court of Appeal (Civil Division). This position is currently held by Lord Denning. The holder receives a life peerage.

Lord Chief Justice. Head of the Court of Appeal (Criminal Division) and of the Queen's Bench Division of the High Court. The current incumbent is Lord Widgery. The holder receives a life peerage. While some of his work involves business before the Court of Appeal, the Lord Chief Justice has an

important function hearing cases presented to the Divisional
Court of the Queen's Bench Division, particularly cases coming through on points of law from summary trial.

In the three divisions of the High Court the respective heads
are:

(1) *Queen's Bench:* the Lord Chief Justice (see above) with
about 40 puisne (High Court) judges. The criminal jurisdiction of the High Court functions entirely through this division.

(2) *Chancery:* technically the Lord Chancellor but, in
practice, the Vice-Chancellor, controlling 10 puisne judges.
The Divisional Court of the Chancery Division hears, in particular, appeals from the county courts on bankruptcy.

(3) *Family:* the President (of what until 1970 was known as
the P.D.A. or Probate, Admiralty and Divorce Division).

While the Lord Chief Justice receives a life peerage, the President and the Vice-Chancellor in the remaining divisions
receive only knighthoods.

Costs

Costs in any court action, civil or criminal, are the iceberg element. Outside the award of damages or a fine, costs represent
the money due for legal advice, representation, witnesses and
the preparation of evidence. In civil cases at the High Court,
the average 1975 costs were about £1,000 for a damages action
taken to court and about £500 for a similar case settled before
court. To defend a dangerous driving charge at the magistrates' court, could cost about £100 and would be more expensive if the charge was taken at the crown court.

A brief outline of rules is set out below. Legal aid, dealt with
in the section which follows, is an attempt by the State to contribute towards the costs of any particular case where the individual qualifies for such help.

Costs in civil cases

The basic rule is that the winner has his legal costs paid for
him by the loser as well as getting his remedy (*i.e.* damages).
This rule, seemingly simple, hides a mass of technicalities and
tactical manoeuvres. One rule is that if a plaintiff recovers less,
in damages, than an amount paid into court before the trial by

the defendant, then he (although the winner) must pay the costs of the action from the date of the payment in. In *Dering* v. *Uris* (1964), a Polish doctor who, in Auschwitz, had taken part in certain experiments, won his libel action against the author Leon Uris and the publishers for references made in the book *Exodus*. The publishers had paid £2 into court, a sum that the doctor could obviously never accept. The jury awarded him contemptuous damages of ½d, however, so Dering had to pay the bulk of the costs in the action.

Costs in criminal cases

The civil rule would be inappropriate here because either:

(a) the defendant being punished has no money to pay the costs of the prosecution against him; or

(b) in the event of an acquittal, this fact does not mean that there were no valid grounds for bringing the prosecution.

In a criminal case the court either orders part or all of the costs to be paid by one of the parties or, more usually, out of central government funds. The rules are complex and will not be explored in any great detail. The position of successful defendants in relation to costs will be noted.

In 1973, the Lord Chief Justice issued a Practice Note, which emphasised that, if the court had power to award costs out of central funds, it should do so to the successful defendant unless there were positive reasons for making a different order. Such reasons could include:

(1) the prosecution acting spitefully or without reasonable cause: in this case the prosecution will be ordered to pay the defendant's costs;

(2) the defendant's own conduct brought suspicion on himself and it was his fault that the prosecution thought the case was stronger than it was: here the defendant pays his own costs;

(3) where there was clear evidence to support a guilty verdict but, because of a procedural error, the defendant was entitled to an acquittal: again, the defendant pays his own costs; and

(4) where the defendant was acquitted on one charge but convicted on another: here the court should make whatever order is appropriate, taking into account the difference between the charges and the general conduct of the defendant.

Legal Aid

Civil

In cases needing court resolution, this aids people with a disposable income not exceeding (currently) £2,085 per annum and disposable capital of under £1,400. The Supplementary Benefits Commission makes the necessary financial assessments, deducting money needed by the person for rent, loan interest, taxes, dependants, etc. For the legal aid to be completely free (*i.e.* a nil contribution from the individual) disposable income must be under £665 per annum and disposable capital below £300. Between these upper and lower limits, the assisted person may be required to contribute up to one-third of the costs. For advice (short of a court battle), the limits are more strict.

The Law Society, in addition to administering the funding of the legal aid scheme, operates a system to give basic advice for a nominal payment known as the "Green Form" scheme. This enables the public to find out whether they have a legal problem and whether the state would give them further assistance.

Within the legal aid scheme, the assisted person can spread any contributions, which are required from him, over 12 months. He can be exempted from paying any or all of them if his income falls below certain levels because of sickness or unemployment.

Criminal

In 1966, a committee chaired by Lord Widgery, the present Lord Chief Justice, recommended that legal aid in criminal cases should be granted (subject to the accused's means) in the following cases:

(1) If the charge could mean the accused losing his liberty or suffering serious damage to his reputation; or

(2) If the charge raises a substantial point of law; or

(3) If the accused might be unable to follow the proceedings and state his own case because of inadequate knowledge of English, mental illness or physical disability; or

(4) If the defence involves tracing and interviewing witnesses or expert cross-examination of prosecution witnesses; or

(5) If legal representation is desirable in the interests of someone other than the accused (*i.e.* in a case where a sexual offence
is alleged against a child, it is undesirable for the accused to
cross-examine the witness in person).

In criminal cases it is the court itself which decides whether
or not the accused will receive legal aid.

(a) *Magistrates' proceedings* (including juvenile courts): aid
can be granted by the clerk but only refused by the magistrates.

(b) *Crown Court:* can be granted by the magistrates' committing for trial (or from whom the appeal is being taken) or by
the Crown Court. This order covers advice on a further appeal
to the Court of Appeal.

(c) *Court of Appeal:* can be granted by a single judge or the
full court. Usually the Registrar of the Criminal Division of
the court is directed to act for the appellant.

(d) *Divisional Court, Queen's Bench Division:* in these cases
(*i.e.* on appeal on a point of law by way of case stated) legal aid
falls under the civil scheme.

Under section 37 of the Criminal Justice Act 1972, it is
unlawful to send unrepresented defendants to prison, borstal
or a detention centre unless they have been specifically told of
this right to apply for legal aid and they have either been
turned down because of their means or they have refused to
apply.

Under section 2 (4) of the Legal Aid Act 1974, magistrates
may assign any solicitor present in court to assist someone
who is unrepresented. The purpose of this is to allow representation where there is a short point (*i.e.* bail on a remand) to be
considered. If the point is more complex, the magistrates
should adjourn the case and make a full legal aid order.

[A Royal commission is currntly (1978) examining the legal
profession, its structure and practices.]

2   The Criminal Process

If a wrong is committed, the courts seek to provide a forum for the injured party to state the grievance publicly and in which it may judge whether the grievance is one that the law will recognise and act upon.

This point is worth noting at the outset in an examination of the criminal courts because a particular act may give rise to both criminal and civil liability. If an individual drives carelessly and injures another, there may be two actions taken against him. The Crown (in the form of the police or the prosecuting solicitor's department for a County Council) may take action against the driver for the criminal offence of careless driving and ask for punishment if the offence is proved beyond all reasonable doubt. The injured person may bring a civil action for the damage he has suffered, without regard to the criminal proceedings, and he will seek to prove his case (in this example, of negligence on the part of the driver) on the balance of probabilities.

In criminal actions, the state argues that the driver's conduct has led to a situation which the law, in principle, will punish because the state has theoretically been injured. In civil actions, the personally injured party asks for the payment of money to remedy his pain and suffering.

While there are a number of different types of criminal offence, there are basically three categories:

(1) *indictable offences:* ones which must be tried at the crown court, even though the accused intends to plead guilty, because the magistrates have no power to deal with such offences. Examples include murder, treason, robbery, wounding with intent and causing death by dangerous driving.

(2) *hybrid offences:* ones which may be tried at the crown court or which may be tried by the magistrates. The accused may resist summary trial if he could go to prison for three months or more and demand a crown court trial with a judge

THE CRIMINAL PROCESS

and, if he is pleading not guilty, a jury. This category includes theft, criminal damage, burglary and assault occasioning actual bodily harm.

(3) *summary offences:* ones which may be dealt with only by the magistrates and where there is no right to demand a crown court trial (though there may be an appeal to the crown court sitting as an appeal court). Parking offences, careless driving and being drunk and disorderly come into this category.

The Criminal Law Act 1977 confirms this classification. By section 23, certain hybrid offences are now only triable summarily if the amount involved is below £200.

Another method of classification is to view criminal offences as either arrestable or non-arrestable. By section 1 (1) of the Criminal Law Act 1967, an arrestable offence is defined as an offence or any attempt to commit an offence for which the sentence is fixed by law or for which the maximum sentence on first conviction is five years or more. For murder (or attempted murder) the sentence of life imprisonment is fixed by law. It is also an indictable offence. For theft (or attempted theft) the maximum term is 10 years' imprisonment. It is a hybrid offence. For a parking offence the sentence is a fine. It is a summary offence. The first two offences above are arrestable, the third is not.

In addition the police have power to arrest:

(1) anyone they suspect, with reasonable cause, to have committed an arrestable offence; or

(2) anyone they suspect, with reasonable cause, to be about to commit an arrestable offence; or

(3) under various Acts of Parliament (*e.g.* arrest following a positive breath test).

Although arrests, as described above, may be justified, they will be unlawful unless the arrested person is told of the reason for his detention. Without an arrest, there is no power, at common law, to require a citizen to reveal his name and address or to make the citizen go to a police station.

Section 62 of the Criminal Law Act 1977 provides that where a person has been arrested and is being held at a police station or other premises, he has the right to inform one person of his choice of this fact. Communication of this should occur without delay or unnecessary delay.

The police have no power to search anyone who has not been arrested, unless they are searching for drugs, firearms or (in certain large cities) for stolen property. After a person has been arrested, the police do have the power to search and seize anything, which may be evidence of the crime for which he has been arrested or of any other crime in which he may be implicated.

Whether the offence is indictable, hybrid or summary, arrestable or non-arrestable, the Crown begins its action by compelling the accused to appear before magistrates.

Magistrates (Justices of the Peace) comprise some 21,000 unpaid persons, with no formal legal training, who are appointed by the Lord Chancellor. In certain large urban areas, there are stipendiary (paid) magistrates, appointed from the ranks of barristers and solicitors of at least seven years' standing. While a stipendiary can sit on his own to dispense summary justice, there must be at least two lay magistrates, and not more than seven, to deal with a summary trial.

Magistrates are assisted by a clerk appointed to each court. The clerk must be a qualified barrister or solicitor of at least five years' standing. His job is to supervise court procedure and to advise the magistrates on the law and their powers of sentence. Clerks should not take part in the decision of guilt or innocence. The magistrates have to decide all questions of fact and, in the event of a not guilty plea, act initially as a small jury.

The offender appears before the court because he has been arrested committing an offence, because a summons has been issued or because a warrant has been issued for his arrest. If the arrest takes place in the commission of an offence, an information is not necessary to start the process: the appearance of the accused in court, when the charge is put to him, serves as the information. For a summons or a warrant to be issued, an information is necessary.

The information: This is the general start to criminal proceedings, where the prosecution allege that a person named has committed some specific offence. The information may be oral but is generally made in writing. The information document must indicate the place, date and nature of the offence. It is a formal statement of the charge against the accused and

4444444

criminal proceedings in a magistrates' court are, in law, the "hearing of an information."

Unless the person has already been arrested and charged, the laying of the information is an *ex parte* action; only the prosecution is involved. From this process follows the issuing of a summons or a warrant.

The summons. In most cases there is no reason to suppose that the accused will not attend court. A summons, requiring his attendance, is sent to him:

(i) by personal delivery; or

(ii) by leaving it with someone for him at his last known address; or

(iii) by posting it by registered or recorded delivery to his last known address.

The warrant. This is the alternative form of process. It directs the police to arrest the person named in the information and to bring that person before the court. A warrant is normally used:

(i) where the charge is serious or, for some other reason, the accused is unlikely to attend court voluntarily; or

(ii) where the police can prove that the summons has been served and the defendant has failed to answer it; or

(iii) where the defendant has been allowed bail by the police but has failed to attend at court.

With the accused before the court, the magistrates have power to deal with the information positively. They may either:

(a) deal with the offence summarily; or

(b) decide whether there is prima facia evidence to commit the accused for trial on indictment at the crown court.

Everything depends on the category of the offence and, in addition, if the offence is hybrid or purely indictable, the wish of the accused.

(A) *Summary Trial*

The general rule is that the accused need not be physically present at any stage of the proceedings, providing the magistrates are satisfied by evidence on oath that the summons was served on the accused, giving him reasonable notice of the proceedings.

The exceptions to this rule are:

(i) if the accused wishes a jury trial, he must claim this right personally in court;

(ii) if he has been bailed to appear, he must actually be present;

(iii) if the offence is hybrid but he wishes it tried summarily; or

(iv) if the court wishes to imprison, suspend a sentence, disqualify or commit the accused to prison for non-payment of a fine.

The exceptions, above, require either the accused's initial attendance or an adjournment until he can attend.

For a number of purely summary offences, the accused may plead guilty by post but exception (iv), above, may operate if the magistrates wish to disqualify him from driving.

(1) *If the accused pleads guilty*

If there is no doubt about this, the court does not need to hear any further evidence before convicting. It is usual for a brief summary of the facts to be presented unsworn by the prosecutor. If the accused is present, he will be asked whether he has anything to say to mitigate (lessen) the sentence. The magistrates may then proceed to sentence.

(2) *If the accused pleads not guilty*

Part, or all, of the following process may be used. It should be understood that proceedings in magistrates' courts are less legally formal than those in the crown court.

(i) Prosecution outline of evidence.

(ii) Prosecution evidence. The witnesses may be examined in chief (with no leading questions from the prosecution), cross-examined by the defence (when leading questions may be asked to test the truth of the witness) and then re-examined by the prosecution.

(iii) A submission by the defence that there is no case to answer. This is a legal argument that the prosecution have proved insufficient facts beyond reasonable doubt to warrant the accused being bothered further and, in particular, perhaps to give evidence on oath on which he may be cross-examined by the prosecution.

(iv) The accused may, if he wishes, make an unsworn statement. He may not be cross-examined on such a statement but, as it is not on oath, it carries less evidential weight.

(v) Evidence for the defence may be presented. If the accused is to give sworn evidence, he must do this before his other witnesses are called. He and his witnesses give evidence in chief, face cross-examination and may be re-examined.

(vi) If the defence has not submitted that there is no case to answer, they may summarise their case. At the conclusion of the evidence, the magistrates must decide whether the accused is guilty or not guilty.

If they decide to convict the accused, a number of further considerations become relevant.

(1) If the offence is purely summary, their powers will generally be limited to a maximum fine not exceeding £400 and/or imprisonment for up to six months. They may sentence to a total of 12 months' imprisonment for two or more offences in certain circumstances.

(2) If the offence is hybrid, but tried summarily because of the provisions of section 23 of the Criminal Law Act 1977 (where under £200 is involved) they may fine up to £1,000. The limit on imprisonment is as above. They may, however, hear evidence about a defendant's character and background, which makes them feel their imprisoning powers under (1) are insufficient. In this situation, under section 29 of the Magistrates' Courts Act 1952, they may commit the defendant (on bail or in custody) to the crown court for sentence. The crown court may then sentence the accused on the indictable penalty scale rather than being bound by the purely summary scale (*i.e.* up to 10 years for theft rather than six months). This section and process may be used only if the accused is over 17.

(3) Magistrates have no power to sentence defendants to borstal training. Under section 28 of the Magistrates' Courts Act 1952, they may commit the defendant aged between 15-21 to the crown court with a recommendation for borstal training. The crown court, if there is a decision not to send the defendant to borstal, may only sentence within the limits by which the magistrates are bound.

Other forms of sentence are dealt with in detail below in the chapter headed "Sentencing."

If the magistrates decide to acquit the accused (or if they decide to convict but the accused wishes to raise this matter) their decision may be challenged on a point of law by requiring them to "state a case" for consideration by the Divisional Court of the Queen's Bench Division of the High Court.

This highlights the fact that an acquittal before the magistrates is in no sense absolute because their interpretation and application of the relevant law may also be challenged by the prosecution by this process. The Divisional Court of the Queen's Bench Division has supervisory jurisdiction over all inferior judicial bodies and may direct the magistrates to reconsider a particular point in such a way that a conviction is inevitable.

This point raises the whole question of appeals, whether they follow from a purely summary conviction or from a conviction where the magistrates are dealing with a hybrid offence summarily.

Appeals Against Summary Conviction

If the accused has pleaded guilty before the magistrates, his appeal may rest on one of two points. In either instance, it will be heard by the crown court sitting as an appeal court.

In certain circumstances, he may argue that the lower court advised him to plead guilty when, in fact, his plea was equivocal and he meant to plead not guilty. In this situation, he may ask the crown court to set aside his conviction, to remit the case back to the magistrates with a direction to enter a plea of "not guilty" and proceed with a summary trial. This area of appeal jurisdiction is far from smothered with authority. If the accused has pleaded guilty and there is nothing in the evidence from the lower court to show a mistake, it appears that the crown court can do nothing. What remains to be decided is whether the crown court could set aside a clear guilty plea which came as a result of undue influence (for instance, police pressure on an unrepresented accused). If, in such circumstances, the crown court refused to act, it is suggested that the

Divisional Court would have power to deal with the problem as a matter of law, in relation to the taking of the plea, and should direct on a case stated from the crown court that the magistrates rehear the case as if the accused had pleaded not guilty. The problem in this area relates to turning questions of fact (the undue influence) into points of law, which the Divisional Court may deal with.

The accused, usually, will argue that the magistrates' sentence was too severe. This appeal exists as of right against every sentence except probation, a conditional discharge or an order for costs. The accused has 21 days to enter this appeal. The crown court, in hearing this appeal, receives details of the accused's background and allows him to present mitigating factors. It may increase the sentence passed, if in unusual circumstances it feels this is warranted, but not beyond the limits which exist in the lower courts.

There is one procedure which may not be adopted. If the offence is a hybrid offence or one for which the crown court could consider borstal training then, on appeal against sentence only, the crown court cannot increase its powers of sentence by considering the matter as one committed through to them for sentence under either section 29 or section 28 of the Magistrates' Courts Act 1952, which would allow them to sentence within the indictable range of penalties.

If the accused has pleaded not guilty before the magistrates, he may, by section 83 of the Magistrates' Courts Act 1952, appeal against conviction to the crown court. This is an appeal on facts found within the case in the lower court which he disputes. The crown court, in this capacity, has power to review the sentence imposed, even though they decide the accused was correctly convicted, within the magistrates' limits.

It should be noted that the prosecution may not appeal against an acquittal on the facts found within a case, but only on a point of law to the Divisional Court.

The accused must serve notice on the clerk to the magistrates and to the prosecution within 21 days of the sentence.

The appeals against sentence or conviction are heard by a circuit judge or recorder sitting with at least two magistrates up to a maximum of four. The magistrates may not be the same as those who originally convicted the accused. Decisions of the crown court sitting as an appeal court are governed by a straight majority. The magistrates have, individually, an equal vote with the circuit judge or recorder. The legally trained person is allowed a casting vote in the event of a tied vote. On an appeal heard by a circuit judge sitting with three magistrates, if the judge and one magistrate decide for acquittal while the other two magistrates decide for conviction, the judge has a casting vote for the accused's acquittal. If, however, he is sitting with four (or two) magistrates and is in the minority, the majority carries the decision.

The form of an appeal against conviction is by way of a total rehearing of the case. All the evidence will be re-examined as if the case was being heard for the first time in the magistrates' court. If the appeal fails against conviction, the court may increase the sentence within the range available to magistrates.

It has already been mentioned that appeals on points of law can be dealt with by the Divisional Court. An appeal on this ground is open to either the prosecution, in the event of an acquittal they challenge on a legal point, or the accused.

One factor, which distinguishes summary proceedings from those taken on indictment, is this prosecution right to challenge the magistrates' interpretation of the law. It follows that an acquittal from summary proceedings is not necessarily absolute or final.

Section 87 of the Magistrates Courts Act 1952 states that either party, in criminal proceedings, before a magistrates' court, may challenge the decision on a point of law by requiring the magistrates to state a case for review by the Divisional Court of the Queen's Bench Division. Both parties have a similar right, by section 10 of the Courts Acts 1971, following an appeal to the crown court sitting as an appeal court.

A point of law might arise from a situation similar to the following example:

X is stopped for a moving traffic offence and breathalysed under the provisions of the Road Traffic Act 1972. The test is positive, as is the second test at the police station. He is then, under section 9 (1) of the Act, required to provide a specimen of blood. Knowing it is an offence to refuse to supply a specimen, X reaches into his coat and produces a sample of his blood in a container, taken at a time when no alcohol was present in his system. He hands this over to the police. He is later prosecuted for failing to provide a specimen.

X's argument is that he did provide the required specimen because the word "provide", which is not defined in the Act, could, in its normal meaning, be complied with by simply handing over the specimen.

The prosecution argument is that "provide " means, implicitly, submitting to a blood sample being taken at the time the request is made.

Neither X nor the prosecution will be arguing about the facts of the incident. The issue turns on the legal meaning of this key word in the Road Traffic Act.

The unsuccessful party in the magistrates' court must give notice in writing within 14 days of the conclusion of the case, asking the court to draw up a statement of the case. The court must do this unless the application is frivolous. The magistrates' clerk (or, on occasions, the parties) prepares a statement detailing the charges against the defendant, the facts on which the magistrates based their decision, the points of law raised before the magistrates and the court's final decision on the law.

The Divisional Court is, in effect, asked whether the court was correct in law. No further evidence may be introduced to the Divisional Court: argument is limited to the legal ground of whether the magistrates were correct. The Divisional Court may affirm, reverse or amend the decision. If a point of law of general public importance is involved, there may be a further appeal to the House of Lords if leave is granted by the Divisional Court or the House itself.

If the magistrates acquitted X, the prosecution would be asking for a direction to the magistrates to convict and proceed to sentence. Legal aid would be granted to the accused for the necessary representation. If the original hearing had resulted in a conviction, then it is this type of summary case which could lead to an appeal all the way up to the House of Lords.

The accused might, instead of asking for a case to be stated immediately, decide to appeal to the crown court for a complete rehearing in the event of a conviction. If the crown court sitting as an appeal court decided for an acquittal, the same process would be open to the prosecution (or the accused if the crown court confirmed the magistrates' view).

There is a further application, which may be made to the Divisional Court of the Queen's Bench Division: it is for the prerogative order of certiorari. This application is outside section 87 of the Magistrates Courts Act and covers a broader field than courts in their usual sense. Certiorari exists to correct the procedural record of inferior tribunals. If the magistrates have mistaken a particular procedure — perhaps by disqualifying a driver, without adjourning to allow him to appear before them — the order may be sought. A modern application is when the magistrates do not observe the rules of natural justice or where there may be a suspicion of bias within the proceedings. One aspect of natural justice is that an individual should not act as a judge in his own cause. A magistrate with a personal interest in a case which he fails to reveal, may find that the bench's decision is questioned by way of this order. A clerk to the magistrates, whose firm had, unbeknown to him, acted for a party to the proceedings, might similarly find the court's decision questioned because he has to advise the court on the law. As Lord Hewart C.J. pointed out "justice should not only be done, but should manifestly and undoubtedly be seen to be done."

There is only one occasion on which the accused may appeal to the Court of Appeal (Criminal Division) following summary proceedings. If the magistrates have convicted the accused but, because they feel their powers are insufficient, have sent him to the crown court for sentence, then the accused can appeal against the severity of the crown court sentence to the Court of Appeal. This situation may arise out of committals under section 28 or section 29 of the Magistrates Courts Act 1952 (where they recommend borstal training or where the offence is hybrid). The committal may, in addition, have resulted because the summary conviction was a breach of a conditional discharge, a probation order or involves activation of a suspended sentence imposed earlier by the crown court.

The appeal to the Court of Appeal will only lie where the crown court sets a sentence above six months' imprisonment or imposes a sentence which the convicting court had no power to make (*e.g.* borstal training) or activates a suspended sentence or orders deportation.

A further requirement is that the Court of Appeal itself must give leave for the appeal: this process is not an appeal as of right. The Court of Appeal will only interfere with the sentence if it is manifestly excessive in the circumstances or wrong in principle. If the Court of Appeal decides the crown court sentence is excessive or wrong, while variation is possible, it must be towards leniency.

(B) *Trial on Indictment*

The process will generally have begun in the same way but the accused is likely to have been either arrested in commission or on suspicion of the offence or arrested on a warrant issued by the magistrates. The offence will either be one which the magistrates have no jurisdiction to deal with or one for which the accused is seeking trial before a jury.

At the initial stage of the accused's appearance before the magistrates they are functioning as examining magistrates and not as summary justices (though, with a hybrid offence, they may revert to this latter role).

The function of examining magistrates is to decide whether there is sufficient evidence to put the accused on trial by jury for any indictable offence. It is not their function to decide whether the accused is guilty or not guilty. They are seeking to establish whether there is a prima facie (apparent) case for the accused to answer. The magistrates here are acting as a filter process to prevent the accused being troubled by a trial which has no legal or evidential substance. It should be understood that, if the magistrates dismiss the prosecution application for committal, this does not amount to an acquittal: similarly, a decision to commit for trial does not equate with a conviction. The whole process is preliminary, to test the strength of the prosecution case. If the case is weak but, after an application for committal has been dismissed, further facts come to light then the prosecution may try again for the committal. The accused is given the chance of seeing and hearing the evidence to be offered against him (or at least a part of it) but he may wait until the trial proper in front of a jury before revealing the defence picture.

There are three basic forms which committals may take. (1)

The full oral form where prosecution witnesses are called to give evidence on oath; (2) the section 2 form where written evidence is permissible; and (3) the "short form" committal under section 1 of the Criminal Justice Act 1967 on agreed written evidence.

[It is also possible to persuade a judge to issue a voluntary Bill of Indictment. Such procedure is rare but, if issued, the Bill brings the accused direct for trial at the Crown Court without the committal process (see *R.* v. *Gay News and Lemon* (1977)]

Full committal

(1) Brief prosecution outline.

(2) Prosecution evidence. Witnesses are examined on oath, cross-examined by the defence and re-examined. The Clerk of the court has this evidence written down and the witness is required to sign this record of his evidence when he finishes. This written record of evidence is called a "deposition." It must be signed by the presiding magistrate or certified as authentic by him.

(3) After hearing this evidence, the defence may submit that it is insufficient to justify committing the accused for trial. This may happen when prosecution evidence is weak, has been discredited or where the prosecution has been unable to provide evidence of a legal requirement within the offence. The magistrates decide whether or not to uphold the defence submission by a majority. If they agree, the accused is discharged; otherwise the proceedings continue.

(4) The charge is then read over to the accused. He will be told that he may remain silent, make an unsworn statement or give evidence on oath (making him liable for cross-examination). Usually the accused will say nothing at all and "reserve his defence" until he appears for trial at the crown court. This reservation should not be taken to suggest guilt. He sees no point in revealing his defence to the prosecution in advance of the trial. While committal proceedings give the defence a chance to see the prosecution case, since 1967 they have been the point at which the accused is warned that, if he wishes to rely on an alibi, he must give the basic details to the prosecution within seven days of the proceedings.

(5) The accused may choose to present evidence if it is strong enough to make the magistrates decide not to commit. The accused's advocate will probably not present an outline because this allows the prosecution to address the court when the defence evidence has finished. Defence evidence, if given, is also recorded in the form of depositions.

(6) At the conclusion of the defence evidence, there may be a further submission that there is insufficient evidence to warrant committal. The magistrates are only considering whether there is a case to answer, not whether the accused is guilty or not guilty.

(7) If the accused is not committed for trial, he is discharged. He may apply for costs which, if awarded, will normally be paid for out of central funds, unless the magistrates decide the prosecution was brought in bad faith by the prosecuting authority, when that authority may be ordered to bear the costs (Costs in Criminal Cases Act 1973, ss. 1 (2) and 2 (4)).

Written evidence

The process above can be extremely lengthy. It is inappropriate in cases where the accused accepts the evidence of a particular witness. Section 2 allows the court to receive a written statement, taking prior to the proceedings to save that witness attending. The written statement is as admissible as oral evidence provided that:

(i) it is signed by the maker of the statement;

(ii) there is a declaration that the maker has told the truth to the best of his knowledge and belief and that he made the statement knowing that, if tendered in evidence, he would be liable to prosecution if he willingly stated anything in it, which he knew to be false or did not believe to be true;

(iii) before being used in evidence, a copy is given to other parties to the proceedings; and

(iv) none of the other parties, before the statement was tendered, objected to it being used under section 2.

Reporting restrictions

Before 1967, the normal course of committal was that the prosecution presented their evidence but the defence, unwilling to reveal important facts at the pre-trial stage, said little more than that the accused denied the offence and would present the denial in full at the eventual trial. Potential jurors could conceivably have been prejudiced by newspaper reports of such proceedings. While the point was never settled clearly, however, and is the subject of a major recommendation from the Phillimore Committee on Contempt of Court, it was thought that a report of open court proceedings might not constitute a contempt of court.

Since the Criminal Justice Act 1967, committal proceedings have been subject to certain restrictions on reportable detail unless the accused asks for the restrictions to be lifted. The provisions of section 3 of the Act approximate to the general provisions which existed in Scotland at the committal stage.

Section 3 is set out below. The scheme of the section is that the restrictions apply, unless the magistrates decide to try an accused summarily or unless they decide not to commit for trial. In addition, the restrictions do not apply if the accused (or one of the accused) asks for the restrictions to be lifted. A defendant must be informed of his right to have the reporting restrictions lifted. Where the court has lifted the reporting restrictions, it should announce this at the beginning of any adjourned hearings. With restrictions in force, only the following details may be used:

(i) the name of the court and the names of the justices;

(ii) the names, ages, addresses and occupations of parties and witnesses;

(iii) names of legal advisers;

(iv) the decision of the court and, in the event of committal, the charges involved; and

(v) whether bail and/or legal aid is granted and details of any adjournment of the proceedings.

Section 3 is worth considering in some detail because there are certain special situations and omissions.

3.—(1) Except as provided by subsections (2) and (3) of this section, it should not be lawful to publish in Great Britain a written report, or to broadcast in Great Britain a report, of any committal proceedings in England and Wales containing any matter other than that permitted by subsection (4) of this section.

(2) A magistrates' court shall, on an application for the purposes

made with reference to any committal proceedings by the defendant or one of the defendants. . . . order that the foregoing subsection shall not apply to those proceedings.

(3) It shall not be unlawful under this section to publish or broadcast a report of committal proceedings containing any matter other than that permitted by the next following subsection,

    (a) where the magistrates' court determines not to commit the defendant or the defendants for trial, after it so determines;

    (b) where the court commits the defendant or any of the defendants for trial, after the conclusion of his trial or, as the case may be, the trial of the last to be tried;

and where at any time during the inquiry the court proceeds to try summarily the case of one or more of the defendants under ss. 18, 19 or 20 of the Magistrates' Courts Act 1952 or section 6 of the Children and Young Persons Act 1969 (summary trial of indictable offences), while committing the other defendant or one or more of the other defendants for trial, it shall not be unlawful under this section to publish or broadcast as part of a report of the summary trial, after the court determines to proceed as aforesaid, a report of so much of the committal proceedings containing any such matter as takes place before the determination.

(4) The following matters may be contained in a report of committal proceedings published or broadcast without an order under subsection (2) of this section before the time authorised by the last foregoing subsection, that is to say —

    (a) the identity of the court and the names of the examining justices;

    (b) the names, addresses and occupations of the parties and witnesses and the ages of the defendant or defendants and witnesses;

    (c) the offence or offences or a summary of them, with which the defendant or defendants is or are charged;

    (d) the names of counsel and solicitors engaged in the proceedings;

    (e) any decision of the court to commit the defendant or any of the defendants for trial, and any decision of the court on the disposal of the case of any defendants not committed;

    (f) where the court commits the defendant or any of the defendants for trial, the charge or charges, or a summary of them, on which he is committed and the court to which he is committed;

    (g) where the committal proceedings are adjourned, the date and place to which they are adjourned;

(*h*) any arrangements as to bail on committal or adjournment;
(*i*) whether legal aid was granted to the defendant or any of the defendants.
(5) If a report is published or broadcast in contravention of this section, the following persons, that is to say —
(*a*) in the case of a publication of a written report as part of a newspaper or periodical, any proprietor, editor or publisher of the newspaper or periodical;
(*b*) in the case of a publication of a written report otherwise than as part of a newspaper or periodical, the person who publishes it;
(*c*) in the case of a broadcast of a report, any body corporate which transmits or provides the programme in which the report is broadcast and any person having functions in relation to the programme corresponding to those of the editor of a newspaper or periodical; shall be liable on summary conviction to a fine not exceeding £500.
(6) Proceedings for an offence under this section shall not, in England and Wales, be instituted otherwise than by or with the consent of the Attorney-General.
(7) Subsection (1) of this section shall be in addition to, and not in derogation from, the provisions of any other enactment with respect to the publication of reports and proceedings of magistrates' and other courts.

This section appears to apply only to committal proceedings rather than remands prior to committal. However, section 35 of the Criminal Justice Act 1967 states that, when an accused person is brought before the magistrates' court charged with an indictable offence, the justices are to be treated as sitting as examining magistrates as soon as the accused appears or is brought before the court. Even at remands, therefore, these restrictions apply unless the accused wants them lifted.

Three men accused of offences under section 2 of the Official Secrets Act 1911 in 1977 (Aubrey, Berry and Campbell) specifically asked for the reporting restrictions to be lifted when they appeared on remand. Two of them were journalists and, in the light of Government promises for revision of section 2, they wished for maximum initial publicity about its continued operation.

If an accused is brought before the court in a rather battered condition and remanded in custody without the restrictions

being lifted, it would be a breach of section (4) to describe the
apparent injuries. However section 3 (6) states that the Attorney-General's consent is required before a newspaper is prosecuted: he might refuse consent where the details revealed
indicate, perhaps, ill-treatment from the police or prison staff.

There appear to have been four prosecutions under section
3. In September 1968, the B.B.C. was fined for a committal
report relating to a girl, who had been indecently assaulted.
The following month, the *Bicester Advertiser* was fined for a
report of a rape committal. In 1972, a Greek language magazine *Kosmos* was fined after publishing a report about a bribery and abortion committal and, in June 1973, the *Eastbourne
Herald* was fined a total of £250 for a report headlined "Organ-
ist for trial on Sex Charges." While this piece of the headline
was safe, it continued: "New Year's Day Bridegroom Bailed."
The copy, about his committal on a charge of unlawful sexual
intercourse with a young girl, described the charge as "serious." It mentioned that he had appeared in court "bespecta-
cled and dressed in a dark suit"; there was a reference to the
conduct of the prosecuting solicitor in the proceedings and the
report stated that the defendant had been married at a named
church on a specific date.

It is sufficient that one of a number of accused asks for the
restrictions to be lifted for unrestricted reporting to operate.
This became clear from *R. v. Russell* (1968) and *R. v. Bow
Street Magistrate, ex p. Kray* (1968) and was extended further
by *R. v. Blackpool Justices, ex p. Beaverbrook Newspapers
Ltd.* (1972).

> In this last case, at a full committal of A, B, C, D and Frederick
> Joseph Sewell for murder, attempted murder and robbery, three
> other accused — E, F and G — faced charges of impeding Sewell's
> arrest. One and a half months earlier, at remand proceedings, E, F
> and G had asked for reporting restrictions to be lifted in respect of
> their charges. At these later committal proceedings proper — with
> all the accused appearing together — the examining justices ruled
> that restrictions should apply.
>   The Divisional Court of the Queen's Bench Division ruled that
> the justices were wrong. The proceedings could be reported in full
> because of the earlier application by E, F and G

As has been noted earlier, the restrictions do not apply if the magistrates decide not to commit the accused for trial. Neither do they apply at the conclusion of the crown court trial. In this latter case, it may be desired to include details of matters not explored at the trial. Use of such material will still carry absolute privilege from the point of view of defamation. Publication will still be contemporaneous because, by law, it could not have occurred earlier.

Section 3 (3) allows an unrestricted report in one further situation: where one accused is dealt with summarily while others are committed for trial. For example:

> X, Y and Z are charged with theft. During the committal proceedings, Z decides to plead guilty to the offence and he asks for summary trial. Evidence has already been presented by the prosecution against all three men. Copy may contain the details and references to X and Y in the coverage of Z's summary trial, but only those details presented up until a summary trial was allowed. X and Y might be charged with an additional offence with which Z had no connection. The wording of subsection (3) suggests that a full report could be used, providing that details of the further charge were revealed before the magistrates decided to deal with Z summarily for theft.

Subsection (7) makes it clear that all the provisions of section 3 toughen up the existing law and inclusion of details about the second offence is obviously coming close to committing at least a technical contempt.

The restrictions on details do not permit the inclusion of material outside the list in section 3 (4). A description of the accused's clothes or the fact that the accused was appearing for committal on his wife's birthday would contravene the requirements of this section. The penalty is a fine not exceeding £500 on the proprietor, editor or publisher.

It should be born in mind that section 3 (4) (h) would not permit details of the evidence brought to oppose bail to appear in copy (for this could prejudice the man's trial and would be a contempt). If bail is granted, however, restrictions placed on the accused may be reported. The accused might have to surrender his passport or report to the police every 24 hours. If bail is refused, only this fact should be given.

Short Form Committals

The discussion about full committal proceedings and proceedings, under section 2, to allow for written evidence may give rather a distorted impression of committal proceedings. The majority of committals take place under section 1 of the Criminal Justice Act 1967, using the short form to speed the matter to trial.

Where the accused is going to plead guilty at the crown court to an offence, which the magistrates could not deal with (*e.g.* robbery) or when he accepts that there is a case to answer, even though he intends to plead not guilty, section 1 has considerably quickened the process through for trial.

There are three basic requirements:

(1) the accused must be legally represented; this is to avoid him agreeing with the prosecution that there is a prima facie case against him when this is not so;

(2) the prosecution must have collected all their evidence under section 2 in writing and given copies of this to the accused; and

(3) the accused must consent to section 1 being used.

An important aspect of a section 1 committal is that the magistrates do not have to decide whether there is a prima facie case against the accused, only that the requirements of section 1 are being complied with. It is not open to them to read through the written evidence and refuse to commit because they feel there is no prima facie case. At no stage is the written evidence made available to the Press.

Remand and Bail

Mention has been made of these two aspects of criminal procedure. After an arrest, the accused must be brought before the magistrates as soon as possible. "Remand" means a decision that the accused either remains in custody or is released on bail.

When remanded in custody, the accused is sent to the local prison but remands, prior to committal to the crown court, cannot be for periods longer than eight clear days. If the prosecution case is not ready, the court may remand the accused in custody for a further eight days. There is no limit on the num-

ber of times this may happen but if the period in custody without trial becomes excessive the accused may apply to the High
Court to be released on bail.

After deciding that the prosecution has produced a prima
facie case against the accused in committal proceedings, the
magistrates may commit the accused in custody to the crown
court for trial.

The accused is bailed when he is released from custody on
his signed undertaking (recognizance) to attend court or a
police station at a specified time and date. Failure to comply
with this undertaking may mean the forfeiting (estreating) of
the notional sum of money the accused has agreed he will owe
the Crown in the event of non-attendance. The undertaking
may be reinforced by sureties (guarantors) who also agree to
forfeit sums of money if the person bailed fails to attend as
promised.

In certain situations, the police may grant bail and the
crown court, during the trial of a case, may also grant bail.

The Bail Act 1976 sets out, in section 4, a general right to
bail. In Schedule 1 to the Act, exceptions to the general right
are listed. In particular, the defendant need not be granted bail
if the court is satisfied that there are substantial grounds for
believing that he, if released (whether subject to conditions or
not), would:

(a) fail to surrender to custody;

(b) commit an offence while on bail; or

(c) interfere with witnesses or otherwise obstruct the course
of justice, either in relation to himself or anyone else.

Other grounds for refusing bail are:

(1) that the defendant needs to be kept in custody for his own
protection (or, if he is a child or young person, for his own wel-
fare);

(2) that the defendant is in custody because of the sentence of
a court;

(3) that the court is satisfied that it has not been possible to
obtain sufficient information to make a decision about release
for lack of time;

(4) that the defendant has been arrested for absconding or
breaking conditions while on bail.

If bail is refused or conditions are imposed, the court must now give the defendant its reasons (s.5 (3)) and, if the defendant is not legally represented and bail is refused by magistrates, he must be told that he may apply to the High Court (or, in some cases, the crown court) for bail (s.5 (6)).

This High Court jurisdiction grew out of, but is distinct from, the writ of habeas corpus. Section 22 (1) of the Criminal Justice Act 1967 gives the High Court power to grant bail or vary conditions where bail has been granted. Application is by summons before a judge in chambers, supported by affidavit evidence (a sworn written statement) from the person wishing bail.

In 1969, over half the people refused bail before the magistrates were either acquitted or not sent to prison. Conditions for remand prisoners are generally worse than those a convicted offender would experience in prison or borstal because there is extensive cell confinement. In the event of conviction, the sentence is reduced by the amount of time spent on remand in custody. At the close of 1976, there was a total prison population of 42,000 compared with 40,808 in 1975.

The crown court

The crown court, which is part of the Supreme Court, has exclusive jurisdiction over trials on indictment and has general jurisdiction over all offences committed in any place in England and Wales. The country is divided into six circuits for administrative purposes (Midland and Oxford, North-Eastern, Northern, South-Eastern, Wales and Chester, and Western).

Each circuit has centres designated as first-tier, second-tier and third-tier. First-tier centres are attended by High Court judges and can deal with criminal and civil business. Second-tier centres are also served by a High Court judge but deal solely with criminal business. Third-tier centres are served only by circuit judges and recorders to hear criminal business. Circuit judges and recorders also work in first and second-tier centres.

Judges. The jurisdiction and powers of the crown court are exercised by a High Court judge, a circuit judge, a recorder or a

deputy judge or a court consisting of any one of these sitting
with justices of the peace. For all trials on indictment the court
sits with a jury in the event of a not guilty plea.

Any judge of the High Court may sit in the crown court.
This allows judges of the Chancery or Family Divisions to sit,
although the judges are normally drawn from the Queen's
Bench Division. Each circuit has one Queen's Bench judge
appointed with special responsibility for the circuit. He is
known as the "presiding judge."

A circuit judge is a permanent judge of the crown court. His
status and jurisdiction is slightly inferior to that of a High
Court judge. Appointment is by the Queen, on the recommendation of the Lord Chancellor, from the ranks of barristers of
at least 10 years' experience or from recorders with at least five
years' experience. County court judges are, by virtue of their
office, also circuit judges (as from January 1, 1972, when the
Courts Acts 1971 came into operation). Circuit judges generally retire at the age of 72 but may serve on until 75, if the Lord
Chancellor so authorises. They may be removed by the Lord
Chancellor for incapacity or misbehaviour.

A recorder is a part-time judge of the crown court. Appointment is by the Queen, on the recommendation of the Lord
Chancellor, from the ranks of barristers or solicitors of at least
10 years' standing. While retaining his private practice as a lawyer, the recorder is required to work a specified number of days
during the year as a judge. Because a recorder of at least five
years' standing may be appointed a circuit judge, solicitors
may, for the first time, become full-time judges of the Supreme
Court after January 1, 1977.

There is an additional back-up system for deputising properly qualified persons on an ad hoc basis. A circuit judge could
be appointed a deputy High Court judge to deal with a particular case; a suitably qualified recorder could be appointed a deputy circuit judge and any barrister or solicitor of 10 years'
standing could be made a deputy recorder to ease a heavy court
list.

Magistrates must sit in a crown court hearing appeals and
committals for sentence from magistrates' courts. They may
not be the same magistrates who sat in the court below. The
"professional" judges in these cases must sit with at least two

magistrates up to a maximum of four. When a judge sits with magistrates, the decision is by a majority; in the event of a tie, the judge has the casting vote. Magistrates may sit with judges at trials on indictment. If they do so, they are given an equal vote.

The crown court sitting in the City of London is known as the Central Criminal Court (The Old Bailey) and, unaltered by the Courts Act 1971, the Lord Mayor and Aldermen of the City of London may sit in all proceedings, not merely those designated as triable by a court made up of justices.

The magistrates have to decide to which particular crown court the accused should be sent for trial. The work of the crown court is allocated on the basis that the High Court judge deals with the more serious and difficult cases and, to establish guidelines, offences have been placed in four categories:

Class 1 Cases which must be tried by a High Court judge: murder, treason, offences committed under section 1 of the Official Secrets Act 1911;

Class II Cases which are normally tried by a High Court judge but which may be released by him to a circuit judge or recorder: manslaughter, infanticide, abortion, rape, sexual intercourse with a girl under 13, incest, sedition, mutiny and piracy;

Class III Cases which may be tried by a High Court judge, a circuit judge or a recorder: robbery, blackmail, unlawful sexual intercourse with a girl under 16; and

Class IV Cases normally tried by a circuit judge or recorder: theft, assault occasioning actual bodily harm, breathalyser offences and causing death by dangerous driving.

If the magistrates think that a Class IV offence should be tried by a High Court judge, they should commit to a place where such a judge is sitting. This might happen where there is an allegation of serious violence or where the accused is in a prominent public position. In *R* v. *Nabarro (No. 2)* (1972), a prominent Member of Parliament was tried by a High Court judge at Winchester Crown Court on a charge of dangerous driving.

[Apart from being required to sit in the crown court for appeals and committal for sentence, magistrates may also hear Class III and IV cases where these are allocated to a court "comprising justices of the peace" (*i.e.* without a professional judge).]

Crown court trial. If either the prosecution or the defence are dissatisfied with the decision of the magistrates to commit to a particular crown court, an application may be made to a High Court judge for variation of the place of trial. This may occur if there is a real likelihood of local prejudice to the accused.

The indictment, the legal document setting out the charge or charges, is drawn up. It may contain extra charges beyond those specified at committal, providing the committal evidence justifies this.

The trial itself begins with the clerk of the court reading out the indictment to the accused and asking him how he pleads. The accused may:

(1) plead guilty to the offences charged or to some lesser offences;

(2) plead that he has already been convicted or acquitted of these charges (see *R.* v. *Coughlan* (1975) reported in *The Times*, February 28, 1976, on appeal to the Court of Appeal on the point of prejudice in newspaper coverage of pre-trial argument: the appeal was dismissed);

(3) remain silent; or

(4) plead not guilty.

Plea of guilty

The physical presence of the accused is necessary. While the accused may be told that a plea of guilty may lessen the possible sentence, the decision to plead guilty must be his own and must not be the result of pressure put on him by, in particular, the judge.

If he chooses to plead not guilty to the major offence but guilty to a lesser offence (*e.g.* not guilty to murder but guilty to manslaughter) the court may at its discretion accept this and a formal not guilty verdict will be entered in respect of the major offence.

Technical objections

There is a basic rule of criminal law that a man may not be

charged twice for the same criminal offence.

> X is accused of murdering Y; prosecution evidence is very circum-
> stantial and X is acquitted. X goes to France where he admits, in an
> interview with a Sunday newspaper, that he did commit the
> offence. He cannot be extradited and re-tried for the offence of mur-
> der (though he would still be liable for the crime of perjury).

The technical pleas are *autrefois acquit* (there has already been
acquittal) or *autrefois convict* (there has already been acquittal).

In *R.* v. *Coughlan* (mentioned above) where an Irishman
charged with conspiracy to cause explosions appeared before
Birmingham Crown Court, the latter plea was offered. He
claimed he was being tried for the same offences for which he
had already been convicted at Manchester.

The judge ruled against him. The jury who had heard the
plea were discharged and warned that the matter should not be
discussed outside the court pending the main trial before a new
jury. The *Birmingham Post* reported the legal arguments
offered on this preliminary issue. The accused was subsequently convicted and jailed.

He argued that the full trial was prejudiced because the jury
might have read of the preliminary argument. The Court of
Appeal did not agree with him.

On the general issue of contempt, Lord Justice Lawton's
comments are of some relevance: "Juries are capable of disre-
garding that which is not properly before them. Juries are
expected to disregard what one accused says about another in
his absence. If they can do that, which is far from easy, they can
disregard what has been said in a newspaper."

The trial judge, Mr. Justice Forbes, had commented: "Of
course I have no power to do anything about it, but one can
only hope that the organ of the Press will observe the principles here."

Lord Justice Lawton observed: "We do not know why this
newspaper acted in the way it did and no explanation was ever
given to the judge. The potential damage was lessened to some
extent by the way the proceedings were reported; not every
reader would appreciate what a plea of *autrefois convict* meant
and there was no mention of the Manchester case. We would

have thought it right to take the appropriate action if we had
been satisfied that this untoward piece of reporting had
resulted in a miscarriage of justice."

Silence

The court must decide whether silence is deliberate (mute of
malice) or due to any other cause, which may raise the issue of
whether the accused is fit to plead. If the accused is deliberately
refusing to plead, a formal not guilty plea is entered on his
behalf. This means that the prosecution is still required to
prove its case. If he cannot plead and a new jury decide that he
is unfit to do so, then the court may direct that the accused be
detained in a mental hospital, selected by the Home Secretary,
even though he has not been convicted of any offence. The general practice is for the court to postpone a decision on this last
matter until the prosecution has presented its evidence, to
allow time for the court to discover whether there is a credible
case to answer.

Not guilty plea

If an accused pleads not guilty (or guilty to some offences but
not guilty to others) then a jury will be empanelled.

The jury

A person is liable to jury service, under section 25 of the Criminal Justice Act 1972, if:
    (a) he is a registered elector; and
    (b) is aged between 18 and 65; and
    (c) has lived in the United Kingdom for at least five years
since his thirteenth birthday; and
    (d) is not ineligible or disqualified from jury service.
    Ineligible. Judges and justices of the peace, lawyers and
policemen, clergymen and the mentally ill.
    Disqualified. Persons who have been sentenced to 5 years'
imprisonment or more or those who, during the last 10 years,
have been sentenced to three months' imprisonment or more
or who have served a borstal term.
    Members of Parliament, service personnel, doctors and mem-
bers of similar professions may apply to be excused from jury

service. A journalist might apply to be excused either because he is aware of the accused's background or because of the amount of time he spends covering court proceedings generally.

A jury of 12 must be empanelled. Each accused may challenge three names called out peremptorily as of right (*i.e.* without showing cause) but, having used up these three challenges, he must then convince the judge that the person he is challenging should not serve for a particular reason (sex, social class, bias, etc.). If insufficient potential jurors have been gathered, then people in the vicinity of the court can be required to serve on the jury. This archaic procedure is called "praying a tales."

The jury is sworn in to try the issue between the Crown and the accused.

The trial

(1) The prosecution begins by presenting an outline of its case. It should be remembered that statements made during this outline are not evidence in the sense that they are proven fact. They are nothing more than claims and allegations which the prosecution hope to be able to prove. For copy to retain absolute privilege and remain fair and accurate, the status of opening quotes used, and they are often dramatic, should be made clear to the reader. "Claimed," "alleged" and "said" are all useful attributive words at this stage.

(2) Prosecution evidence (as on p. 173).

(3) Defence submission of no case to answer (if applicable).

(4) Defence outline (if the accused is going to give evidence as to the facts).

(5) Defence evidence and witnesses. If the accused is going to give evidence on oath, he may not be cross-examined as to his credit (about his background) unless:

(a) to show a system in committing the crime charged;

(b) he has attacked prosecution witnesses to try to establish his good character; or

(c) he has attacked the character of his co-accused in evidence.

These three exceptions to the general rule, that previous convictions are not revealed to the jury in advance of their decision, will be telegraphed to the judge by a prosecution request to "make a submission." The jury will be asked to leave the court but the Press may stay and hear the legal argument. Such argument may be reported at the end of the case (subject to the provisions of the Rehabilitation of Offenders Act 1974 if "spent" convictions are involved). If the judge agrees with the prosecution submission, the jury will probably receive a summary of what they have missed, plus evidence which is now admissible. Any summary by the judge, of what the jury have not heard at this stage, may be safely used with the defamation protection of privilege. If the judge rules that the prosecution submission is inadmissible, then use of the material, immediately, could constitute a contempt of court.

At the conclusion of the evidence, first the prosecution and then defence counsel sum up their respective cases to the jury. The judge then sums up both sides, directs the jury on relevant points of law, and must emphasise that there should be no conviction unless the jury are satisfied beyond reasonable doubt that the prosecution have proved their case. He must further make it clear to the jury that they are the judges of fact in the trial. The jury will be told to try to reach a unanimous verdict. After at least two hours and 10 minutes have pased, if there is no immediate prospect of a unanimous verdict, section 13 of the Criminal Justice Act 1967 allows the court to accept a majority verdict within the following figures:

$\left. \begin{array}{l} 11\text{-}1 \\ 10\text{-}2 \end{array} \right\}$ with a jury of 12

$\left. \begin{array}{l} 11\text{-}0 \\ 10\text{-}1 \\ 9\text{-}2 \end{array} \right\}$ if the jury has dropped to 11

$\left. \begin{array}{l} 10\text{-}0 \\ 9\text{-}1 \end{array} \right\}$ if the jury has dropped to 10

$9\text{-}0 \left\{ \right.$ if the jury has reached its minimum number: majority verdicts are not possible at this figure.

If the majority verdict is "guilty," the jury foreman must state the voting figures, and such details may be reported. However, the form of the questions to the jury foreman are such that a majority "not guilty" verdict (and the voting figures) should not become apparent and should, if known unofficially, not be reported. Two trials in 1976 (the Linda Lovelace "Deep Throat" obscenity trial and the Peter Hain robbery trial) led to revelations of majority not guilty decisions. A practice direction, issued by the Lord Chief Justice in 1967, stressed that majority acquittals should be reported only as aquittals.

If, after a reasonable time, the jury cannot arrive at a majority decision, they will be discharged and the accused may be retried.

In the event of a conviction, the accused may present a plea in mitigation of sentence which will, effectively, ask the judge to be as lenient as possible. The topic of sentencing is dealt with separately.

Appeals from the crown court

Following trial on indictment, the line of appeal is to the Court of Appeal, Criminal Division. This court hears appeals against conviction and/or sentence. If the accused has been acquitted, the prosecution cannot appeal to the Court of Appeal. Unlike the procedure in a summary trial, where the prosecution may appeal, on a point of law, to the Divisional Court of the Queen's Bench Division, an acquittal at a trial on indictment is absolute.

The prosecution may wish to challenge the ruling of a judge on an important point of law. Since the Criminal Justice Act 1972 (s.36), the Attorney-General may refer a case to the Court of Appeal for their advisory opinion. This process cannot overturn an acquittal. If the Court of Appeal feels that the trial judge was in error, in stating their opinion, they prevent future accused persons being acquitted on the relevant point of law.

The composition of the Criminal Division is broad. Any judge of the Court of Appeal (Lords Justices of Appeal) may sit, as may any High Court judge. Any number of courts may sit at the same time. A full court consists of an uneven number of judges, the minimum figure being three. In general, only one judgment is delivered although, on a difficult question of law, there may be separate judgments. Since 1966, no High Court judge who dealt with the case at crown court level can sit on the appeal.

(a) *Appeal against conviction.* The situation here depends on whether the appeal is based on a point of law only or whether the appeal also involves disputed facts.

(1) *Point of law only:* no permission is required in this situation and the appeal lies as of right. Notice of appeal must be given within 28 days of conviction or there must be an application for extension of time, giving reasons for the delay. Appeals under this head would include questions of whether the jury heard inadmissible evidence or whether the judge correctly defined an offence to the jury.

(2) *Fact:* permission is required if the appeal is on a point of fact or mixed fact and law. Either the Court of Appeal gives leave to appeal or the trial judge issues a certificate that the case is fit for appeal. Notice of appeal or an application for leave must be given within 28 days. A single judge of the Court of Appeal or a full court may hear an application for leave to appeal. In the latter case, if the court rejects the application, this decision is final. A recent example of this situation was the unsuccessful application for leave to appeal made by George Davis.

Under section 2 (1) of the Criminal Appeal Act 1968, the only grounds for appeal against conviction are:

(i) that the conviction of the jury should be set aside on the ground that, under all the circumstances of the case, it is unsafe or unsatisfactory; or

(ii) that the judgment of the court of trial should be set aside on the ground of a wrong decision of any question of law; or

(iii) that there was a material irregularity in the course of the trial.

There is, however, a caveat within the Criminal Appeal Act enabling the Court of Appeal to dismiss an appeal, despite the appellant showing one of the above grounds to have been satisfied, if they consider that no miscarriage of justice has actually occurred. The "proviso" (as it is known) effectively prevents appellants escaping by finding trivial errors or unimportant technical mistakes within the proceedings at trial.

A request may be made for permission to introduce fresh evidence not called at the original trial. Such evidence must be credible and admissible and there must be an explanation which is reasonable as to why it was not introduced at the original trial. If the Court of Appeal decides to hear such evidence, it may either quash the conviction or order a new trial.

(b) *Appeal against sentence.* Leave from the Court of Appeal is always necessary for an appeal against sentence. If the Court decides to hear such an appeal, it may never, in any way, increase the sentence imposed by the Crown Court but lesser penalties may be substituted.

Appeal to the House of Lords

Either the defendant or the prosecution may apply for leave to appeal to the House of Lords. The prosecution, while they cannot effectively challenge an outright acquittal, may challenge the quashing of a conviction by the Court of Appeal. Permission from the Court of Appeal or the House of Lords is always necessary and the Court of Appeal must, in addition, certify that there is a point of law of general public importance involved. The appellant has 14 days to give notice of such an appeal and, if the Court of Appeal does not grant leave, then the Appeals Committee of the House of Lords (consisting of three Lords of Appeal in Ordinary, popularly known as Law Lords) may hear the request for permission.

If permission is granted and the Court of Appeal (or the Divisional Court of the Queen's Bench Division if the case originated from a summary trial) has issued the certificate of the point of law of general public importance, then the appeal will be heard by five Law Lords. In rare cases, more may sit. While there is oral argument, both sides must submit their "cases" before the hearing. The "cases" are bound in book form and accompany the other relevant documents (*i.e.* the trial transcript and the transcript of the Court of Appeal hearing).

Each Law Lord may deliver a judgment and decisions are by a majority. Decisions are not delivered immediately but judgment is reserved, written down and given to each of counsel in draft before the House of Lords holds the final hearing where the result is publicly announced. The House of Lords can deal with any appeal in the same way as the Court of Appeal in respect of variation of sentence, although an appeal against the severity of sentence, as this is not a point of law, should never reach the House of Lords.

A final point, which relates to all courts, criminal or civil, concerns photographs of people involved in court proceedings.

Section 41 (1) of the Criminal Justice Act 1925 states:

> "No person shall (a) take or attempt to take in any court any photograph, or, with a view to publication, make or attempt to make in any court any portrait or sketch of any person, being a judge of the court, or a juror or a witness in, or a party to, any proceedings before the court, whether civil or criminal, or (b) publish any photograph, portrait or sketch taken or made in contravention of this section, or any reproduction thereof."

"Court" includes the court room or the building or precincts in which the court is held. It is an offence to make a photograph, portrait or sketch of anyone entering or leaving the court room, building or precincts. It is advisable to find out from the clerk to the court (in the case of magistrates' courts) or the court administrator (in other cases) exactly what area the court regards as its precincts. Very technically, to include the court building in a photograph contravenes the section but many officials do not object, providing entrances and exits to the court itself are not cluttered up by photographers and television camera crews.

"Judge" includes recorder, registrar, magistrate, justice or coroner.

ADULT TRIAL AND APPEALS

Trial on Indictment   Summary Trial

HOUSE OF LORDS
Appeals only on point of law of
general public importance.

COURT OF APPEAL
(CRIMINAL DIVISION)

Appeals against   Only against severity   DIVISIONAL
conviction (fact)   of sentence, where   COURT, Q.B.D.
and/or sentence   accused convicted   Prosecution or
and appeals on   by magistrates and   defence may
point of law.   sent to Crown Court   appeal on point
                           for sentence.   of law only (case
                                                        stated).

CROWN COURT

Trial before High Court judge,   Crown Court as appeal court,
circuit judge or recorder (and   with circuit judge or recorder
jury if accused pleading not   and two-four magistrates.
guilty). Serious crimes which   Case reheard in full if
magistrates not empowered to   original plea was not guilty.
deal with or where alleged   If plea was guilty, appeal
offence is one for which   against severity of sentence.
accused may elect to be tried   Magistrates may also convict
on indictment before a jury.   and refer to this court for
                                        sentence beyond their
                                        powers. They have equal
                                        vote with judge.

MAGISTRATES' COURT

Examining justices decide   Summary justices, two-seven,
whether prima facie case   or stipendiary who may sit
exists justifying trial in   alone. Fines up to £1000,
Crown Court. Not acquittal   imprisonment up to six
if they dismiss this com-   months for one offence,
mittal application since it is   twelve months for two or
examination not trial.   more offences. Not legally
                                        qualified, save for stipen-
                                        diaries.

3 The Courts, the Press and Juveniles

Juvenile offenders aged between 10 and 16 inclusive are normally dealt with summarily by magistrates sitting as a Juvenile Court.

The age of the offender has a particular bearing on the process in this area. The following age scale illustrates some of the major classifications.

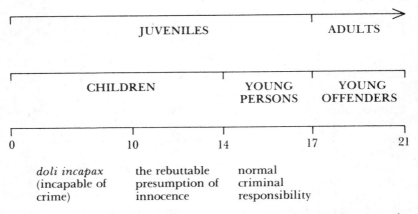

As may be seen from the scale above, adult criminal responsibility begins at the offender's seventeenth birthday. It is the age of the accused at the time of the alleged offence which determines the trial venue, however for offences after the seventeenth birthday, the accused will be tried either in the normal magistrates' court or at the Crown Court on indictment.

Doli Incapax

From birth until the child's tenth birthday (or eighth in Scotland) there is an absolute presumption in law that the child is incapable of committing a crime. Care proceedings may be taken (see the chapter concerning sentencing, below) but a child within the terms of this presumption may never be prosecuted. If an adult uses a child under 10 to commit a crime for him, the adult will be prosecuted as the only offender.

Recently three nine-year-old girls were taken into care for running a brothel in one part of London. No criminal proceedings could be brought against them. A further extention of the *doli incapax* rule is that a boy under 14 cannot be prosecuted for rape or any major sexual indecency. This anomaly does not prevent prosecution being brought against 10 to 14 year-old males for indecent assault or for aiding and abetting such offences.

Under the Children and Young Persons Act 1969, the Home Secretary has power to raise the age limit for this presumption in stages from 10 to 14. When, eventually, this power is exercised, there will be an interim period when children between 10 and 12 will not face criminal prosecution and then the presumption will be spread through to cover those up to 14. Care proceedings will be used exclusively within these age ranges. It will be some time before a Home Secretary exercises this power: there are insufficient local authority facilities at the moment and the economic climate has not speeded their provision. In any event, the proposal has met with extensive criticism from certain magistrates in juvenile courts, who feel that criminal responsibility is progressing down the age scale and who want tougher measures to deal with troublesome children.

The Rebuttable Presumption

This might be termed the "twilight zone" and may eventually disappear completely, as described above. From the age of 10 to the child's fourteenth birthday there may be a prosecution for a crime. There is a presumption that the child is incapable, in law, of committing a crime: but this presumption may be rebutted (proved otherwise).

The prosecution must show two fundamentals:

(1) that the child committed the offence beyond all reasonable doubt; and

(2) that the child knew that what he was doing was wrong.

Proof of (1) only will not secure a conviction and the burden of proving (2) is on the prosecution, not the child. An 11-year-old child, accused of stealing apples, might answer in evidence "I thought it was okay . . . . my Dad said there was nothing wrong" and might be acquitted if the court was satisfied that the child genuinely saw nothing wrong in his action.

Once a child is 10 he may be tried on indictment (*i.e.* before a judge and jury at the crown court) if charged with murder or manslaughter, but the prosecution will face the same double hurdle in evidence. In addition, a child in this age range may be tried jointly with an adult (aged 17 or over) in an adult court. In this case, the court must consider that it is in the interests of justice that the juvenile and adult should be tried together. Trial of the juvenile and adult offender together in the adult court will, generally, be in the interests of justice because one court then has the task of assessing the guilt or innocence of the individuals. If the parties are dealt with separately, anomalies may occur. The adult may be acquitted in the adult court but the juvenile, on exactly the same facts before the juvenile court, may be judged to have committed the offence.

The adult courts (magistrates' and the crown court) have a general power to remit juveniles tried jointly with adults for sentence to the juvenile court if there is a finding of guilt in the adult court. This power must be exercised unless

(a) the court is satisfied that it would be undesirable to do so; and

(b) the court proposes to deal with the juvenile, other than in a limited number of ways (see the section on sentencing, below).

[Section 34 of the Criminal Law Act 1977 adds a slight variation. If the adult accused pleads guilty *or* if th magistrates' dismiss the charge against the adult or commit him for trial, they can remit the case against the juvenile to a juvenile court if if he pleads not guilty.]

Young Persons

From the age of 14 to the seventeenth birthday, juveniles in this age range are fully responsible in criminal law. The prosecution need only prove that the offence was committed by the accused beyond all reasonable doubt.

Children (10-14) and young persons (14-17) must be tried summarily before a juvenile court unless:

(a) charged jointly with an adult (as explained above); or

(b) the offender is a young person and the offence, if committed by an adult, is punishable with 14 years' imprisonment or more and the court considers that, if the young person is found guilty, he should be detained for the period an adult might face; or

(c) the juvenile is charged with homicide (murder or manslaughter or, it is thought, causing death by dangerous driving under section 1 of the Road Traffic Act, 1972).

In (a), trial might be at the magistrates' court or the crown court; in (b) and (c), trial must be at the crown court. Magistrates may commit a juvenile accused for crown court trial under (b) and (c) "without consideration of the evidence" *i.e.* under section 1 of the Criminal Justice Act 1967.

An example of (b) is *R.* v. *Storey* (1973), the Birmingham mugging case. Paul Storey, aged 16, together with two other young persons aged 15 and 14, were accused of attempted murder and robbery. They had attacked a 50-year-old drunken man on Guy Fawkes night, 1972. Storey was sentenced to a 20-year term for this especially vicious attack: the other accused received 10 year terms. The Court of Appeal did not regard the crown court sentences as too severe on a subsequent appeal.

Terminology

In reporting juvenile court cases and cases where juveniles are tried jointly, and summarily, with adults, the following terminology should be adopted. The accused admits (rather than pleads guilty) or denies (pleads not guilty); if the court finds the case proved, this means a finding of guilt (rather than a conviction) and the court makes an order (rather than sentencing). The phrases are cumbersome but the purpose is to stress the protected position of the juvenile facing summary justice. The terminology does not apply where a juvenile appears on his own (or with an adult) for a trial on indictment in the Crown Court.

Restrictions

While the juvenile court is just a special type of magistrates' court, extra restrictions apply to make the criminal proceedings less formidable for the accused.

(1) A juvenile court may not be held in the same court room within one hour of the proceedings there of an adult magistrates' court. This allows time for the adult accused, witnesses and the public to disperse.

(2) There are restrictions on those who may attend juvenile court proceedings. The following are permitted:

(a) members and officers of the court;
(b) parties to the case before the court, their solicitors and counsel, witnesses and other persons directly concerned with the case (*i.e.* probation officers);
(c) reporters; and
(d) others whom the court specially authorises.

(3) Reports of cases in juvenile courts may not reveal:

(a) the name, address or school of the accused;
(b) any particulars calculated to identify any person under 17 who is either the accused or a witness or anyone under 18, who is the subject of care proceedings; or
(c) photographs of the accused or witnesses under 17 (or under 18 if the subject of care proceedings).

There is a £500 fine for the summary offences listed above.

To avoid injustice to a child or young person before the court, the court or the Home Secretary may, in appropriate cases, lift the restrictions in (3) above. It should be noted that this discretion (from s.49 of the Children and Young Persons Act 1933 as amended by s.10 of the Children and Young Persons Act 1969) does not allow the court to suggest publicity for offender X to avoid Y — of the same age and living in the same small village but who is not before the court — being suspected of the offence. Neither should it be used to add the sting of publicity as part of any order of the court (sentence). If, however, X is a 14-year-old living in a small community and the court feels that the accusation against him was totally without foundation, it would be open to them to operate their discretion within this section.

From the author's experience, certain juvenile courts mis-

understand the basis for the exercise of their discretion to
identify and treat the matter as a reserve sentencing element
(which it is not) or use it generally for the wrong reasons.

A reporter, faced with a situation where a juvenile court
makes an order allowing identification, should consider noting his copy with a message to the subs that the court appears
to have misunderstood the law, if he thinks this is the case. A
full quote from the chairman of the bench would help to clarify any doubts as to the reason for identification both inter-
nally, to speed an editorial decision, and externally to allow
readers to grasp what the court is attempting to do.

While a newspaper report identifying a juvenile as a result
of a "sentencing" order for publicity could not lead to a prosecution, the idea that a judicial mistake means no mistake can
only lead to irresponsible journalism. Reporters are admitted
to juvenile courts as part of a special category of permitted persons. The admission to the proceedings is not a licence to leave
their common sense or knowledge on the Press bench when the
proceedings are completed.

The restrictions described above relate to juvenile court proceedings. There are other restrictions which may apply to proceedings in the adult magistrates' court or the crown court. By
section 39 (1) of the Children and Young Persons Act 1933 any
court, civil or criminal, may order that reports of its proceedings "shall not reveal the name, address or school or otherwise
give information which might identify any child or young person concerned in the proceedings" on penalty of a £500 fine.
[The fine used to be £50 but was raised to £500 by section 31 of
the Criminal Law Act 1977 and Schedule 6 of that Act.)] If such
a direction is made, it can cover any juvenile involved as prosecutor, defendant, litigant or witness; pictures of such juveniles
may also be prohibited under section 39 (1) (b).

Adult magistrates' courts, the crown court dealing with a
trial on indictment, the county court or the High Court all
have power to order anonymity for juveniles.

As the result of a Home Office direction (17/1964), the clerk
to the magistrates is asked to remind the bench of their powers
under section 39 in relevant cases. The police, in a Home
Office circular (18/1956), were asked to warn the clerk when
juveniles were to be called as prosecution witnesses in adult

proceedings. The clerk should give the reminder:
(1) if a juvenile is being charged jointly with an adult; or
(2) if the proceedings relate to an offence against or conduct
contrary to decency or morality (when the bench should also
be reminded of their power to exclude the general public).

If a juvenile alone, or a juvenile charged jointly with an
adult, is committed through to the crown court for trial on
indictment, the magistrates will, in most cases, make a section
39 order. In any event, there is extra protection given by the
Children and Young Persons Act 1969 (s.10 (3)). Following
committal proceedings, the court is required to display a statutory notice. Where juveniles are concerned, the notice will not
reveal the name and address of the juvenile in the proceedings
unless the magistrates decide he should be named to avoid
injustice to him. This might occur if the prosecution tries
unsuccessfully for a committal and the magistrates feel proceedings should never have been set in motion.

In addition to these general reporting restrictions, when a
child or young person (*i.e.* someone under 17) is called as a witness in proceedings, which relate to an offence involving conduct contrary to decency or morality, then any court (civil or
criminal) can direct that the public be excluded. While this
allows the evidence to be taken more privately, the Press is permitted to remain: a section 39 direction could then be made to
prevent identification in the Press reports.

There is one further (though perhaps obvious) restriction. If
a juvenile appeals from a juvenile court hearing against conviction and/or sentence to the crown court sitting as an appeal
court, then the juvenile court restrictions on identification
automatically apply.

A summary of the restrictions on identification of juveniles
on trial or involved in court proceedings (criminal or civil)
may be of assistance.

If proceedings are in:

Juvenile Court: no-one under 17, or 18 if the subject of care
proceedings, may be identified unless magistrates direct this to
avoid injustice to anyone concerned in the proceedings;

Adult Magistrates' Court: juveniles may be identified unless
magistrates direct otherwise under section 39 of the Children
and Young Persons Act 1933. This direction is generally made

and, if not given, the newspaper's house rules will probably prevent identification;

Crown Court: on appeal from juvenile court, restrictions apply; on appeal from adult magistrates' court (if juvenile has been tried jointly with adult summarily) then restrictions apply if the magistrates made a section 39 direction; if juvenile is being tried on indictment (either on his own or jointly with an adult) juvenile may be named unless the court makes a section 39 order or does not rescind a section 39 order made by the court committing through for trial;

County Court or High Court: juveniles may be named unless the court makes a section 39 direction.

JUVENILE TRIAL AND APPEAL

Trial on Indictment   **Summary Trial**

HOUSE OF LORDS
Appeals only on point of law of
general public importance.

COURT OF APPEAL
(CRIMINAL DIVISION)

C.A. will hear appeals against
conviction (fact) and/or
sentence AND on points of law.

DIVISIONAL
COURT, Q.B.D.

Prosecution or defence may
appeal on point of law only.

CROWN COURT

Before High Court judge,
circuit judge or recorder and
(if pleading not guilty) a jury.
No identification if trial judge
or committing magistrates
made section 39 order.

Juvenile can appeal to
Crown Court sitting as
appeal court against conviction and/or sentence. If the
former, complete hearing
of case. No jury, circuit
judge or recorder with at
least two magistrates from
a juvenile court. Juvenile
not identified.

MAGISTRATES' JUVENILE COURT

Committed for trial by this
court if not charged jointly
with adult. Examines case to
see if prima facie case exists
to send for trial to Crown
Court.

Summary trial from ages 10
to 17. No identification of
anyone under 17 in copy. If
charged with adult, juvenile
may appear in adult magistrates' court, but he may be
named unless magistrates
direct otherwise. [Maximum
fines £50 (from 10 to 14),
£200 (14 to 17).]

4 The "Open Court" Rule and the Sexual Offences (Amendment) Act 1976.

There is a basic principle that courts must administer justice in public. In practical terms, this means allowing the Press to attend and report the proceedings as representatives of the public.

Certain statutes specifically erode this rule for particular situations. Detailed reference is made elsewhere to these provisions but a brief summary follows

(1) Juvenile proceedings: public not permitted to attend but the Press may. Reports may not identify juveniles, or any person under 18, in care proceedings.

(2) Domestic proceedings: public not permitted to attend but Press may. They may be excluded during the taking of evidence relating to indecent acts if this is in the interests of justice or public decency. Reportable details are restricted.

(3) Committal proceedings: public may attend, as may the press, but, unless reporting restrictions are lifted, limited details only may be published. The magistrates may exclude the Press and the public "where it appears to them, as respects the whole or any part of the committal proceedings, that the ends of justice would not be served by their sitting in open court." (s.6 (1) of the Criminal Justice Act 1967.)

(4) Official Secrets Act cases: Press and public may attend but may be excluded if the court operates section 8 (4) of the Official Secrets Act 1920. This permits evidence to be taken *in camera* (*i.e.* with the Press and public excluded) if the court agrees with a prosecution application that publication would prejudice national safety. If the court operates this section, sentencing must still take place in public.

In addition to these statutory powers, there is a House of Lords' decision in 1913 (*Scott* v. *Scott*) that a court may sit *in camera* in exceptional circumstances if justice could not be done by allowing the case to proceed in public. What has yet to be established is the effect of this ruling on hearings in magistrates' courts.

As far as magistrates' courts are concerned, two statutory requirements emphasise the need for justice at this level to be conducted in public.

Section 98 (4) of the Magistrates' Courts Act 1952 requires justices to sit in open court when trying informations and complaints. Section 6 (1) of the Criminal Justice Act 1967, mentioned above, requires the magistrates to sit in open court except when the ends of justice would not be served during committal proceedings.

The *Scott* v. *Scott* rule appears to have received statutory confirmation as regards committal proceedings: the problem is whether section 98 (4) governs all other situations. As all the powers of magistrates' courts come from Acts of Parliament it is said they can do nothing which is not expressly enacted. The full effect of such an argument would be that magistrates could not exclude the public when trying informations or complaints.

There are three arguments which may be set against this proposition:

(a) magistrates do have power to exclude the public or witnesses if they think the proceedings may be disrupted and this is a common law power, independent of statute;

(b) there are various elements of procedural practice in magistrates' courts which are not regulated by statute and the power to sit *in camera* in the interests of justice may be one such element; and

(c) common law exceptions may apply without the need for a statute to elaborate on them.

The arguments need specific examples to bring them to life.

X is the son of a well-known politician. He is accused of a minor theft and elects for summary trial. The magistrates, aware that interest in the case will rest almost solely on the father's public position, decide that justice cannot be done if the case is heard in public. They exclude the Press and the public for the totality of the case. [In this instance, the court would appear to have exceeded its powers.]

That example differs from the next.

A, B and C are accused of murdering seven people and of conspiracy to cause explosions. They have Irish surnames and addresses in a provincial English city. At remand proceedings, the magistrates direct that the public shall be excluded but that the Press may remain providing they do not reveal the names and addresses of the accused (to prevent reprisals on their families) nor the names of the justices. Bail applications are refused and the accused are remanded in custody.

What has occurred in this example results from a combination of section 35 and section 6 (1) of the Criminal Justice Act 1967. As mentioned in the chapter on *The Criminal Process,* section 35 makes remands for indictable offences a situation in which the magistrates are sitting as examining justices. As such, they may then operate section 6 (1): the ends of justice would arguably not be served if identification of the accused might lead to reprisals on their families at this initial stage of the proceedings.

The governing effect of section 98 (4) for summary trials did receive some clarification by the Divisional Court in *R.* v. *Denbigh Justices, ex p. Williams and Evans* (1975).

Two members of the Welsh Language Society were each fined £15 by Denbigh Justices for television licence offences. They unsuccessfully argued that the fines should be quashed because the case was heard with only five members of the public permitted to sit in the court room. The accused had between 20 and 30 relatives and supporters who wished to hear the case but the court room was small. A reporter, however, was present.

Lord Widgery, the Lord Chief Justice, remarked that while it was easy to say that a hearing must be in open court, it was not so easy to define the characteristics which really made a court open as opposed to one conducted in private. As the public obtained their news of how justice was administered from the Press, the presence or absence of the Press was a vital factor in deciding whether or not a hearing was in open court. He felt it would be difficult to imagine a case which could be said to be held publicly if the Press had been actively excluded.

While this case does not resolve the basic problem, there is significant emphasis on the overriding requirement of open justice coupled with the attendance of the Press as representatives of the public.

This latter aspect received some further elaboration in a

Court of Appeal case, *R*. v. *Waterfield* (1975), but in relation to a crown court trial involving "blue" films.

At a trial involving importation of indecent material, the prosecution wished the jury to see 22 "blue" films. The judge announced that the court would be closed and ruled that the Press should leave as well. The jury then watched the films for seven hours and the court reopened.

Lord Justice Lawton, although he dismissed the accused's appeal, felt that the public depended on the Press for information on which to base their opinions. If allegedly indecent films were always shown in closed courtrooms, then the Press could not give the public the information which it might want and which was necessary for the forming of public opinion. There was a danger that pornographers might be able to convince people that prosecuting authorities were using standards, via censorship, which were out of date. He felt that, in such cases, Press representatives should be present at the showing of the evidence. No harm could be done by doing so and some good might result.

These two recent cases emphasise the special position of the Press in reporting court matters generally and underline judicial acceptance of the necessity for open justice wherever possible.

While magistrates trying cases summarily may have a right to exclude the Press and the public in the interests of justice, this will only receive approval in very exceptional cases and is not a general discretionary power. It is even possible that the House of Lords might now decide that *Scott* v. *Scott* was incorrectly decided and that courts cannot sit *in camera* merely because the judge feels that justice could not be done otherwise.

The Younger Committee on Privacy were urged to recommend that magistrates should be able to direct that publicity should not be given to particular cases. The arguments were:

(1) publicity is a further penalty out of all proportion to the conventional penalties, which may have been imposed by the court;

(2) its effect is haphazard: the consequences for someone living in a small community are likely to be greater than for some-

one living in an anonymous urban setting;
(3) the effect on people with socially different backgrounds is haphazard; and
(4) space and individual editorial policy may affect whether the report appears or not.

The committee rejected these arguments because suppression of identities in court reports is contrary to the principle of open justice. "Where legal proceedings are open and therefore public events, it is a grave interference with the freedom of the Press to prohibit reports of them," the committee concluded.

Since 1972, when the report appeared, there has been a major alteration to, and erosion of, the principle in the Sexual Offences (Amendment) Act 1976.

Sexual Offences (Amendment) Act 1976

This Act was a Private Member's measure, promoted by Mr. Robin Corbett, M.P. The Government aided its passage during the autumn of 1976 by providing the necessary legislative time.

Portions of the Act examined here introduce, for the first time in English law, the concept of adult anonymity for the accused facing a rape accusation and for the female complainant.

The Act came into force on December 22, 1976, but accusations of a rape offence made prior to this date may be reported without the restrictions described below.

(1) *Anonymity of defendants in rape cases* (s. 6)

(1) After a man is accused of a rape offence, no matter, likely to help the public to identify him with the accusation, can be broadcast or published:
  (a) unless he is convicted of the offence at a crown court trial (s.6 (1) (a)); or
  (b) unless the accusation occurs in legal proceedings other than those dealing with a rape offence (or committal or appeal proceedings for a rape offence) (s.4 (7) (a)).
(2) It is open to the man to ask for identification at committal proceedings. At the crown court trial, even if he has not

asked for identification, it may be permitted if either:
  (a) he requests it; or
  (b) the judge feels that the identification restrictions impose
      a substantial and unreasonable block on reporting the
      court case and that it is in the public interest to lift the
      restriction on identifying him (s.6 (2) (a) and (b)).

(3) Before the crown court trial, if there is more than one
defendant, a crown court judge may hear an application for
identification of another accused. He may permit identification of the other accused if he feels:
  (a) it is necessary to get witnesses to come forward who may
      be needed at the trial; and
  (b) the applicant's trial defence may be substantially pre-
      judiced if the direction is not given (s.6 (3)).

(2) Anonymity of complainants in rape cases (s. 4)

(1) After a woman makes a rape accusation, no matter likely
to lead members of the public to identify her as the complainant may be broadcast or published unless the accusation
occurs in legal proceedings other than those dealing with a
rape offence (or committal or appeal proceedings for a rape
offence) or one of the directions described below is made (s.4
(1)).

(2) She may be identified if, before the crown court trial, the
accused or one of the people against whom she may give evidence applies to a crown court judge. He may permit identification of her if he is satisfied:
  (a) this is necessary to get witnesses to come forward who
      may be needed at the trial; and
  (b) the man's trial defence may be substantially prejudiced if
      the direction is not given (s.4 (2)).

(3) At the crown court trial, if the judge feels that the identification restrictions impose a substantial and unreasonable
block on reporting the court case and it is in the public interest
to lift the restriction on identifying her, he may do so (s. 4 (3)).

(4) Following a conviction, the Court of Appeal may permit
the woman to be identified if the accused convinces it that this
will help him obtain further evidence for the appeal and that,
otherwise, he would suffer substantial injustice (s.4 (4)).

If a complainant is identified outside these provisions, then the editor and publisher (or their equivalents in broadcasting situations) may be fined up to £500 following summary conviction. There is no corresponding provision relating to unauthorised identification of accused but such identification would appear to constitute a contempt of court, carrying potentially heavier penalties. [It could be argued that, even given a flagrant breach of this provision, the maximum penalty should not be greater than a £500 fine. As the Act sought to protect the anonymity of complainants, and set a maximum fine, this maximum should apply by implication to unlawful identification of the accused. On the other hand, for a flagrant identification of a complainant, the court might take the view that this was *also* a contempt.]

It is important to understand the technical meaning of a man being "accused of a rape offence" and, further, to define what is and what is not a "rape offence."

(3) *Rape accusations* (s.4 (6))

A person is accused of a rape offence:

    (a) when an information is laid alleging this;

    (b) when he is charged before a court with this;

    (c) when he is committed for trial on a new charge involving this; or

    (d) when a bill of indictment is preferred against him at the Crown Court alleging this.

(4) *Rape offences* (s.7 (2))

Offences, which are the subject of this Act, are:

    (a) rape;

    (b) attempted rape;

    (c) aiding, abetting, counselling or procuring rape; or

    (d) incitement to rape.

The restrictions (relating to both parties) begin to apply at committal proceedings, unless the man asks to be named, or when an information is laid that a person has committed a rape offence.

An information can be laid in the accused's absence to obtain a warrant for his arrest. While the accused is not pres-

ent, the effect of the restrictions would be to prevent a report
that the police had obtained a warrant for a named wanted rapist's arrest. Neither could a report indicate, even though the
man was not named, that, following the alleged rape of an
identified woman, a warrant had been issued for someone's
arrest. The first instance could be a contempt; the second could
lead to a fine of up to £500.

However, in affiliation proceedings or other legal proceedings which are not ones involving the defined rape offences,
there may be identification of the man and the woman. Criminal charges like indecent assault or buggery, because they do
not fall within section 7 (2), do not attract the anonymity provisions. There are occasions when what might seem like a rape
accusation could lead to a burglary charge. Section 9 of the
Theft Act 1968 details a number of ways in which burglary
may be committed. Section 9 (2) covers situations where a person enters property as a trespasser with the intention of raping
any woman there: proceedings on this type of charge would be
clear of restrictions. If the man was charged with *both* burglary
and rape, restrictions would apply.

As a result of the provisions of the Sexual Offences (Amendment) Act 1976, the following rules apply:

(i) No identification of the accused or the complainant after
a warrant has been issued for the man's arrest.

(ii) No identification of the complainant at committal proceedings. The man may be identified if he requests this. There
is no power for the examining justices, if they dismiss the committal application, to permit identification of the man or
woman.

(iii) The woman may be identified before the crown court
trial if a Crown Court judge so permits.

(iv) A man may be identified before the crown court trial if
another person charged obtains permission for this.

(v) At the crown court, the man may be identified if he so
requests. The judge at the crown court trial may lift identification provisions relating to the accused, the woman or both at
any time during the case if the Press are severely hampered by
the restrictions in reporting the case and if identifications in
the public interest.

(vi) If the accused is convicted, he may be identified.

(vii) If the accused is convicted and appeals, the Court of Appeal may permit identification of the woman if this may produce evidence necessary for the accused's appeal.

Although one purpose of the Act was to remove the fear of undue publicity given to rape victims in contested cases, that has not been completely achieved, although some reassurance may have been given.

While commital proceedings could already be subject to reporting restrictions, unless provisions within the Criminal Justice Act 1967 operate, these new provisions have created a specially restricted class of such proceedings. Witnesses in blackmail cases may receive the cloak of anonymity from the Common law (see the chapter on "Contempt") but there is no Act of Parliament which gives the alleged blackmailer automatic protection at the start of the proceedings. Domestic proceedings and matrimonial cases may be subject to restrictions — by statute — but none so sweeping as those contained in this Act.

The principle of open justice, which can only function effectively when the public are aware of who is accused of what, has been fundamental to the English judicial system.

This Act and the Rehabilitation of Offenders Act 1974 demonstrate that recent Private Members' legislation has eroded certain basic principles and may, indeed, have created the base for further changes.

One final point: the provisions of this Act only apply to written publications available to the public or broadcast in England and Wales. The Scottish Press are not bound by it. This creates at least one rather anomalous situation. If a well-known Scottish celebrity was accused of a rape offence in England, if the restrictions were not lifted and he was aquitted, then the English Press would be unable to reveal his identity while the Scottish Press could give the trial full publicity. (See also Appendix B.)

5 Sentencing

A knowledge of sentencing terms and procedures is necessary to avoid misrepresenting the effect of the court's punishment. Variations or restrictions may occur because of the age of the offender. For this reason, three groups of offenders are considered:

(1) those aged 21 or over;
(2) those aged 17 to 20 inclusive; and
(3) those under 17.

In each group, there is a subdivision between non-custodial sentences and custodial terms.

The procedure leading up to sentence is summarised for emphasis at this stage.

(i) The accused will either have pleaded not guilty and been convicted or have pleaded guilty.

(ii) Police give evidence about his previous convictions and general character.

(iii) The accused may ask for other outstanding offences to be taken into consideration.

(iv) The court may hear social enquiry and other reports.

(v) The court hears a plea in mitigation of sentence from the accused.

(vi) Sentence.

(1) *Non-custodial Sentences: Offender aged 21 or Over*

Absolute discharge/conditional discharge. Used where the court feels that no punishment is necessary and probation is inappropriate. An absolute discharge carries no further penalty. A conditional discharge, where the period of the condition may be up to three years, carries with it the possibility that, if the offender commits a further offence during the period of the condition, he may be brought back before the court and dealt with for the original and the new offence. It

220

should be emphasised that these orders are convictions and are, in no sense, acquittals.

Binding over orders. These orders cover two distinct situations. A person may be bound over in a certain sum to keep the peace and be of good behaviour. Justices were first given this power in 1361 to deal with "offenders, rioters and other barators" and superior courts have a similar power. If the person fails to comply, his recognizance will be estreated (the notional debt he has agreed exists between the Crown and himself becomes payable). This form is commonly used in proceedings put before magistrates and which are essentially civil in character. It may be used even in cases where there is no conviction. The other situation relates to binding over to come up for judgment, if called upon, normally for breach of a particular condition. In essence, this is a form of conditional discharge at Common law.

R. v. Moore (1963): M was sentenced to six months' imprisonment for stealing a radio from a car. He had been to borstal 12 years before and had stayed out of trouble until this offence. He wanted the radio for his wife, who was bedridden. The sentence was varied to a binding over order on condition that he kept the peace for three years.

Fines. Unless a maximum fine is fixed by statute for a particular offence, there is no limit on the amount which may be imposed.

(i) At magistrates' courts, nearly every summary offence has a fixed maximum. If an hybrid offence is tried summarily (*e.g.* theft) then the court may not fine more than £1,000 for each offence. If the individual refuses to pay, he can be sent to prison for seven days (£25 fine), 14 days (£50 fine), 30 days (£200 fine), 60 days (£500 fine) or 90 days (above £500) in default. The court may also order compensation of up to £1,000 to be paid by the accused to the injured party where there is summary trial of an indictable offence. A similar power exists where there is a summary conviction for criminal damage. Such orders are enforced as if they were orders for costs and may be added to discharge or probation orders. [These financial limits have been raised by sections 59 and 60 of the Criminal Law Act 1977.]

(ii) At the crown court, the situation is similar, without the magistrates' general limit, subject to statutory restrictions. The fine, as in the lower courts, may be imposed in addition to or instead of any other punishment. The crown court may order up to 12 months' imprisonment for non-payment of a fine but all courts should take into account the offender's means and either allow time to pay or order payment by instalments.

The fine, whether imposed by the magistrates or at the crown court, may not accompany a probation order or discharge. These latter sentences may only be used where punishment is inappropriate.

Probation. This can only be ordered if:
(i) the offender is over 17;
(ii) the offender has been convicted
(iii) the court feels that "having regard to the circumstances, including the nature of the offence and the character of the offender, it is expedient to do so"; and
(iv) the offender agrees to comply with the order.

The order is in lieu of any other sentence (but not of compensation orders). It may run for a minimum period of at least a year up to a maximum of three years. Conditions may be attached to the probation order but residence in a probation home or hostel can never be specified for more than 12 months. Breach of probation can occur either because the offender fails to comply with a condition or commits a further offence. In either case, the offender may be brought back before the court and dealt with for the original offence. In the first situation, breach of a probation condition, the court may either sentence him as if he had just been convicted (which discharges the probation order) or may fine him up to £50 and allow the order to continue. If the accused has committed a further offence, the court may deal with him for the probation offence as well or send him to be dealt with by the court which issued the original probation order.

Linked to probation orders may be requirements for attendance at a training centre for up to 12 months, as a patient in a non-security hospital, as an out-patient in a specified institution or on attachment to a particular doctor.

Community service orders. Offenders who are over 17 may, instead of being punished, be ordered to perform specified unpaid work for the benefit of the community for a certain number of hours (not below 40 or above 240) during a 12-month period. Such orders are usually supervised by probation officers. Failure to comply with the order gives the court two basic options:

(i) a fine of up to £50 and a continuation of the order; or
(ii) punishment for the original offence.

Suspended sentences. These may be used if the court imposes a prison sentence of two years or less. The court may order that such sentence should not come into effect if the offender stays out of trouble during a stated period. A suspended sentence may only be passed if the court is satisfied that no other form of custodial sentence is appropriate. The court must reach the stage of deciding that prison is the only method of dealing with the offender and then it may suspend the sentence. The suspension period must be for not less than one year and not more than two years. If the offender does commit a further offence during the suspension period, then the sentence must be brought into effect to run consecutive to any other sentence of imprisonment imposed for the new offence. In very exceptional cases, this may not be enforced. The courts often find reasons not to impose a prison sentence for the new offence, using a fine or probation, to avoid activating a suspended term. Probation does not rank as a conviction within the provisions for suspended sentences.

Providing the term suspended is for six months or more, the order may be linked with a supervision order. The supervising officer, usually a probation officer, has slightly more limited powers than under a probation order.

(2) *Custodial Sentences: Offender aged 21 or Over*

Prison. When courts are dealing with offenders in this category who have not previously been to prison, such a sentence should only be imposed if the court feels there is no other way of dealing with the offender. Offenders should not be sent to prison unless they are legally represented or have been given the opportunity to apply for legal aid but have failed to do so.

Magistrates can generally only sentence to a maximum term of six months for one offence or up to 12 months for two or more offences.

The crown court's maximum powers are normally set out in the statute creating the offence. In the case of a conviction for murder, the court is obliged to sentence to life imprisonment; the judge may recommend the minimum period the offender should serve before the Home Secretary considers release on licence. A selection of statutory maximum sentences is given below.

OFFENCE	MAXIMUM TERM
Manslaughter	life
Wounding with intent to maim, disfigure or cause grievous bodily harm	life
Unlawful wounding or causing grievous bodily harm	5 years
Assault occasioning actual bodily harm	5 years
Common assault	1 year
Assault on police	2 years
Robbery	life
Burglary	14 years
Theft	10 years
Obtaining property by deception	10 years
Obtaining a pecuniary advantage by deception	5 years
Handling stolen goods	14 years
Criminal damage	10 years
Arson	life
Rape	life
Unlawful intercourse with girl under 16	2 years
Unlawful intercourse with girl under 13	life
Possession of class A controlled drug (mascaline, opium, LSD)	7 years

Possession of class B drug (cannabis or amphetamine)	5 years
Possession of class A or B drug with intent to supply others or supplying the same	14 years

If the conviction is for an attempt to commit a crime, the sentence passed should not be greater than if the full offence was committed. Convictions for conspiracy in relation to crimes had no maximum limits until the Criminal Law Act 1977, s. 3. Now the maximum sentence should not exceed that for the substantive offence.

> *R. v. Wilson and others (1965):* the Court of Appeal upheld sentences of 30 years on the Great Train Robbery leaders for robbery and of 25 years, concurrent, for conspiracy to rob.

Once sentenced, the prison selection is a matter for the Home Office and the Prison Service. Short term prisoners will spend their time in local prisons; offenders facing longer sentences will be classified in the local prison and ultimately sent to long term prisons.

All prisoners automatically receive one-third remission of sentence for good conduct but may lose this in the event of misconduct.

After serving one third of the sentence, the Home Secretary may release the prisoner on licence, which runs until the time he would normally have qualified for release. This parole system, under supervision, bridges the gap between pure custody and total freedom. If the offender breaks the terms of the licence by being uncooperative with the supervising officer or by committing a further offence, the licence may be revoked.

The crown court has power to impose extended sentences if the statutory maximum is inappropriate and the offender falls into a specified class of recidivists (persistent criminals). The effect of an extended sentence is to ensure that, if released, the licence period operates for longer.

[Section 47 of the Criminal Law Act 1977 has introduced a new form of sentence. If someone who is 21 or over is sentenced to more than six months' imprisonment but less than two years' then the court may order that part of the sentence be served in prison, the remainder being held in suspense. The suspended portion cannot be more than three quarters and not less than one quarter of the whole term. If a further offence is committed, there are provisions to activate the unserved portion.]

Hospital orders. If three conditions are satisfied, the crown court and magistrates' courts have power to order compulsory admission of the offender to a mental hospital. The conditions are:

(i) Two doctors (one an approved psychiatrist) must certify to the court that the offender is suffering from a mental illness or disorder of a kind to warrant detention;

(ii) A hospital must be willing to admit the offender within 28 days;

(iii) The court must be satisfied that this order is the most suitable way of dealing with the case.

The offender is then committed to hospital. The order lapses after 12 months unless it is renewed by the managers of the hospital. The offender, or his relative, may apply to have the order or its renewal discharged.

If the offender is dangerous or violent, the order may direct detention in a special hospital (Broadmoor, Moss Side or Rampton) but this requires a restriction order. Such an order can only be issued by the crown court; if the magistrates feel it would be appropriate, they must commit the offender to the crown court for that court to consider the situation.

If an accused is found by a crown court jury to be unfit to plead or not guilty by reason of insanity, the court must order that he be admitted to a hospital nominated by the Home Secretary. If the accused is dangerous, this will be a special hospital; otherwise it will be a psychiatric hospital in his own area.

(3) *Non-custodial Sentences: Offender aged 17 and under 21*

These are similar to those already discussed under (1), above.

(4) *Custodial Sentences: Offender aged 17 and under 21*

Prison. The minimum age at which a person may be sentenced to prison is 17. The sentence may only be used on some-

one under 21 if there is no other appropriate way of dealing
with the offender.

Magistrates face a general limit, as already discussed, of six
months' but they may not aggregate sentences above 12
months for two or more offences. If they consider their powers
to be inadequate, they may commit the offender to the crown
court for sentence (if the offence is hybrid) or with a recommendation for borstal training.

The crown court faces certain restrictions. They may usually only sentence for up to six months' imprisonment or for a
term of three years or more. The exceptions within these two
boundary areas are as follows:

(i) if the offender has already served a prison term of six
months or more *or* has previously served a term of borstal training, then the court can sentence to 18 months' imprisonment
or more; and

(ii) if the offender is serving a prison term at the time of the
current court appearance, no limits apply.

The crown court generally only operates its powers within
these exceptions where the young offender has been involved
in a serious crime like robbery or rape.

Detention centre. Both magistrates and the crown court may
commit male offenders between 14 and 21 to a detention centre
for not less than three months and not more than six months.
The offender will face a period of intensive discipline and
training. The normal sentence is for three months with automatic rmission of one month on reception. Misbehaviour may
mean the full term is served. The discipline resembles the
regime in basic training for the armed services. A detention centre causes a minimum of disruption to the individual's home
life (as the average term there is only two months). The sentence is followed by a year of supervision, during which the
offender may be recalled in the event of misbehaviour.

Borstal training. This form of sentence may be used for offenders aged between 15 and 21. The sentence has a variable effect
because it must run for a minimum of six months' training but
may not exceed two years. The release date is decided by the
Home Office in consultation with the Borstal governor. After

release, there is a supervision period of two years, with the prospect of recall for misbehaviour. There are closed Borstals for serious offenders and open Borstals where the regime is more relaxed. The success rate, checked during a three year period up to 1970, was only 30 per cent. when judged by the number of subsequent reconvictions.

Only the crown court may order this type of training. If Magistrates, following conviction, feel it may be suitable, they must commit the offender to the crown court with a recommendation for borstal training. If the crown court disagree with the recommendation, they may only sentence the offender within the range of punishments available to the magistrates.

Attendance centres. Magistrates have power to order offenders under the age of 21 to attend a specified centre for a set number of hours (usually 12) spread over any number of weeks for character training. Such centres are usually run by police officers on Saturday afternoons and involve physical training, craftwork and lectures on social affairs. Such centres are of particular use in dealing with soccer hooligans. The Children and Young Persons Act 1969 seeks to phase out such centres for offenders under 17.

(5) *Non-custodial Sentences: Offender Under 17*

It should be understood that the bulk of powers relating to juveniles, whether children (under 14) or young persons (under 17), are exercisable only via the juvenile courts. Absolute and conditional discharges may be imposed. Fines are limited to a £50 maximum in the case of an offender under 14 and £200 if under 17. The court must in the case of a child and may, in the case of a young person, order the fine to be paid by the parent (who has a right of appeal). Juveniles may also cause their parents to be bound over to take proper care and exercise control over the offender: failure to enter into such an agreement would mean the court would have to consider taking the child out of the parents' control and into care. As a juvenile can never be sentenced to imprisonment, suspended sentences have no relevance here. Probation may only be used if the offender is over 17. In the non-custodial sense, supervision orders are the closest analogy to probation for offenders under 17.

Supervision order. The Children and Young Persons Act 1969 permits the court to place a child or young person under the supervision of a child-care officer. The effect of this is that a trained social worker assumes general responsibility for seeing that the offender keeps out of trouble and integrates within the community. The consent of the child is not required, there is no automatic punishment for breach of a condition within the supervision order and the supervising officer is connected with the local Social Services department.

The following requirements may be included in the order:

(i) residence with an individual named in the order (a close relative);

(ii) intermediate treatment (*i.e.* character training away from home) to be directed by the supervising officer; and

(iii) that the offender receives either in-patient or out-patient treatment for a psychiatric disorder.

(6) *Custodial Sentences: Offenders Under 17*

No child or young person can ever be sentenced to imprisonment. A young person (14 or over) convicted on indictment of a crime so grave that an adult could be sent to prison for 14 years or more (or a child convicted of manslaughter or attempted murder) may be sentenced to detention for a specified period. The Home Secretary has power to release the offender on licence.

Anyone under the age of 18 convicted of murder is not sentenced to life imprisonment. The juvenile equivalent is a sentence that the offender be detained at Her Majesty's pleasure. The sentence is for an indeterminate period and the Home Secretary may allow release after consultation with the Lord Chief Justice and, if possible, the trial judge.

Borstal may be used if the young person is aged 15 or over; detention centre orders for the 14-17 age-group would include full-time schooling.

(7) *Care Proceedings*

Since 1969, if a juvenile court feels that any of the following conditions are satisfied in relation to someone under 17, it may make an order committing the juvenile into the care of a local authority.

The conditions are that the juvenile is being neglected, is in moral danger, is beyond parental control, is of school age but not receiving full-time education or is guilty of an offence excluding homicide (which must be tried on indictment if the child is over 10). This last "offence" condition can lead to a care order being made in quasi-criminal proceedings. The court is making a decision that the child is in need of care and control, rather than punishment, which he is unlikely to receive unless the order is made. The local authority is bound to review the order every six months and the child's parents may challenge the renewal.

6   Coroners' Courts

Outside the general system of courts — magistrates', the crown court, etc. — there exist the coroners' courts. A brief examination of their historical origin and continued existence is necessary.

The office of coroner dates, at least in name, from the time of King Alfred (871 - 910) and became formalised in 1194. The coroner's primary duty was to protect the financial interests of the Crown in relation to criminal proceedings (*custos placitorum coronas*). He was generally a knight of considerable wealth; this was the Crown's insurance against his possible misbehaviour as his lands could be confiscated.

From the beginning, coroners had to enquire into deaths which were sudden, violent or unexpected or when a body was found in the open and the cause of death was unknown. To encourage the public to report such deaths, particularly if they were homicides, there was a procedure known as "presentment of Englishry." Kinsmen of the deceased had to appear before the coroner and prove their relationship to the deceased: failure to do this meant the local community had to face a "murdrum" fine. This fine was developed after the Norman invasion to discourage the elimination of the conquerors. If the body could be proved to be English, there was no fine: otherwise, the community faced a financial penalty. It was also the coroner's duty to ensure the arrest of anyone indicted at an inquest of a homicide (murder or manslaughter) and he issued a warrant for this purpose.

During the fifteenth and sixteenth centuries, the coroner was an unpopular official because much of his work involved financial extortion. It was not until 1751 that any attempt was made to give dignity or purpose to the office. The statute which tried to improve matters, however, only created a conflict between coroners and judicial authorities as to what constituted a "duly held" inquest.

By 1860, coroners were being appointed by counties and paid salaries. By 1887, the coroner's job was to provide a service for investigating deaths and their surrounding circumstances, and had moved away from protecting the financial interests of the Crown.

In 1926, the Coroners (Amendment) Act was passed giving the Lord Chancellor power to make rules to guide the work of coroners. This power was not taken up fully until 1953, when the Coroners Rules were issued.

A coroner is an "independent judicial officer who is solely responsible, subject to the requirements of the law, for the conduct of his duties." He is appointed for life and paid by a local authority which, thereafter, has no control over his actions. No government Minister can give him directions, call him to account or review his work.

He is a judicial officer because he presides over court proceedings known as inquests. Such proceedings lead to a legal conclusion in the form of a verdict. When in court, he has power to refer someone for contempt of court. Statements in his court (and fair, accurate and contemporaneous reports of coroner's court proceedings) carry absolute privilege.

He is solely responsible in that he takes his own decisions and such proceedings can only be reviewed, on a point of law, by the Divisional Court of the Queen's Bench Division.

An example of such a review occurred in *R. v. City of London Coroner, ex p. Barber* (1975). The case has an additional relevance because it emphasises the High Court's determination that suicide verdicts should only be reached where there is absolutely clear evidence that this is the case. Borderline situations should result in open verdicts (see below).

Mr. and Mrs. Barber had been out for a lunchtime drink and returned home. Mr. Barber went on to the flat roof above the three-storey office block at which he was the caretaker, fell and died. A post-mortem revealed his blood-alcohol level at 258 milligrammes of alcohol in 100 millilitres of blood. There were railings round the roof. Mrs. Barber had told the coroner that he usually went up on to the roof and she thought he was chasing the cat around. Otherwise, he appeared to be behaving perfectly normally. The coroner concluded the case was one of suicide. The Divisional Court quashed his verdict and ordered a new inquest before a different coroner.

Lord Widgery stated: "... coroners should bear in mind in cases of this class ... that suicide must never be presumed. If a person dies a violent death, the possibility of suicide may be there for all to see, but it must not be presumed merely because it seems on the face of it to be a likely explanation. Suicide must be proved by evidence, and if it is not proved by evidence, it is the duty of the coroner not to find suicide but to find an open verdict."

A coroner's action is restricted by law and the 1953 rules provide certain mandatory requirements. From the Press point of view, the most important rules are:

(a) Every inquest must be held in public, unless the coroner deems it to be in the interests of national security to exclude the public (Rule 14). If an inquest has to be held at short notice and the Press are unable to attend, coroners have been asked to provide the Press with the relevant details.

(b) No verdict should be framed in such a way as to determine civil liability (Rule 33). The recommended forms of verdict (which do not, in fact, totally avoid implications of civil liability) are:

death from natural causes
death from the industrial disease of . . .
death from want of attention at birth
death from chronic alcoholism or addiction to drugs
the cause of death was aggravated by lack of care/or self-neglect/or killed himself (while the balance of his mind was disturbed)
death as a result of an accident or misadventure
death as a result of an attempted or self-induced abortion
execution of sentence of death
killing was justifiable or excusable
open verdict (*i.e.* no conclusive evidence to record other verdicts).

(c) Evidence at an inquest should only be directed to establishing:

(i) who the deceased was;
(ii) how, when and where he came by his death;
(iii) the person, if any, to be charged if the jury find a named person caused the death by dangerous driving; and

(iv) the particulars required for registration of the death. This is the effect of Rule 26.

In addition, the rules also contain protection for individuals, because no person is obliged to answer a question, which might incriminate him (though the jury may be tempted to speculate about reasons for silence or evasion) and because interested parties may examine any witness at an inquest, if the coroner so permits (Rule 16).

The basic situation is that a coroner will now investigate all deaths, the cause of which is not known or which is in serious doubt, where death has been violent or unnatural or has taken place in prison.

If a coroner feels it is unnecessary to hold an inquest (whether after a post mortem or without one) he will use Form 100, completing Part A or B as appropriate.

If the coroner does decide to hold an inquest, then Form 99 is used.

Apart from the Judicial Proceedings (Regulation of Reports) Act 1926, which prohibits the publication of indecent medical, surgical or other details calculated to injure public morals, press reporting in a coroner's court is unrestricted. In practice, most coroners refrain from reading out the details of suicide notes and some coroners ask the Press not to publish particular details. When reasonable, such requests are usually observed. The corollary of this restriction is that, in certain cases, coroners ask for publicity to be given to dangerous circumstances (usually expressed in their "riders" to verdicts) and press co-operation is generally forthcoming.

The coroner must sit with a jury, if there is reason to suspect that death:

(a) occurred in prison; or

(b) occurred in circumstances which, if continued, could prejudice the health or safety of the public (s.13 of the Coroners (Amendment) Act 1926).

In 1969, only 31 per cent. of all inquests were held with juries. The jury must consist of at least seven and not more than 11 people and majority verdicts are possible. The coroner's jury returns a verdict; sitting on his own, a coroner records a verdict.

Reference has already been made to the jury's power to name

a person they felt was responsible for the murder, man-slaughter or infanticide of the deceased. In this situation, if a person was named, the coroner issued a warrant for his arrest. When arrested, the warrant acted as a direct committal of the accused for trial on indictment at the crown court. Between 1961 and 1970, some 105 people were committed for trial, solely on a coroner's warrant: not one was convicted on the basis of the warrant alone.

The most recent example of note was the warrant issued by the coroner following the naming by the jury of Lord Lucan for the murder of his children's nanny (see the section on Contempt).

The peculiar power of the jury was also demonstrated in October 1976 at an inquest in Durham.

A boxing coach, Mr. Liddle Towers, was found drunk and disorderly outside a Durham club in January 1976. Police were called and Mr. Towers refused to co-operate. While trying to arrest him, a policeman was grabbed in the groin and pulled on top of Mr. Towers. The policeman told the inquest that he was in pain and had knelt on Mr. Towers several times during the struggle. Mr. Towers later died from internal injuries. The jury returned a verdict that the cause of the death was justifiable. At one stage in the inquest, eight policemen had refused to be cross-examined on voluntary statements read to the jury by the coroner (as they were quite entitled to do under the Coroners Rules).

In practice, coroners only rarely found themselves holding inquests in full on deaths from suspected homicides and the use of the power to commit for trial was even less frequent.

Generally, when a coroner dealt with a murder case, he simply opened the inquest, took evidence of identification, medical evidence of the cause of death and the other particulars required for the registration of the death. He then adjourned the inquest until the result of the criminal proceedings in the criminal courts was known.

When the result of the criminal proceedings was known, even if the magistrates had found no case to answer, the inquest was not, in practice, resumed. Instead, the coroner sent the Registrar a certificate, in which he recorded the findings of the criminal court.

It was only if the suspected murderer was dead, or when the Director of Public Prosecutions felt there was insufficient evidence to justify a charge against a living person, that an inquest in this category proceeded. The exception, of course, occured in the *Lucan* case, where the suspect had disappeared.

In instances where a coroner's jury named a person but the prosecuting authorities (generally the office of the Director of Public Prosecutions) felt there was insufficient evidence, the procedure was for the prosecution at the crown court trial formally to offer no evidence against the accused, who was then released.

The Brodrick Committee, which looked at the role of coroners and reported in 1971, recommended the abolition of the jury's power to name a person, forcing the issue of a warrant and resulting in such automatic, and confusing, committals.

The Criminal Law Act 1977 took up the Brodrick Committee recommendation in section 56. Pressure developed for change in the process in the wake of the Lord Lucan saga.

Section 56 states that inquests into a person's death shall not include, as part of the proceedings, a finding that another individual is guilty of murder, manslaughter or infanticide. A coroner's inquest shall not charge anyone with those offences.

In addition, the coroner will no longer be obliged to summon a jury is he thinks the death arose from murder, manslaughter infanticide or death from an accident with a vehicle on the roads. He retains a discretion to sit with a jury in these cases if he so wishes, but this is no longer a mandatory requirement. Schedule 10 to the Act redrafts section 20 of the Coroners (Amendment) Act 1920. The purpose of this is to make the adjournment of inquests, when other proceedings are pending, more simple.

Section 56 (4) of the Criminal Law Act 1977 abolished the power of coroners in the City of London to hold inquests into fires in the City. Under the City of London Fire Inquests Act 1888, juries could find a verdict of arson against a named person, who was then committed for trial at the Old Bailey. This has been completely repealed.

Coroners also have jurisdiction over treasure trove. This area runs directly back to provisions of a statute in the fourth year of the reign of Edward I. The sums gained for the Crown through treasure trove were an important supplement to the revenue of the sovereign.

The only definition which exists is one from 1820 where, in Chitty's *Prerogatives of the Crown,* treasure trove is described as:

> "Any gold or silver in coin, plate or bullion found concealed in a house, or in the earth, or in a private place, the owner thereof being unknown, in which the treasure belongs to the Queen . . . but if he that made it be known or afterwards discovered the owner, and not the Queen, is entitled to it, this prerogative right only applying in the absence of an owner to claim the property."

A find will normally only be regarded as treasure trove if:

(1) the articles are of gold or silver;

(2) the ownership is unknown;

(3) it was hidden in the ground or in a building with the intention of subsequent recovery.

If the coroner decides that the articles are treasure trove, they become the property of the Crown. Normally an *ex gratia* payment, equivalent to the full market value of the find, is made to encourage prompt disclosure. If the find is held not to be treasure trove, it is normal for the inquest to say who is the owner (the finder or the owner of the land on which it was found) but such decision is open to challenge in the civil courts.

The Brodrick Committee recognised that the procedure was archaic and defective in certain respects. Only gold and silver finds fell within the coroner's jurisdiction yet, from the archaeological point of view, other items might be of considerable value and interest (like the containers of the gold and silver). In addition, the coroner has no jurisdiction over items deliberately buried in graves (which are not hidden with a view to subsequent recovery). The Committee found the issue to be almost outside its terms of reference and ultimately recommended no change in the present system.

7 Military Law and Courts-Martial

Members of Her Majesty's armed forces do not escape liability under domestic (civilian) law for their criminal or civil acts. Military obligations are in addition to the normal rights and duties of United Kingdom citizens. During peace time, however, most criminal offences committed by service personnel are dealt with in the civilian courts at the discretion of the military authorities. The individual could, generally, be dealt with by court-martial exclusively and, in time of war, may well be.

The serious offences of treason, murder, manslaughter and rape must, however, be tried by the crown court and cannot generally be dealt with by the court-martial procedure.

There are some purely military offences, which are the province solely of courts-martial. These include looting, mutiny, insubordination, disobedience to lawful orders, desertion, absence without leave, offences relating to public or service property, flying offences and cowardice. An officer who behaves in a scandalous manner, unbecoming the conduct of an officer and gentleman, may be dismissed from the service with disgrace (this replaces the sentence of "cashiering"). Any person who is guilty of any act, conduct, disorder or neglect to the prejudice of good order and military discipline faces up to two years' imprisonment.

The administration of military law by courts-martial composed of serving officers is supervised by the Judge Advocate General, who must be a barrister of at least 10 years' standing. On his staff there are a Vice Judge Advocate General, Assistant Judge Advocates General and Deputy Judge Advocates. The Judge Advocate General, who is appointed by the Crown on the recommendation of the Lord Chancellor, is a judicial officer. From his staff, he provides a judge advocate for all trials held by general court-martial in the United Kingdom and for important trials held abroad by general or field general court-martial. It should be understood that a judge advocate attends

238

the court in an advisory capacity, to ensure that formalities and procedures are observed.

For minor infringements of discipline, an officer of the equivalent rank of captain in the Army may order up to seven days' confinement to camp and admonishment. An officer of field rank (major) may order up to 28 days' detention, usually served in the guard room.

The lowest court proper in the military scale is the court of the commanding officer, normally of the equivalent rank of lieutenant-colonel commanding a battalion or regiment. Non-commissioned officers and soldiers charged with military offences are brought before this court having been remanded by their company or battery commanders.

This court resembles a magistrates' court sitting with a stipendiary. After hearing the evidence, the commanding officer may dismiss the charge or, if minor, punish with up to 28 days' detention. If the charge is serious, he will order a summary of evidence (similar to magistrates hearing evidence at a full committal) or receive an abstract of evidence (similar to the s.1 procedure of the Criminal Justice Act 1967). The accused has a right to trial by court-martial if the commanding officer orders detention or forfeiture of pay. If a prima facie case is revealed from the summary or abstract of evidence, the papers go forward to the headquarters' staff where the officer decides on the type of charge.

There are three forms of trial by court-martial:

A General Court-Martial, which must consist of at least five officers, can try any military offence whether committed by an officer or a member of the other ranks.

A District Court-Martial cannot try an officer and is restricted to sentences of up to two years' imprisonment. There must be at least three officers present at this court.

A Field General Court-Martial operates for offences committed on active service when it would be impossible to convene either of the two courts named above.

Trial by court-martial resembles an ordinary criminal trial. There is a presumption of innocence. It will be held in public but may sit *in camera* with the Press and public excluded, if this is necessary for the administration of justice. The findings must be announced in open court and the sentences declared as soon as they are determined.

The accused may ask for an officer to be appointed to defend him and civilian lawyers may take part in this portion of the proceedings. In the case of an accused officer, the persons appointed to sit in the court must be of a higher rank.

A judge advocate may (and in the case of a general court-martial must) be appointed to advise the court on the law and to summarise the facts. He will not, however, retire with the court to consider guilt or innocence (matters of fact) but will retire when a sentence has to be considered. By this process, the other members of the court-martial act, in effect, as the jury. The difference between these proceedings and civilian juries is that the decision is arrived at by a simple majority and need not be unanimous or within the terms of acceptable majority verdicts (*i.e.* 10-2). In addition, the court fixes the sentence (subject to confirmation) at a court-martial: a civilian jury has discharged its duty once it has found on the facts.

Mention has been made of the sentence being subject to confirmation. In Army and R.A.F. courts-martial, the sentence must be confirmed by higher military authority before it is completely effective and copy, at the conclusion of the court-martial proceedings, should state that the sentence is subject to confirmation. The reporter should liaise with headquarters' staff to make certain the sentence has not been modified or the conviction quashed. While awaiting confirmation, the case is *sub judice* and comment on it (rather than straightforward copy from the trial) could amount to a contempt of court. In Naval courts-martial (sometimes called tribunals) the finding operates immediately, enabling the reporter to comment freely, but the papers are sent through to the Naval Department of the Ministry of Defence to be checked from the procedural and legal point of view. The Minister responsible for the Navy may quash or modify the sentence.

If the accused is acquitted by a court-martial this is final: the finding cannot be reversed and needs no confirmation.

Service personnel tried for an offence by court-martial or dealt with summarily by the commanding officer may not, subsequently, be tried by a civilian court for what amounts to substantially the same offence. (Armed Forces Act 1966, s.25). A person acquitted or convicted by a civilian court cannot be tried by court-martial for the same offence.

The sentences and proceedings of all courts-martial are reviewed at the Judge Advocate General's office to check for miscarriages of justice. In addition, the person sentenced may petition for review. If he wishes to appeal, he must wait for confirmation of the sentence and for rejection of his petition for review. If this process produces nothing, he may appeal to the Courts-Martial Appeal Court for permission to have the case heard there on appeal.

The judges of the Courts-Martial Appeal Court consist of the Lord Chief Justice and High Court judges (generally from the Queen's Bench Division). This court, like the Court of Appeal (Criminal Division) sits with an uneven number of judges, normally in London. There is no appeal against sentence only; leave to appeal can only be granted by the court itself against the facts and/or questions of law.

If the Courts-Martial Appeal Court does grant leave but the appeal is unsuccessful, a final appeal to the House of Lords on a point of law of general public importance is possible.

8 The Civil Courts

The civil jurisdiction of the courts and certain restrictions on reports of proceedings are examined in this section. In ascending order of seniority, the courts reviewed are the magistrates' courts, the county courts, the High Court, the Court of Appeal (Civil Division) and the House of Lords.

Magistrates' Courts

Apart from the general criminal jurisdiction of the magistrates' courts, there is a substantial amount of work at this level in the non-criminal area under the general heading of "domestic proceedings."

This work can be divided into four main areas:

(1) matrimonial proceedings (not to be confused with matrimonial causes, which are divorce petitions) where one party wants separation from the other linked, perhaps, with maintenance and/or custody of the children;

(2) guardianship proceedings, where one party wants custody of and maintenance for a child;

(3) affiliation proceedings, where a woman is seeking maintenance from the father of her illegitimate child; and

(4) consent to marry applications, where minors (aged between 16 and 18) seek the court's permission to marry because their parents refuse to grant consent.

The public are not admitted to domestic proceedings but the Press may attend (s.57 of the Magistrates Courts Act 1952). The court may exclude the Press during the taking of indecent evidence but only where this is necessary in the interests of justice or of public decency. In guardianship and consent to marry applications, the Press may be excluded if the court considers that the application should be heard *in camera* in the interests of the minor.

The following details only may be published in domestic proceedings (s.58 of the Magistrates' Courts Act 1952):

(a) names, addresses and occupations of the parties and witnesses;

(b) the grounds of the application and a concise statement of the charges and counter charges in support of which evidence is given;

(c) submissions on points of law in the proceedings and the court's decision on such submissions; and

(d) the decision of the court and any observations made by the court in giving it.

Extra details make the paper liable for a fine of up to £100 and/or imprisonment of the editor, proprietor or publisher for up to four months. Curiously, there is no apparent prohibition on broadcasting additional details. The consent of the Attorney-General is required before there is a prosecution.

The age of the parties is not, apparently, a permissible detail and could only be revealed if contained under (b) above. The whole wording of (b) is so ambiguous, however, that many papers prefer not to cover such proceedings because of the uncertainty of how much detail is permitted. A precis of evidential points is permissible but details of unsupported allegations would not be safe. Interviews with the parties after consent to marry applications are dangerous as they might reveal extra details of the domestic proceedings.

The restrictions apply only to domestic proceedings and not, automatically, to enforcement of such proceedings. A person summonsed to appear for non-payment of maintenance, or applying to the court for a variation of a maintenance order, is before the normal magistrates' court unless and until the court classifies the proceedings as domestic ones, when restrictions would apply.

Apart from the fact that the rules are complex and unclear in this area, many courts often do not make certain that their domestic proceedings are clearly separated from normal business. For example:

X appears for non-payment of maintenance to his wife. This is normal business and X may go to prison for the non-payment. All details could be fully reported unless the court decided to declare

the matter domestic, at which stage the public could be excluded
and the restrictions mentioned above would apply. It is unlikely
that non-payment of maintenance would raise indecent evidence
but, if it did, then the Press could be excluded.

The sad fact is that, because of the general confusion, these
courts are rarely even monitored by the Press, yet they may, on
occasions, produce copy of national significance. The magistrates in Newcastle who, in 1972, allowed a French father custody of his child set off a process, which ran for many months
when the child was taken to France.

When magistrates hold their general annual licensing meeting, they must sit in public and, if proper notice has been
given, listen to objections. There are similar requirements for
meetings of betting and gaming licensing committees (Betting, Gaming and Lotteries Act 1963, s.1; Gaming Act 1968,
s.2).

County Courts

These courts, with purely civil jurisdiction, were set up in 1846
to provide convenient and cheaper forms of dealing with
limited claims. There are over 400 county courts throughout
the country, grouped into circuits. At least one circuit judge is
assigned to each circuit and courts must be held at least once a
month.

The administrative business of the county court is dealt with
by the Registrar, who is a solicitor of at least seven years' standing and who is usually also District Registrar for the High
Court (acting as a local administrative agent for this senior
court).

The Registrar also has a judicial function. He deals with all
preliminary matters and is responsible for "taxing" the costs
of the county court actions. This means that he checks the
legal expenses of the winning party and decides which items
the losing side must pay. With the circuit judge's permission,
he has all the powers of a county court judge:

(a) if the defendant in the action does not appear; or
(b) when a claim is admitted.

If the parties do not object, he can try any action in which the claim does not exceed £200 while, with their consent, he can try any other actions. He has an important function in judging small claims, using an even less formal procedure than in normal county court business.

The general jurisdiction of the county court follows in outline:

(1) Actions in contract and tort (civil wrongs) where the claim is limited to £2,000. The exception is that defamation actions cannot be tried in the county court unless it is declared a sitting of the High Court for the hearing of a particular case. The Faulks' Committee recommend there should be a change to allow trials of such actions in the county court, where the damages claimed are limited to £1,000.

(2) Actions for the recovery of land where the rateable value is limited to £1,000.

(3) Equity actions limited to £15,000 (*i.e.* small trusts).

(4) Disputes on wills where the estate is worth under £1,000.

(5) Divorces in certain nominated courts (see below: matrimonial causes in the Family Division of the High Court). In such cases, the Judicial Proceedings (Regulation of Reports) Act 1926 lays down reporting restrictions. These are identical to the domestic proceedings restrictions discussed earlier.

The county court can hear any matter remitted to it by the High Court (an example is the original *Horrocks* v. *Lowe* trial: see *Defamation*).

County court actions are less formal than those in the High Court and the county courts deal with over 90 per cent. of civil matters, particularly hire purchase claims, landlord and tenant matters and consumer claims against the suppliers of faulty goods.

Solicitors have an equal audience in the county court with barristers. Jury trials are a possibility (but extremely rare) if there is an allegation of fraud, false imprisonment or malicious prosecution: the jury consists of eight people.

Appeal, on a point of law, lies generally to the Court of Appeal (Civil Division) but the county court judge decides all questions of fact.

Apart from (5) above, the only restriction is that the judge can direct that any case or part of a case shall be heard in private, if publicity would prevent justice being done. Certain

matters must be dealt with in private (such as applications to
adopt children) and if a judge declares that, rather than hearing matters like this "in chambers", he will sit in court but
treat the court hearing as in chambers, the proceedings are
totally private. It makes no difference that a reporter is aware
of the details: to use them would constitute a contempt of
court.

There are two further areas of jurisdiction: proceedings
brought under the Sex Discrimination Act 1975 or the Race
Relations Act 1976 where settlements of certain matters
between parties cannot be reached. The case of *Relf*, in 1976,
resulted in a county court order to the defendant to remove a
sign indicating that a house was for sale to an English family
only. Refusal to obey this order resulted in the defendant being
committed to prison for civil contempt.

Bankruptcy and winding up

While actions in this area may appear either in the High Court
or the county court, the County Court Registrar in fact deals
with the bulk of the work. The effects of such proceedings and
related orders, together with the reporting hazards, are of considerable significance during this decade. Both at local and
national level, the proceedings are of more than peripheral
interest. The public deserve to know in accurate detail how
and why individuals and companies are failing and the stated
reasons for such failures. There is a degree of sophistication in
business life, however, which makes an understanding of the
reporting of this area difficult and, at times, dangerous.

Bankruptcy involves the state taking possession of the property of the debtor by appointing an Official Receiver, who
pays over to the creditors such sums as can be managed.

Example: X has debts totalling £80,000.
He owns a house worth £25,000 and a car worth £5,000. He earns
£10,000.
He has, therefore, realisable assets worth £30,000 and an income.
When declared bankrupt, the Official Receiver controls the fixed
assets, any savings and the income X can bring in. He would sell
the fixed assets and make an initial distribution to the creditors. X
might well be encouraged to continue working and allowed to
retain certain property until the bulk of the debts had been repaid,

when he could apply to have his bankruptcy discharged to give him control of his own affairs again.

If the debtor is a company, the same basic procedure is used to allow, if possible, for the firm to be run under court or state control until the debts are eliminated. The Department of Trade is in overall administrative control and this procedure is called winding up.

Proceedings in either area may be started either by the individual (or company) asking the state to take over control or because creditors ask the court to authorise this.

When the proceedings begin, the debtor must present a statement of the financial situation, actual and in prospect. The assets, debts and liabilities must be set out. The Official Receiver then calls the creditors together for a meeting with the debtor to decide whether a less formal method of repayment is possible: at this stage the debtor is not bankrupt, nor a company wound up. The Press have no automatic right of admission to these meetings but may be permitted to attend at the discretion of the Official Receiver. If they are allowed in, defamation protection is that of qualified privilege, subject to explanation or contradiction from the injured party. Care should be taken over the contents of the "reply" statement in case it defames a third party.

The next stage is the public examination of the debtor (if no compromise is possible) and this falls within the protection given to judicial proceedings (*i.e.* absolute privilege).

Apart from the public examination, certain other matters and applications in bankruptcy must be heard and decided in open court:

(1) Proposals for payment, which would avoid the debtor being declared bankrupt.

(2) Opposed applications for discharge of bankruptcy: unopposed applications may be heard in chambers.

(3) Appeals from the Department of Trade to the High Court (in winding up actions).

(4) Applications to decide who owns particular property and, if necessary, the use of a jury to decide questions of fact.

(5) Applications for permission to act as a director of a company or to take part in the management of a company (see X's possible situation in the last example).

(6) Applications to commit someone to prison for contempt (this may occur if the debtor, or officers of a company, are refusing to co-operate with the Official Receiver in working out the financial liabilities which exist).

When the debtor is judged bankrupt and this fact has been published in the *London Gazette,* creditors will receive repayments of the debt in "dividends" of so much in the £.

After the debtor has repaid at least 50p in the £, he may apply to have his bankruptcy discharged.

It should be noted that, unless a debtor is filing a petition in bankruptcy himself, there should be no report that bankruptcy proceedings are being filed until a notice of this appears in the *London Gazette.* This rule applies even though the information comes from other court proceedings or elsewhere.

The High Court

The jurisdiction of the High Court, created last century, is virtually unlimited in civil actions although, where actions relate to small claims, they will be brought in the county court.

The High Court is divided into three divisions of equal standing. The nature of the claim or issue governs the choice of division for the bringing of the action. Matrimonial causes (*i.e.* divorce) may only be heard in the Family Division, for instance. There are cases where there may be an overlap of issues. As the divisions are not separate courts, any High Court judge is competent to deal with related matters outside his normal divisional work. For instance, a Family Division judge may decide a property dispute in a divorce case, although property cases are normally dealt with in the Chancery Division.

To be appointed a High Court judge, the individual must have been a barrister of at least 10 years' standing. This time period is regarded as the bare minimum for appointment and most High Court judges, in practice, have at least twenty years' experience. High Court appointments are generally made from the ranks of Queen's Counsel although, since the Courts Act 1971, circuit judges may be appointed with greater frequency. Appointment is to a particular division, depending on the practice which the appointee had at the Bar prior to appointment.

The three divisions consist of:

(1) Chancery. Staffed by about 10 judges, headed by the Vice-Chancellor, and normally hearing business in London. This work relates to trusts, land matters, bankruptcy and winding up, revenue matters (tax), disputes over wills and, when sitting as the Court of Protection, the management of the property and affairs of mental patients.

The divisional court of the Chancery Division (sitting with at least two of the judges from this division) hears matters like appeals from county courts in bankruptcy.

(2) Family. Staffed by about 14 judges, headed by the President of the Family Division. Business relates to divorces, dissolution of marriage, declarations of legitimacy, validity of marriage, wardship, adoptions, guardianship, etc.

The divisional court of the Family Division (sitting with at least two judges from the division) hears appeals from the magistrates' courts and county courts in guardianship, from the magistrates' courts in adoption and separation matters and from the crown court in affiliation proceedings.

The relationship between wardship matters and contempt of court has already been discussed see *Re F.* (1976)). The following case, another wardship matter, also relates to the law of publications and shows some of the work done by the Family Division outside straightforward matrimonial matters.

Re X. (a minor) (Wardship: restriction on publication) (1975): a 14-year-old girl, who was psychologically fragile and highly-strung, had been brought up to respect the memory of her father. He had died in 1967 and her mother had remarried in 1970. A friend of X's father had written a book about him. The first chapter described X's father as a man utterly depraved sexually, who indulged in sordid and degrading conduct, who was obscene and who drank to excess. Just before publication, X.'s step-father got to hear of the book. He feared that this account of her father would be grossly damaging psychologically to such a sensitive child. X. was declared a ward of court and an injunction issued by Latey J. in the Family Division.

He held that the duty to protect minors from injury gave the court unlimited powers in the exercise of its wardship jurisdiction. This duty had to be balanced against the duty to protect freedom of publication. In this case, the danger to X. was so grave that offending passages in the book should be barred.

The publishers of the book appealed to the Court of Appeal against the injunction. The Court of Appeal unanimously removed the injunction to permit undoctored publication.

The judgment of Lord Denning M.R. touches on many of the issues which have been mentioned in this book and highlights the difficult balancing factors which have to be considered in the preservation and protection of the principle of freedom of publication:

"On the one hand, there is the freedom of the Press to consider; on the other hand, the protection of a young child from harm. The judge seems to have balanced the one against the other and to have held that the interest of the child shall prevail.

If the function of the judges was simply a balancing function — to balance the competing interests — there would be much to be said for this view. To quote some of the adjectives used about the passages in the book, they are: 'bizarre,' 'salacious,' 'scandalous' and 'revolting.' It is difficult to see that there is any public interest to be served by their publication. But this is where freedom of speech comes in. It means freedom, not only for the statements of opinion of which we approve, but also for those of which we most heartily disapprove. Take some aspects of the law which are relevant in this very case. For instance, is there any remedy in the law of defamation? Suppose the mother of the child were to bring an action for defamation on the ground that the passages were untrue and a gross libel on her dead husband. Many might think she should be able to prevent the publication, especially as it would bring such grief and distress to his relatives and, in addition, emotional damage to his child. But the law of defamation does not permit any such proceeding. It says simply that no action lies for a libel on a dead man; on the ground that on balance it is in the public interest that no such action should lie. . . . Again, is there any remedy in the law as to infringement of privacy? Suppose the dead man were still alive. The passages describe conduct by him which was done in private and which he would wish to keep private and not disclosed to anyone except his close friends. They expose his depravity to the view of the whole world. He could not sue for libel; or, if he did, he would fail because the words are true. But could he sue for infringement of privacy? Many might think that he should be able to do so; he should be able to prevent his public exposure. But again, as I understand it, it would be difficult to give him any remedy. We have as yet no general remedy for infringement of privacy; the reason given being that on balance it is not in the public interest that there should be, see the Report of the Committee on Privacy in 1972.

The reason why, in these cases, the law gives no remedy is because of the importance it attaches to the freedom of the Press; or, better put, the importance in a free society of the circulation of true information. The metes and bounds of this are already staked out by the rules of law. The law of libel stops that which is untrue on living persons. The law of contempt stops that which is prejudicial to a fair trial. The law of obscenity stops that which tends to deprave and corrupt. It would be a mistake to extend these so as to give the judges a power to stop publication of true matter whenever the judges, or any particular judge, thought that it was in the interests of a child to do so.

It is on this account that I do not think the wardship jurisdiction should be extended so as to enable the court to stop publication of this book. The relatives of the child must do their best to protect her by doing all they can to see that the book does not come into her hands. It is a better way of protection than the court can give. In my opinion it would be extending the wardship jurisdiction too far and infringing too much on the freedom of the press for us to grant an injunction in this case."

Roskill L.J. commented:

"There is in this country — and it is right that it should be restated in the clearest terms and never more so than at this stage of the twentieth century — a right of free speech and a right of free publication. That right is at least as important — some may think more important — as the right of individuals, whether adults or minors, whether wards or not."

Matrimonial causes

These proceedings, normally relating to divorce, are noted in outline for information. As mentioned previously, the Judicial Proceedings (Regulation of Reports) Act 1926 restricts the details which may be reported in terms identical to those repeated in s.58 of the Magistrates Courts Act 1952. Contravention may lead to a term of imprisonment not exceeding four months, a fine up to a maximum of £500 or both.

The Domestic and Appellate Proceedings (Restriction of Publicity) Act 1968, s.2, as amended by the Matrimonial

Causes Act 1973, extends the reporting restrictions to proceedings involving declarations of legitimacy or financial provisions for a spouse.

Petitions for divorce, judicial separation and nullity must generally be heard in open court. An exception to this occurs in nullity petitions. A decree of nullity is a declaration that the "marriage" is invalid. The marriage may be void (because one of the parties was already married, under age or because the parties are too closely related) or voidable (because of a spouse's incapacity or wilful refusal to consummate the marriage). Section 48 (2) of the Matrimonial Causes Act 1973 provides that evidence of sexual capacity in nullity petitions is to be heard *in camera*.

If a divorce petitioner prior to the hearing of the full petition, wants a court order to exclude the other spouse from the matrimonial home or to restrain assaults or molestation, feared from the other spouse, there will be an application to the Family Division for an interlocutory injunction. Such matters are dealt with in chambers unless the judge, for special reasons, directs that the hearing shall be in open court. If a spouse is in danger of going to prison for breach of such an injunction, the hearing must be in open court. (In county courts with divorce jurisdiction, the above also applies.)

Since 1973, divorce cases are no longer allocated on the basis of whether they are defended or undefended. The Family Division takes the longer cases and those where the custody of children is involved; shorter hearings (often involving uncontested divorces) are dealt with at the county court.

While, since 1969, there has only been one ground for a divorce petition — irretrievable breakdown of the marriage — any of the following factors may be used to show such a breakdown. Unless there are exceptional circumstances, the marriage must have been in existence for three years before the petition is presented.

Factors

(a) The respondent has committed adultery and the petitioner finds it intolerable to live with him or her. In this area, a single act of adultery, without further evidence of the effect of this on the breakdown of the marriage, may not necessarily be sufficient to show irretrievable breakdown.

(b) The respondent has behaved in such a way that the petitioner can no longer reasonably be expected to live with him or her. This absorbs the old ground of cruelty.

(c) The respondent has deserted the petitioner for a continuous period of at least two years prior to the petition.

(d) The parties have lived apart for two years prior to the petition and the respondent consents to the decree. This factor allows, in effect, for an amicable divorce and, if used as the petitioning factor in uncomplicated situations, can reduce the costs of the whole petition.

(e) The parties have lived apart for at least five years. The respondent may resist the decree if this factor is used by arguing that the divorce could result in grave financial or other hardship.

Under the Matrimonial Proceedings and Property Act 1970, the court has wide powers to direct terms of financial settlements and arrangements about property. The aim is to "place the parties so far as is practicable and, having regard to their conduct, just to do so, in the financial position in which they would have been if the marriage had not broken down and each had properly discharged his or her financial responsibilities to the other."

If the court decides to grant the petition, a decree nisi (a provisional decree) is issued. The "nisi" period is generally six weeks and, during this the parties are not free to remarry. When this period is complete, the decree may be made absolute on the application of one of the parties and they are then free to remarry.

The nisi period gives a chance for reconciliation which, if effective, will result in the parties asking for the decree nisi to be set aside. An official, called the Queen's Proctor, can use this period to investigate the background to the petition and check whether there has been any dishonesty in obtaining the decree nisi.

If the husband is petitioning, he may name a third party alleging adultery. The named adulterer is known as the co-respondent. If the wife is petitioning, the adulteress is referred to as "the woman named." The purpose of this is to allow these third parties to appear and, if relevant, clear themselves of involvement.

(3) Queen's Bench. This division deals with a wider variety of work than Chancery or Family and consists of some 44 judges headed by the Lord Chief Justice. This division has civil, criminal and supervisory jurisdiction.

(a) *Civil business:* actions relating to contracts and to torts (civil wrongs). Defamation, for instance, is a tort as are such things as trespass, negligence, nuisance, injurious falsehood and "passing off." Within the division are two special courts: admiralty, which deals with salvage and shipping matters, and the commercial court, covering such things as insurance, banking and mercantile documents. Trial is before a single Queen's Bench judge.

(b) *Criminal and supervisory jurisdiction:* this is undertaken by the Divisional Court of the Queen's Bench made up, normally, of three judges (often the Lord Chief Justice sitting with two Queen's Bench judges in the Lord Chief Justice's court). This court hears appeals by way of "case stated" from the magistrates' courts and the crown court sitting as an appeal court (see the section on Criminal Process).

It is this court which hears complaints of contempt referred to it (*i.e.* The *Sunday Times* thalidomide reference and Paul Foot's identification of blackmail witnesses).

It can issue the prerogative writ of habeas corpus and make the orders of mandamus, prohibition and certiorari to compel inferior courts, tribunals and authorities to use their powers properly and to stop them from exceeding their jurisdiction.

Disputed parliamentary elections are decided by an election court made up of two Queen's Bench judges.

The judges from this division play an important part in the trying of serious and difficult indictable cases in the Crown Court (see the section of Criminal Process). The judges spend about half their time dealing with work in the Royal Courts of Justice in the Strand (*i.e.* (a) and (b)) and half their time "on circuit" in the crown court system.

Court of Appeal (Civil Division)

This is presided over by the Master of the Rolls and there are nine Lord Justices of Appeal. This court, together with the High Court and the Crown Court, forms the Supreme Court of Judicature. Our Supreme Court, unlike the American one, is not the final court of appeal because appeals on points of law of general public importance may go to the House of Lords.

The Court of Appeal hears appeals from the county courts and the High Court. There are normally three judges. While decisions are generally reached on the basis of transcript evidence from the lower court, fresh evidence may, in limited situations, be taken. Decisions are by a majority.

House of Lords

As already noted, the House of Lords can only hear appeals on points of law certified to be of general public importance. The Lord Chancellor is the chief judge and there are some nine Lords of Appeal in Ordinary, who receive life peerages. Only these members of the House of Lords and peers who have held high judicial office (*i.e.* previous Lord Chancellors) may sit to deal with the judicial work of the House. Decisions are by a majority, the court usually sitting with five members.

Appeals which may be heard in private

There is one further situation which must be considered. If the court, originally dealing with a matter, had power to sit in private, the appeal, or any part of it, may also be heard in private. This is the effect of section 1 (1) of the Domestic and Appellate Proceedings (Restriction of Publicity) Act 1968.

If this occurs, the appeal court must still give its decision in public, unless there is "good and sufficient" reason for this taking place in private. Even then, the court must publicly state what the "good and sufficient" reasons are.

When an application is made for an appeal court to sit in private, the application itself will be heard in private, unless the court directs otherwise (s.1 (5)).

Appeals from the Court of Appeal, the High Court, county courts and magistrates courts are covered by the Act.

Part 3

Associated Matters

1 Parliamentary Privilege

In discussion of the structure of the courts in the United Kingdom, no mention has been made of the High Court of Parliament.

There are a number of sources of English Law. Common law, developed over the centuries by the judges on the basis of principles declared in precedents (previous cases) is one source. Legislation (statute law) is another. If a parliamentary Bill passes through all the required stages within a session, it receives the Royal Assent and becomes an Act of Parliament. The Act may alter the common law on a specific point or may introduce a completely new legal concept. It is then up to the courts to interpret and construe parliamentary legislation, applying the law as set out in the Acts.

Legislation may be introduced either in the House of Commons or in the House of Lords. The upper House has an additional function because it also acts as a judicial body, hearing appeals on points of law of general public importance, sitting with the Lords of Appeal in Ordinary (the "law lords").

In addition, each House has the right to regulate its own procedure and has certain common law privileges. Neither House can create new privileges, except by legislation, but they have the sole right to judge cases falling within existing privileges.

It should be understood that the reference to privilege in this context is not the same as privilege in relation to the defences of defamation. There is one similarity which has already been mentioned: members of either House are protected absolutely from legal proceedings arising out of statements made in Parliament. This will be discussed in more detail. The privileges of Parliament extend beyond this, however, and either House has power to punish for contempt if there is a breach of privilege.

The privileges exist to enable members to carry out their work and the object is to safeguard the dignity of each House,

259

allowing members to perform their duties without fear or favour. Over the centuries, there has been conflict between the courts and the House of Commons as to which body should determine the extent of a particular privilege or its actual existence. These battles diminished after 1840.

The privileges of the House of Commons are formally claimed from the Crown at the opening of each session by the Speaker.

(1) *Freedom from arrest.* This protects a member from civil arrest for 40 days before a meeting of Parliament until 40 days afterwards. It does not prevent arrest on a criminal charge (the arrest of Mr. John Stonehouse being one recent example) but Parliament maintains a right to receive immediate information of the reasons for the imprisonment or detention of any member.

(2) *Freedom of speech.* This is the only substantial modern privilege and covers an area which is most easily described by examples. A member may speak freely within Parliament but if he publishes his remarks outside such proceedings, he may be liable in defamation. In 1938, Mr. Duncan Sandys, M.P. sent a draft question to a Minister and was then threatened with a prosecution under the Official Secrets Act if he failed to disclose his source of information. The House resolved that this threat was a breach of privilege. In 1958, Mr. George Strauss, M.P. wrote to the Postmaster General alleging fraud in the disposal of scrap cable. The Minister sent in a copy of this letter to the L.E.B. and Mr. Strauss was threatened with a libel action by them unless he withdrew his allegation. He complained to the Committee of Privileges, who decided that there had been a breach as the letter was originally a proceeding in Parliament: the House decided, on a free vote, not to accept this conclusion (and, eventually, it turned out there was no substance to the allegations).

Letters to members from their constitutents or other people are not protected by this privilege but may attract the defamation defence of qualified privilege. Statements made by persons to members within the precincts of the House are not protected by parliamentary privilege.

(3) *The right to expel.* In 1947, Garry Allighan, Member of Parliament for Gravesend, was expelled having been found guilty by the House of dishonourable conduct and gross contempt. He had falsely suggested in a newspaper article that other members were leaking confidential information about parliamentary party meetings either for money or because they were happy to accept drinks and became indiscreet.

(4) *The right to regulate proceedings.* In 1970, a person, who threw two smoke bombs from the public gallery, was handed over to the Metropolitan Police for trial in the magistrates' court although the House could have dealt with the matter of the interruption.

(5) *The power to punish for contempt.* The House has the right to decide whether a particular act is a contempt. This applies to acts by members and "strangers" (*i.e.* members of the public). The contempt generally consists of conduct which offends against the authority or dignity of the House.

Some examples illustrate the scope of such conduct:

(a) In 1935, the League for the Prohibition of Cruel Sports wrote to a number of Members of Parliament asking them to state their views on blood sports and indicated that if no reply was forthcoming, the League would let constituents know the Members of Parliament had no objection to cruel sports.

(b) In 1951, the National Union of Mineworkers threatened to remove Mr. Aneurin Bevan from its list of sponsored Members of Parliament if he resigned from the Government. There were echoes of this conduct in another N.U.M. case involving Mr. Arthur Scargill in 1975.

(c) In 1956, the *Sunday Graphic* criticised a question tabled by Mr. Arthur Lewis, M.P. about whether money from the Hungarian Relief Fund would be used to help Eqyptians made homeless by bombing in the Suez crisis. They gave his telephone number and asked readers to ring him if they disagreed with him. Mr. Lewis was bombarded with calls, many abusive, at all hours during the following few days.

(d) In 1975, the Committee of Privileges attempted to ban the editor of *The Economist* and a member of his staff for leaking the conclusions of a Select Committee. They recommended the ban should operate for a six month period but, on debate by the whole House, the sanction of banning was rejected although the contempt was upheld. The House expressed a desire to have the right to fine in such cases.

This final example raises the whole problem of punishment for contempt of Parliament. A member may be admonished, suspended or expelled. "Strangers" may be admonished, reprimanded or, theoretically, detained in the precincts of the House until the end of the parliamentary session (traditionally in the Clock Tower, but this place has not been used for such custody this century).

The pattern over the last two decades has been for the Committee of Privileges, given a reasonable complaint, to recommend to the House that there has been a contempt. If the House accepts this view, there is the ridiculous spectacle of an editor being summoned to the Bar of the House and offering an apology for his temerity in suitably obedient terms in order to purge his contempt. *The Economist* episode raised issues which, should Parliament have time, may subsequently lead to legislation with the right to fine. A Select Committee, which examined the whole issue of parliamentary privilege, reported in 1968 and recommended that the House should concern itself with its rights and immunities and contempt rather than the archaic phraseology of "rights and privileges" and "breach of privilege". The House has yet to find the time to put the Committee's recommendations into a more positive form, however.

The procedure, if a member believes there has been a breach of privilege, is outlined below:

(1) The member brings the matter to the Speaker's notice as soon as possible.

(2) The Speaker must rule as soon as possible on the matter: he has 24 hours to decide whether there is a prima facie case. If he decides that such a case does exist, the House is asked to refer the matter to the Committee of Privileges (composed of senior members from all parties). If the Speaker decides there is no prima facie case, the member may still attempt a reference through to the Committee via a debate of the full House.

(3) If the matter goes through to the Committee, it will be dealt with in private but the Committee has the power to call witnesses (refusal to testify amounting to contempt). Its report returns to the House in the form of a recommendation.

(4) The House then resolves what action should be taken on the Committee's report, normally on a free vote.

The privileges of the House of Lords are substantially similar to those already described. For contempt, however, committal may be for a period extending beyond a parliamentary session. The House of Lords had a right to summon judges for advice on points of law: this is now a formality, preserved at the opening of Parliament. The right of a peer to demand trial in the House of Lords by his fellows no longer exists.

The Upper House, like the Commons, has a right to decide who is eligible to sit and who is not. A very recent example of this occurred in the Ampthill Peerage claim (*House of Lords Committee of Privileges* (1976) 2 W.L.R. 777).

> John Russell, son of the third Baron Ampthill, argued he should be able to take his father's place in the House of Lords. A counter-petition was lodged by Geoffrey Russell, born to the Baron's first wife but never accepted by the Baron as his legitimate son. Geoffrey had, however, been declared legitimate under an Act of Parliament. The other son argued that this Act of Parliament need not be binding on the House of Lords in giving advice to Her Majesty about who should take the seat. The Committee held that it was bound by the Act of Parliament (legislation rather than common law) and advised that Geoffrey Russell should take the seat.

(There is an interesting side-note to this case. The Judicial Proceedings (Regulation of Reports) Act 1926 owed its existence to the coverage given by the Press in the mid 20s to the third Baron's legal battle with Geoffrey Russell's mother over the circumstances of conception. The Act once passed, however, did not regulate reports of proceedings before the Committee of Privileges, although it certainly covers other judicial proceedings.)

Election Law

This topic, which relates both to parliamentary and local government elections, is covered here because elections can lead newspapers inadvertently into the commission of criminal offences.

By section 91 of the Representation of the People Act 1949, it is a summary offence to make a false statement of fact about a candidate. This relates to the person's character or conduct and must be for the purposes of affecting his return. This illegal practice can lead to a fine of up to £100 and disqualification as an elector for up to five years. Where a newspaper company commits the offence, the directors may bear the fine and disqualification.

It is not sufficient that the falsity exists in an expression of opinion: it must be contained in a statement of fact. It is a defence for the person charged to show that he had reasonable grounds for believing the statement to be true.

There is a distinction between news copy favouring the views of a particular candidate or party and advertisements (other than those authorised by the candidate or agent) promoting the particular candidate. Bona fide news copy is permitted but, as the candidate's expenses are limited, supporters are committing a corrupt practice if they try to incur expenses without his permission. General propaganda material, which does not favour a particular candidate, is permissible, as was shown in the case of *R. v. Tronoh Mines Ltd.* (1952):

> The company, six days before a general election, took an advertisement in *The Times*. It criticised the Labour Party and stated "the nation . . . cannot survive if the worm of socialism is permitted to eat into the very core of its economic life. . . . The coming general election will give us all an opportunity of saving the country from being reduced through the policies of the Socialist Government to a bankrupt Welfare State."
>
> The company, its secretary and *The Times* were prosecuted for unlawfully incurring expenses in relation to the Conservative candidate for one particular constituency.
>
> The judge dismissed the case because no particular candidate was attacked or aided.

It is section 63 which states that expenses cannot be incurred with a view to procuring the election of a candidate at a parliamentary or local government election, except with the permission of the candidate or his agent. Expenses must be accounted for. There is no infringement of this section if publication of the candidate's views, the nature and extent of his backing or attacks on a candidate appear in a newspaper or other periodical.

In *D.P.P.* v. *Luft* (1976), distribution of literature, urging people not to vote for National Front candidates in three constituencies in which they were standing, was held by the House of Lords to contravene section 63. Expenditure, which was directed at opposing one type of candidate, benefitted others.

One final point: there is no privilege attaching to a statement in an election address nor to any reports of such statements (s.10 Defamation Act 1952).

2 Copyright

Copyright protection is not given to ideas or mechanical systems. The protection, when it is gained, relates to the material presentation. If, therefore, an individual wishes to gain copyright protection, he must reduce his idea to a material form (*i.e.* write it down or record the material). It is a feature of the system of protection in this country that, beyond this, no formalities are required. There is no need for the author to register his copyright at a central office (as he would have to do if he wished to patent a process or system). He does not actually have to publish the work or denote the material "copyright reserved." The moment the words are written, the sketch penned or the melody transcribed, copyright comes into existence.

The Copyright Act 1956 protects "literary, dramatic and artistic works." The word "literary" sounds imposing but has been held to cover any work expressed in print or writing, providing it is long enough to involve some skill or labour in composition. This interpretation spreads to widen the scope of what is classed as dramatic or artistic. The effect of this broad coverage means that football fixture lists, Stock Exchange Lists and advertisements composed by a newspaper's "Dial-an-Ad" department are protected by copyright.

Titles of books or newspapers are normally too short to be protected by copyright; similarly, there is no copyright in a pseudonym. However, if a title or pseudonym is used by someone else in such a way as to confuse the public into believing that the second work is, in fact, the first, then a "passing off" action may be brought. If the author has been contributing to a particular publication under a pen name which he invented, when he ceases to contribute (unless there is an agreement to the contrary) he can take his pen name with him as part of his stock in trade and the publication may not continue to use it.

Copyright generally protects the author. There is a varia-

tion of this, when the work is produced in the course of employment by journalists, which will be discussed shortly. The
general rule is fairly simple to apply in the case of a writer or
artist. In the case of photographs, the copyright belongs to the
person who, when the photograph is taken, owns the material
on which the photograph is taken. If the photograph or portrait is commissioned and paid for, the client obtains the copyright.

Where the material is produced for publication in a
newspaper by someone under a contract of service for the publication, then the newspaper proprietor has the copyright for
this type of publication. If a staff journalist wrote a feature, his
employer could sell this to other newspapers but the journalist
would be free to adapt the information to make a documentary
or a play or a novel. One thing is quite clear: if a journalist
writes copy outside working hours (and this may require careful examination of the terms of the contract of employment) he
retains the full copyright for all purposes.

The next consideration is the duration of the copyright
period. The time period depends on whether the work is
published during the life of the author, after his death or
whether the work is a photograph.

(1) *Works published during the life of the author.* Copyright
runs for the life of the author plus 50 years from the end of the
calendar year in which he died.

(2) *Works published after the death of the author.* Copyright
runs for 50 years from the end of the calendar year in which the
work is published, broadcast or performed in public.

(3) *Photographs.* Copyright runs for 50 years from the end of
the calendar year, in which the photograph was first
published.

It should be understood that copyright is, in effect, a right in
property (albeit, property which can only be protected for a
limited period as described above). As a property right, it may
be the subject of an assignment or of a licence.

Assignment

This must be made in writing and signed by the assignor.
Assignment may relate to specific areas or for limited periods.

An author might assign the copyright of a book to X (thus allowing X to deal with the property in its written form) but might retain the copyright for any film or theatrical adaptation. Future copyright (an agreement to allow X rights over, as yet, unwritten work) can only be assigned on the signature of both the author and X.

Licences

These differ from assignments because the person permitted to do certain acts by the author is more restricted. Unless the licence is exclusive, it need not be in writing. The author is permitting X, perhaps, to perform the work or publish it in a 'one-off' or very limited form.

An example may clarify this area. A writes a successful novel. He assigns the copyright of the book in its written form to B, retaining all other rights and only after allowing C an exclusive licence to publish an abridgement of the novel in an evening newspaper over a limited two-week period. He may then assign the copyright in theatrical adaptations of the novel to D and retain the copyright for filming for himself.

Someone holding an exclusive licence can sue the infringer of the copyright in his own name; someone with a general licence cannot. Licencees (and assignees) are permitted to make alterations in the work unless the express terms forbid this.

Infringement

If any substantial part of a copyright work is reproduced without the permission of the copyright owner, infringement has occurred. The judicial test does not rest on the quantity of what is reproduced so much as its importance in relation to the copyright work. A few bars of the essential melody of a tune may result in an infringement, likewise the key lines to a poem. A translation or adaptation of the work, without permission, would similarly be an infringement.

It is also a civil wrong for anyone to deliberately sell unlawful copies. In this area, there is a fine distinction between an infringer and a converter: in the latter case, an action for conversion would recover the sum potentially lost but, with an infringing distributor, it is necessary to prove that he knew that what he was doing was wrong.

The rules in this area would be unduly harsh if there were no provisions for fair dealing. If the work is used for private study or research, there is no infringement. If the work is used for the purposes of criticism, there is no infringement if the work and the author are identified: this would be permitted as fair dealing. It would not be fair dealing to quote so extensively in criticism that the bulk of the work was revealed. The Publishers Association and the Society of Authors regard it as fair dealing when, for the purposes of criticism or review, a single extract of up to 400 words or a series of extracts (none of which exceeds 300 words) up to a total of 800 words are taken from prose works. The guideline for poems is up to 40 lines provided that this does not mean an extract of more than one quarter of the poem.

The remedies for infringement of copyright are outlined below. They include:

(a) an injunction;
(b) damages;
(c) an account for profits;
(d) a criminal prosecution.

(a) *Injunction*

This is a court order telling the infringer to stop repeating the breach of copyright. If the infringer persists he would, among other things, be in contempt of court (see the chapter on Contempt).

(b) *Damages*

The copyright owner will be seeking to recover the money he has lost by the infringer's acts. A "pirate" version of a book might have resulted in the true owner being unable to sell as many copies as he would have without the infringement. If the infringer can prove that he was unaware and had no reason of suspecting that the work was the subject of copyright, damages cannot be awarded. This defence will succeed only in rare instances: as every work enjoys copyright without registration formalities, it will be difficult to prove that the work was reasonably thought to be out of copyright (except, perhaps, in borderline time cases).

Damages can also be recovered for the tort (civil wrong) of conversion. If damages are claimed for conversion, the relevant sum is the value of the infringing work not the sum lost to the copyright owner. Again, if the infringer can show no knowledge of copyright or reasonable belief that it no longer existed, this operates as a valid (if exceptionally difficult) defence.

(c) *Account for profits*

The true owner here will be claiming the amount of profit made by the infringer, not the value of the infringing material. Of all the practical remedies, this is the most useful because the owner is entitled to the infringer's profit even though the infringer was unaware that copyright existed in the work.

(d) *Criminal prosecution*

Under section 21 of the Copyright Act 1956, a summary prosecution is a possibility. The offence relates to anyone who, when copyright exists in a work, makes or sells or shows any article he knows to be infringing copy. The section also catches people deliberately trading in "pirate" copies or deliberately performing copyright works in public without consent.

On first conviction, the infringer may be fined up to £50; on second or subsequent convictions, in addition to the £50 fine, he faces the alternative penalty of up to two months' imprisonment. The court, whether he is convicted or not, can order the destruction of anything used to infringe the copyright or order that the material be handed over to the copyright owner.

The case of *Beloff* v. *Pressdram* (1973) provides a useful example of some of the issues and remedies at work. The case has the additional relevance of involving journalists and (almost inevitably) *Private Eye*.

Nora Beloff was the *Observer*'s political and lobby correspondent. Paul Foot was a regular contributor to *Private Eye*. He had been investigating the relationship between Reginald

Maudling and one Jerome Hoffman. Hoffman's property transactions resulted in him receiving a prison sentence in America for fraud. Foot wrote a series of articles in *Private Eye* attacking Maudling.

Beloff had written a memorandum to her editor and other *Observer* staff about a conversation with William Whitelaw. It had been made clear to her that if the then Prime Minister (Edward Heath) were "to run under a bus," Maudling would take over as Prime Minister. As a result of her suggestion that she should do a profile on Maudling, the *Observer* later ran such a piece, which also attacked *Private Eye*'s attitude to him as a smear campaign and "pure fabrication." Someone on the *Observer*'s staff "leaked" a copy of Beloff's memorandum to *Private Eye*. It was then published in full in an insulting article about Beloff.

The *Observer*'s editor then purported to assign the copyright in the memorandum from Observer Ltd. (the proprietors and therefore the owners of work done during the course of employment) to Beloff. She then claimed infringement of copyright (because it had supposedly been assigned to her) in the memorandum plus aggravated and exemplary damages.

Ungoed-Thomas J. held that her claim failed because:

(1) Copyright in the memorandum belonged to the Observer Ltd.

(2) The editor had no authority to assign it to Beloff on behalf of the company to give her a cause of action.

(3) If her claim had been successful, *Private Eye* could not have used the defence that publication was in the public interest. This defence would only work when the disclosures involved matters such as conspiracies against the state, fraud, misdeeds or matter medically dangerous to the public.

(4) The defence of "fair dealing" for the purposes of criticism or review would not have succeeded. The "leaking" of the memorandum made it clear that publication was unjustifiable and not for authorised review and was, therefore, dealing with the work which was not fair.

(5) If Beloff's claim had succeeded, she could not have recovered exemplary damages. She could, however, have received additional damages because of the insulting terms and the personal distress caused to her.

This case is mentioned in some detail because, from the author's experience, there appear to be many misunderstandings about the nature of the case and its result. This particular action was not a defamation action (although there was a defa-

mation action on different facts which Miss Beloff won).
Despite *Private Eye*'s heading of the actionable piece as "The
Ballsoff Memorandum," this fact was only used to indicate the
generally insulting terms adopted. The judge said: "Counsel
for the plaintiff strongly attacked the nickname, although the
plaintiff herself seemed to be less concerned about it and did
not take the obvious advantage of exaggerating or emphasising her feelings about it." In any event, had she sued for libel
over the nickname she would have had to prove that reasonable people thought less well of her as a result of the libel.
Given that *Private Eye* is a satirical magazine, prone to lam-
pooning public figures, this might have been a very difficult
task.

The claim for exemplary damages relied heavily on the libel
case of *Broome* v. *Cassell* (1972). While the application of this
case was rejected, the judge seems to have allowed the idea to
creep into the result by another route. "Flagrancy of the
infringement and its benefit to the defendants are of course
expressly mentioned as material; but 'in addition to all other
material considerations.' These include such matters as the
defendants' conduct with regard to the infringement and
motive for it, injury to the plaintiff's feeling for suffering
insults, indignities and the like; and also the plaintiff's own
corresponding behaviour. The damages go largely to compensation for the plaintiff's suffering from injured feelings and distress and strain . . . ," he said. In the event, however, as the
copyright had not be assigned to her, she could not benefit
from this dicta.

At the risk of stressing the obvious, journalists should
beware of breaching copyright in the publication of "confidential" memoranda or reports to local authorities or corpora-
tions. While the defence of public interest exists to resist
breach of confidence and breach of copyright claims, the
"interest" in the latter area must be potentially seriously
affected (see (3), above).

A further matter to be considered is section 43 (2) of the
Copyright Act 1956. This aims to prevent the use of another
person's name on work which he has not written, ("or in or on
a reproduction of such work in such a way as to imply that the
other person is the author of the work") without licence.

In *Moore* v. *News of the World* (1972), discussed in the chapter on defamation, there was a further issue:

The plaintiff recovered £100 damages for breach of copyright under section 43 (2) when the newspaper attributed words to her, following an interview, which she claimed she had never said. The Court of Appeal held that the trial judge had been correct in directing the jury that the right of action given by the section was not limited to professional authors.

In *Jenkins* v. *Socialist Worker* (1977), Clive Jenkins, the General Secretary of the Association of Scientific, Technical and Managerial Staff, recovered £1,000 copyright damages. The publication of a satirical letter with his facsimile signature led to this award.

Miscellaneous

Copyright law functions to protect a person's time, labour and skill in producing a piece of copy. If a piece of news copy is broadcast without the copyright owner's consent, this is an infringement. From the journalist's point of view, his employer has (via s.4 (2) of the Copyright Act 1956) the world newspaper and magazine rights but, if a local radio station lifts news copy, this seems to be a prima facie infringement of the writer's residual copyright. On the other side of the coin, reporters, writing copy during the course of their employment and then telephoning it over on a lineage basis to a national newspaper or a rival local paper, are infringing their employer's copyright. Generally no objection will be taken to this providing the employer is given the first run of the story but this is often a grace and favour situation and could backfire. If the copy comes from time outside employment, this restriction does not exist (unless there is a restrictive term in the journalist's contract of employment giving the employer a contractual first option on such copy).

A freelance, even though he receives a retainer, is not an employee and retains the full rights over his copy, subject to publication negotiations.

A reader's letter is regarded as being sent to the editor under an implied licence for a single publication without payment. Any further printing of the letter would require writer's consent.

The implied licence situation does not carry over to copy submitted "on spec" which should be treated as if it has been submitted for the editor's consideration prior to negotiations about a fee. This situation serves to highlight the difference between licences and assignments generally. If the editor wants a licence to publish the contribution for a payment, this can be agreed orally (say, over the telephone). If he decides the copy is of greater potential value, he may wish to have the copyright assigned to the newspaper. In this case, the assignment must be in writing and signed by the author.

The United Kingdom has treaties with almost every country (one notable exception being China) relating to copyright. A foreign work receives exactly the same protection in the United Kingdom as if it has originated here. A work produced here receives virtually reciprocal treatment abroad.

In some countries, copyright can only be gained by complying with the country's formalities (particularly, in certain South American countries, by local registration). As far as the United States is concerned, the Universal Copyright Convention clears up many former problems. British works, written but unpublished, are protected to the same extent as they are in Britain. British published works are protected providing they bear the international copyright symbol — © plus the name of the copyright proprietor and the year of publication (*i.e.* © R. Callender Smith 1978).

Whitford Committee on Copyright (Cmnd. 6732 (1977))

In 1973, a committee, chaired by Mr. Justice Whitford, was given the task of looking at the law of copyright and recommending proposals for change. The review appeared in 1977 and contains the following recommendations of interest to the Press:

(1) The structure of the Copyright Act 1956 should be revised to put the law on a plain and uniform basis. Matters of principle should be declared and then followed by exceptions; there should be a comprehensive definition section at the beginning of the Act and descriptive words should resemble those commonly used.

(2) Creators of copyright works should have the copyright in their creations unless a contract specifically states otherwise or — in the absence of a contract — unless exceptions apply. Among exceptions recommended are:

(a) where work is produced by an employee in the course of employment, copyright should vest in the employer unless the exploitation was not within the contemplation of the employer and employee at the time of producing the work;

(b) if the work is commissioned, copyright should belong to the author, but:

(i) the commissioner should have an exclusive licence for all purposes which could reasonably be said to have been within the contemplation of the parties at the time of commission; and

(ii) the commissioner should have power to prevent exploitation for other purposes against which he could reasonably take exception.

(3) If the material originates from a speech or lecture delivered extempore and is noted permanently by someone other than the speaker, whether the speaker knows this or not, copyright in the material should be the speaker's (and separate from any copyright in the recording or transcript).

(4) Fair dealing which does not conflict with the copyright owner's legitimate interests should not be a breach of copyright.

(5) Material reproduced for judicial proceedings, statutory administrative enquiries — and official reports of these proceedings — should involve no breach of copyright.

(6) Damages for breach of copyright should be damages for infringement and the remedies of conversion and detention should be abolished.

(7) The provision for exemplary damages should be strengthened. For a flagrant infringement of copyright, the court should have a complete discretion to award such damages as seem appropriate.

(8) Section 21 (dealing with summary criminal offences) should be altered so that:

(a) "possession in the course of trade" should be an offence;

(b) proof of guilty knowledge by the possessor that the mat-

ter infringes copyright should be abolished: there should
be a defence if the accused can prove he was not aware and
had no reasonable grounds for suspecting that he was dealing with infringing copies;
(c) the penalties should be increased and kept in line with
those for offences against property generally: on second
conviction, the court should be able to impose a prison
sentence.

(9) If a defendant claims he has innocently infringed copyright, he should have to prove that he believed and had reasonable grounds for believing that he was not infringing
copyright.

3 Admission to Local Authority Meetings

There has been constant and often highly justified criticism of limitations on the Press's right to attend and report the meetings and deliberations of local authorities and their committees. The law securing the right to attend is only achieving a limited effect.

Briefly, what various Acts of Parliament have tried to achieve by letting the Press and the public in has, successively, been circumvented by many local authorities.

Legislation in 1882 laid down rules governing council meetings but said nothing about admitting the Press or public. In 1908, the Local Authority (Admission of the Press to Meetings) Act allowed the Press into full council meetings and those of education committees. Exclusion was permitted if, in the opinion of the majority of members, this would be in the public interest. This power was misapplied and, in 1960, Mrs. Margaret Thatcher succeeded with a backbench Bill which became the Public Bodies (Admission to Meetings) Act.

This Act applied to full council meetings, to the Education Committees and to all committees on which all members of the council sat. Two major flaws were:

(1) most of the Education Committees' work is conducted by sub-committees, and

(2) it was a simple matter to make sure that other committees were not made up of all members of the council.

The Press and the public could be excluded via section 1 (2). This subsection, which is still operative, deserves detailed noting:

A body may, by resolution, exclude the public from a meeting (whether during the whole or part of the proceedings) whenever publicity would be prejudicial to the public interest by reason of the confidential nature of the business to be transacted or for other special reasons stated in the resolution and arising from the nature of that business or of the proceedings; and where such a resolution is passed, this Act shall not require the meeting to be open for the public during proceedings to which the resolution applies.

So a resolution is needed before exclusion, but it is the resolving body which decides (in subjective terms) whether the public interest will be prejudiced. They may feel the matter is confidential or another reason may be stated in the resolution, providing it is relevant to the item to be discussed.

Under section 1 (3), exclusion may take place if the body wants to hear from an outsider who is going to present them with recommendations or advice. This situation, without in any way restricting the previous sub-section, qualifies as being a "special reason why publicity would be prejudicial to the public interest."

Perhaps the only saving feature of section 1 is the requirement for a resolution before exclusion. If the initial motion to exclude is opposed, then debate on the motion (which may contain at least the outline, from the opposer, of the material sought to be discussed in secret) may be reported. The remarks, until exclusion takes place, will carry qualified privilege and, if reported fairly and accurately, may be printed providing a defamed party is allowed space to explain or contradict the material should he so wish. This resistance tactic, however, is used only exceptionally.

One common tactic to prevent such public resistance was for the authority to pass a resolution each year that certain portions of meetings would be held in camera.

Schedule 12 paragraph 39 (1) to the Local Government Act 1972 states that ".... all questions coming before a local authority shall be decided by a majority of the members of the authority present and voting thereon at a meeting of the authority." The purpose of this might have been to require exclusion resolutions to be taken at each relevant meeting. However, the wording of the Schedule is ambiguous because of the use of the indefinite article in the phrase ".... *a* meeting of the authority." This is being interpreted by many local authorities as including the annual meeting and *carte blanche* exculsion for matters under specified heads, in advance of their actual consideration at individual meetings, continues.

The 1972 Act extended the right of the public to attend "....

all meetings of committees of local authorities as well as to meeting of local authorities themselves . . . ." subject to the resolution to exclude. The failure, in the 1972 Act, to alter the powers of exclusion in more positive terms, has meant that, while the public may attend more of the general business of the local authority, it can still be ejected almost at will on contentious points.

Subject to resolutions to exclude, the Press and public must be admitted to the meetings of the following bodies and their committees: county councils, district councils, city councils, borough councils, the G.L.C. and London boroughs, the Land Authority for Wales, parish councils, parish meetings, community councils and community meetings (in Wales), regional health authorities, area health authorities, community health councils, water authorities, education committees and any bodies, other than police authorities, with power to levy a rate.

In *R.* v. *Liverpool City Council, ex p. Liverpool Taxi Fleet Operators Association* (1974), the Divisional Court had to consider whether a body had validly excluded the public under section 1 (2).

A committee meeting of the council was to consider the issuing of taxi licences. The committee room had 55 seats: 22 were for members of the council, 17 were for officials and two were for the police (*i.e.* 41 seats). The remainder were for the Press and the public (*i.e.* 14 seats). At the start of the meeting about 40 members of the public were waiting to get in. The committee resolved that members of the public — apart from the Press — should be excluded. The reason specified in the resolution was the lack of space and so that the committee business could be effectively carried out. The Lord Chief Justice, Lord Widgery, held that the resolution was valid, because the requirement that special reasons be shown in the resolution was directory only rather than mandatory. As no special injury had been proved, the court would not interfere.

Lord Widgery did make the following point: "It is, I think, important to stress that authorities, arranging committee meetings and other meetings to which the Act applies, must have regard to their duty to the public. That means they must have regard when making the arrangements for the committee to the provision of reasonable accommodation for the public. If a committee was minded to choose to meet in a very small room and turned round and 'We cannot have the public in because there is no room,' it would be acting in bad faith and would not be beyond the long arm of this court."

He added that the case was an example of a body finding its arrangements swamped by the number of people wishing to attend.

The conclusion to be drawn from this judgement is that, should special injury be proved in similar cases, the Divisional Court may step in to overturn such resolutions.

Some general points from the remainder of section 1 of the 1960 Act deserve mention.

(1) If the public are permitted to attend the meeting, notice of the meeting should be displayed, where possible, at the local authority office three days prior to the meeting.

(2) Newspapers should receive advance copies of the agenda as supplied to the members ("but excluding, if thought fit, any item during which the meeting is likely not to be open to the public" (s.1 (4) (b))) and any reports or documents supplied to members.

(3) While the meeting is open to the public, reporters attending ".... so far as practicable (shall) be afforded reasonable facilities for taking their report and, unless the meeting is held in premises not belonging to the body or not on the telephone, for telephoning the report at their own expense".

(4) Matters printed in material circulated to the Press (the agenda, reports, etc.) carry qualified privilege unless the publication is proved to have been made with malice.

4 Disciplinary Bodies

A number of professional disciplinary bodies exist, under Acts of Parliament, to maintain standards and codes of conduct. The right of Press access and the degrees of defamation protection attached to reports of proceedings, vary considerably, as do the routes for appeal.

(A) *The Legal Profession*

(i) *Solicitors*

The Disciplinary Tribunal of the Law Society, established under the Solicitors Acts, investigates complaints against solicitors. The tribunal may strike a solicitor off the rolls, suspend him from practice or fine him for professional misconduct. If the solicitor is struck off, his name is removed from the Roll of Solicitors of the Supreme Court and he cannot practice.

The tribunal hears all applications in private but does announce its findings in the presence of the Press and public. The findings are set out in a document, which is read out by the chairman. The document contains a balanced summary of the case as heard in private, including mitigating factors offered on behalf of the solicitor. This document is known as the findings and order: the Press present receive copies of it and, from the point of view of defamation, it attracts absolute privilege.

Since 1975, the tribunal has sat in panels, consisting of three members, two solicitors and a lay member of the public. A solicitor has 14 days to appeal to the Divisional Court of the Queen's Bench. He may give notice of appeal at the time the tribunal have reached their decision and, if this occurs, the tribunal will suspend the findings and order until the result of the appeal is known.

If the solicitor does appeal to the Divisional Court unsuccessfully he may, with permission, take the matter through to the Court of Appeal and ultimately, on a point of law of general public importance, to the House of Lords. Throughout this period, his identity will be concealed, the Cause Lists referring to him as "a solicitor."

Not every solicitor is taken off the Roll for misconduct. He may apply to be removed from the Roll because he wishes, for instance, to become a barrister. In this situation, the words "at his own request" are vital to avoid an indefensible defamatory innuendo.

(ii) *Barristers*

The Senate of the Inns of Court, through a disciplinary committee, hears and determines complaints against barristers. The committee is composed entirely of barristers and the individual's Inn must abide by the decision of the committee.

The committee may censure the barrister, suspend him for a period or disbar him (depriving him of his right to audience in the courts and, effectively, his right to practice).

In 1969, a barrister who had been disbarred by his Inn, following a Senate committee hearing, appealed to five judges of the Queen's Bench sitting as visitors to his Inn. He argued that the benchers of the Inn had no right to transfer their disciplinary powers to the Senate because they had received the power to call and disbar from the judges and should have preserved this. The visiting judges rejected this on the grounds that the Senate procedure was merely a change in the manner by which judges decided who should and who should not have the right of audience. The visitors did, however, substitute suspension for 12 months in place of an order for disbarment.

The Senate committee hearings are held in private unless the chairman, at the request of the barrister charged, directs that it should be held in public. If disbarment or suspension is ordered, the charges, finding and sentence are published in the barrister's Inn. In other cases, they are published only if the barrister so requests or the President of the Senate so recommends; if the charges are dismissed, they are only published if the barrister so requests.

The proceedings of the disciplinary committee are subject to an appeal to the Lord Chancellor and the judges of the High Court, the latter forming a panel of judges, as mentioned above, described as "visitors."

The findings on appeal will be posted at the barrister's Inn in relevant cases and the Press should add nothing to the details as given.

A barrister may apply to have himself disbarred if, for example, he wishes to become a solicitor. The words "at his request" will appear on the relevant notice and must be included in any copy mentioning this.

(B) *The Medical Profession*

Disciplinary committees exist for doctors (General Medical Council), dentists (General Dental Council), opticians (General Optical Council), vets (Royal College of Veterinary Surgeons) and pharmacists (Pharmaceutical Society).

These bodies deal with members who have been convicted of offences, which reflect on their professional standing, who have transgressed guidelines in professional codes or who have acted in a way which is "infamous or disgraceful in a professional respect" (*i.e.* a doctor having an affair with a patient).

The committee for veterinary surgeons always meets in public; those for dentists and opticians generally do so and the disciplinary committee of the General Medical Council normally does so unless, for special reasons, it decides to sit in private. The ultimate penalty is removal of the individual's name from the relevant register, making subsequent legitimate practice impossible.

The general procedure is that the individual has 28 days in which to lodge an appeal with the Privy Council; for veterinary surgeons, appeal is to the High Court and no decision takes effect until the end of the three-month period allowed in this case.

The procedure of the Disciplinary Committee of the General Medical Council will be examined briefly, the other bodies having similar formats.

There is a "programme" of items to be considered which is

marked confidential. Any charge or part of a charge on the programme, which is not read in public, should not be reported. It
is permissible to mention witnesses names if they are identified
in public. Where they remain anonymous, nothing likely to
identify them should appear in the report.

Accounts of the proceedings should be fair and balanced and
the name, address and qualifications of the individual, appearing before the committee, should correspond to the form set
out in the programme.

A decision to remove a practitioner from the Register is not
effective during the period permitted for appeal and copy
should indicate this fact.

(C) *Other Bodies*

Sporting bodies, trade and industrial associations and certain
non-statutory professional bodies have power to discipline
members. Generally, such proceedings are conducted in private. Part II of the Schedule to the Defamation Act 1952 gives
qualified privilege, subject to explanation or contradiction, to
certain fair and accurate reports. These include the findings or
decisions of United Kingdom associations with the control
over the conduct of members if the association:

(i) promotes or encourages art, science, religion or learning;

(ii) promotes or safeguards the interests of any trade, business, profession or industry; or

(iii) promotes or safeguards the interests of any game, sport
or pastime carried on in public.

This defamation protection can only operate if the Press are
permitted to attend or are given details of the findings or
decisions.

5   The Theft Act 1968 and Race Relations Act 1976

Brief reference is made to the Theft Act 1968 because, while this is substantive criminal law rather than fundamental Press law, the Act provides a major source of criminal prosecutions which are reported.

Theft (stealing)

The dishonest appropriation of property belonging to another with the intention of permanently depriving the other of it (s.1). If tried on indictment the maximum penalty on conviction is 10 years' imprisonment (s.7). The offence is triable summarily with the consent of the accused (s.29 (2)).

Robbery

Stealing when, immediately before or at the time of the offence and in order to commit the crime, the accused uses force on anyone or makes them fear force will be used there and then. This offence is only triable on indictment and carries a maximum penalty of life imprisonment (s.8).

Burglary

The entering of a building as a trespasser with intent to:
(a) steal;
(b) inflict grievous bodily harm on anyone there;
(c) rape any woman there; or
(d) do unlawful damage there (s.9).
If a person, having entered the building as a trespasser, then steals or attempts to steal or inflicts or attempts to inflict grievous bodily harm on any person there, this is also an offence. If tried on indictment, the maximum penalty is 14 years' imprisonment. The offence is triable summarily with the consent of the accused (s.29 (2)).

Aggravated burglary

As above, but when the accused has with him any firearm or imitation firearm, any offensive weapon or any explosive.

This offence is only triable on indictment and the maximum penalty is life imprisonment (s.10)

Obtaining property by deception

The use of deception to obtain property belonging to another with the intention of permanently depriving him of it.

If tried on indictment, the maximum penalty is 10 years' imprisonment (s.15). The offence is triable summarily with the consent of the accused (s.29 (2)).

Obtaining pecuniary advantage by deception

The use of deception to obtain some kind of monetary advantage (evasion of debts, borrowing, etc.).

If tried on indictment, the maximum penalty is 5 years' imprisonment (s.16). The offence is triable summarily with the consent of the accused (s.29 (2)).

Blackmail

The making of any unwarranted demand with menaces for gain to the blackmailer or loss to the victim.

The demand is not blackmail if:

(a) the accused had reasonable grounds for making the demand; and

(b) the use of menaces was a proper means of reinforcing the demand.

The offence is triable, only on indictment and carries up to 14 years' imprisonment (s.21).

Handling

A person handles stolen goods if, other than in the course of stealing, when knowing or believing them to be stolen he:

(a) dishonestly receives them: or

(b) dishonestly helps in their retention, removal, disposal or sale by someone else, or if he arranges to do so.

If tried on indictment, the maximum penalty is 14 years' imprisonment (s.22). The offence may be tried summarily with the consent of the accused (s.29(2)).

Advertising rewards

If any public advertisement of a reward for the return of stolen goods uses words suggesting that no questions will be asked or that the person producing the goods will be safe from further investigation or that money already paid for the goods will be reimbursed, the advertiser, printer and publisher face summary trial with a maximum penalty of a £100 fine on conviction (s.23).

Reporters and sub-editors should note that burglary offences, which encompass a number of differing situations, may be condensed in headlines and introductions to "burglary" and that section 15 and section 16 offences can be referred to as "frauds." "Handling" can cover a variety of situations and carries a greater potential penalty on conviction if tried on indictment than theft. The rationale behind the Act seeks to discourage more severely the marketers of stolen goods for, without the market outlets, organised theft rests in a vacuum. Care should be taken over advertisements which may contravene section 23.

Race Relations Act 1976

Race Relations legislation, which began in 1965, received a major revision in the Race Relations Act 1976. This new Act repealed the whole of the 1968 Act and most of the 1965 Act.

There were unsuccessful attempts in the House of Lords to amend section 70 of the new Act, which imposes very much more stringent liability on publishers of matter which may stir up racial hatred.

Section 70 adds a new section (s.5A) to the Public Order Act 1936. Prosecutions may take place under the 1936 Act, as amended, as follows:

(1) The offence is committed if a person:
(a) publishes or distributes written matter, which is threatening, abusive or insulting; or
(b) uses in a public place or at any public meeting words which are threatening, abusive or insulting,

in situations where hatred is likely to be stirred up against any racial group in Great Britain by the matter or the words.

(2) If, however, the matter occurs in:
(a) fair, accurate and contemporaneous court or tribunal pro-
    ceedings exercising judicial authority; or
(b) fair and accurate reports of Parliamentary proceedings,
then no offence is committed. If the court copy cannot be
published because it would be unlawful (*i.e.* because the matter originates at committal proceedings at which reporting
restrictions were not lifted) it may still be published lawfully
when the report itself would be lawful (*i.e.* at the Crown Court
trial).

(3) There is a defence in relation to the publication or distribution of written matter, if the accused can prove that he was
unaware of the content of the matter in question and did not
suspect or had no reason to suspect that is was threatening,
abusive or insulting.

(4) The penalties are up to 6 months' imprisonment and/or
a fine of up to £400 on summary conviction or up to 2 years'
imprisonment and/or an unlimited fine if convicted on indictment.

(5) Prosecutions can only be brought with the consent of the
Attorney General.

Publication and distribution are deemed to be to the public
unless it takes place only to members of an association of
which the publisher/distributor is a member.

A racial group means any group of people identified by their
colour, race, nationality (including citizenship) or ethnic or
national origins.

Written matter includes writing, signs or any visible representation.

The whole section is much more specific than the old section 6 (1) of the Race Relations Act 1965. That section required
the intent to stir up hatred to be proved. The new offence is one
of strict liability. The prosecution do not need to prove a definite personal intention in the accused, only that the matter is
likely to stir up hatred. In criminal law terms, proof of the
guilty mind (*mens rea*) is unnecessary: it is sufficient to prove
the guilty act (*actus reus*) which is mere publication.

It is quite clear from the new section 5A that, for the first
time, a newspaper carrying a report of an inflammatory speech
relating to race would be as liable as the speaker himself to

prosecution.

Newspapers have to consider carefully the possible effect of words reported from particular meetings. Reporters submitting copy may have to consider careful paraphrasing of what might otherwise have been used as a direct quote. In any event, such copy should at least be marked so that a sub-editor's attention is drawn to the problem and, preferably, should receive some senior editorial consideration. The reporter, editor, proprietor, printer, publisher and distributors could all be held liable on such reports (though innocent parties like distributors may be able to use the s.5A (3) defence).

It will be interesting to see whether making the Press potentially liable for reporting accurately what is said at particular meetings achieves a desirable result. One protection is that prosecutions require the consent of the Attorney General.

The defence in s.5A (3) can have but a very limited effect for the Press. It might be of assistance if a newspaper published an advertisement in a foreign language which is believed to be inoffensive but which, in true translation, was intended to stir up hatred among a particular section of the community.

Court and tribunal reports, within the requirements of the defamation defence of absolute privilege, are completely protected. Trials of accused charged with offences under this section may be safely reported if the requirements are satisfied (as may speeches made in Parliament).

Appendix A: Blasphemous Libel

The *Gay News* Case (1977)

The case came to trial at the Old Bailey in July 1977 as the result of a private prosecution which was never, despite certain reports, taken over by the Crown. It was the first for 55 years. In *R.* v. *Gott* (1922) a pamphleteer, who had described Christ looking like a circus clown as he entered Jerusalem on a donkey, went to prison for nine months.

Gay News was fined £1,000 on conviction; the editor, Mr. Dennis Lemon, was sentenced to nine months' imprisonment, suspended for two years, and fined £500. The matters appear certain to come before the Court of Appeal: the trial judge, Mr. Justice King-Hamilton, took a robust view of legal issues much as the likelihood of a breach of the peace and the use, in the trial, of expert witnesses. His summing-up to the trial jury included remarks like:

> "Although I sometimes read poetry and, as a rule, like what I read, I do not profess to be a judge of it and therefore would not presume to express an opinion as to whether this particular poem is a good one, a bad one or an indifferent one. But I have no doubt whatever that this poem is quite appalling."

The prosecution had alleged that the theme of the poem and cartoon was that Christ was a practising homosexual and utterly promiscuous. The jury's attention was drawn to the prosecution view that the poem:

1. suggested Christ had engaged in buggery with 15 individuals;
2. suggested there had been groups and orgies with the apostles; and
3. that salvation, joy and the resurrection were taken to refer to further homosexual acts of love.

Following the result in the trial, there was considerable

290

debate about the substance of the action, the reasons for bringing the prosecution and a suggestion to the jury that they were
setting standards for the next 50 years.

As many of these matters will be thoroughly explored on
appeal, it is not proposed to deal with them at any length. The
issues, legal and moral, would benefit from clarification by the
Court of Appeal.

Appendix B: Royal Commission on the Press

This Commission, established in 1974, reported in July 1977 (HMSO: Cmnd 6810). A previous Royal Commission had looked at the Press in 1961-62.

Among other matters, the 1977 report considered legal constraints on the Press together with the function and freedom of the Press and the position of the Press Council.

1. *Legal Constraints on the Press*

"Discussion would be advanced if the Government published a single green paper, or a white paper with green edges, setting out their policy on all the recommendations of all the committees, including the Franks Committee (Official Secrets) which have reported in the last five years. All are closely related and all bear directly upon freedom of expression and hence upon the freedom of the Press. In this way, a composite view would be presented and the public debate on proposed changes could be conducted within a coherent framework."

Reporting of minor offences

While there was not complete agreement, the Commission disagreed with the line taken by the Younger Committee on Privacy that anonymity for accused in magistrates' courts should not be extended.

On the subject of accused facing trial on minor offences, the Commission stated: "We received evidence on the subject from Dr Marjorie Jones, and read her book *Justice and Journalism* (1974), which argues that the reporting of names of individuals in minor proceedings before magistrates' courts has become a haphazard way of adding to the punishment of offenders, and should cease."

Some members of the Commission felt it was wrong to use the fear of random publicity as a deterrent. This group noted that countries with schemes allowing anonymity for accused in minor crimes did not seem to have suffered "deleterious consequences." This group hoped for a voluntary system, directed by the Press Council, "to ensure that the names of defendants in magistrates' courts are not reported."

There are an equal number of members of the Commission opposed to any further restrictions on reporting. They felt that publicity was some kind of deterrent, even if the actual reporting of cases was random.

The Commission's eventual recommendation was that the Government should appoint a committee to consider the rights to anonymity of people accused, whether found guilty or not, and the rights of the Press and the public to information about such cases.

"This has become urgent in the light of restrictions on reporting the names of both the complainant and the accused in cases of rape — which is not a minor offence," they note.

It was suggested, at the conclusion of the chapter on the "Open Court" in this book, that recent Private Members' legislation may have created the basis for further changes in the English legal system. The proof has come rapidly. The exception of anonymity for juvenile accused, once extended to cover those accused of rape offences, has become a collection of "rights to anonymity of people accused, whether found guilty or not" in the view of the Commission.

Official Secrets

Some of the Commission were concerned that the Franks Committee proposals to change section 2 of the Official Secrets Act 1911 were inadequate; others felt that the government in this country is conducted "in excessive secrecy."

The Commission eventually recommended that there should be a commission of inquiry to look into the whole matter. On this commission, civil service and local government interests should be represented, but only in the minority of members. Such a commission should work to a Government

time limit because the Commission considered the whole subject a "matter of urgency."

Defamation, contempt and criminal libel

On defamation and contempt there was no serious disagree-
ment with the Faulks or Phillimore Committees. The
Commission did, however, disagree about criminal libel.
They felt that such prosecutions should cease to be possible privately and that they should only be brought by the Director of
Public Prosecutions. While making no recommendations on
obscene, blasphemous or seditious libels (because these areas
were considered to be outside their purview) they felt that the
same rules should apply as for criminal libel (*i.e.* prosecution
only by the D.P.P.).

2. *The Press Council*

The Commission felt that the Press Council, as opposed to just
the Complaints Committee of the Press Council, should have
an equal number of lay and Press representatives.
    Among other suggestions were:
    The appointment of a Conciliator, for pre-Complaints Com-
        mittee matters.
    An extension of the "right of reply" doctrine where there has
        been inaccurate newspaper criticism.
    The Press Council should draw up a code of behaviour
        based on its adjudications.
    The Press Council should attempt to get agreement on the
        publication of adjudications which uphold the com-
        plaint on the front page of the newspaper in question.
    The Press Council should be prepared to undertake a wider
        review than it normally does of the record of the publica-
        tion or journalist concerned in a complaint.

Index

defences, 91
offences, elements of, 90
other statutes, and, 91
Truth. *See* Justification.

Unintentional Defamation
  See also Apology; Defamation;
  Express Malice; Faulks
  Committee.
Unintentional Defamation, 18-20
  affidavit, use of, 19
  changes, proposals for, 20
  defects, 19-20
  innocent publication, meaning
  of, 18
  offer of amends, 18-19
  publisher, meaning of, 18

Volenti Non Fit Injuria. *See*
  Consent.

Warrant, 171
Winding up, 246-248

Young Persons. *See* Juvenile
  Offenders.